Personal
Publishing
with
PC PageMaker®

# HOWARD W. SAMS & COMPANY/HAYDEN BOOKS

## Related Titles

**Personal Publishing with the Macintosh, Second Edition**
Terry Ulick

**The Best Book of: WordStar, Second Edition**
Vincent Alfieri

**Mastering WordStar®**
Vincent Alfieri

**Best Book of: WordPerfect®**
Vincent Alfieri

**dBASE III PLUS™ Programmer's Reference Guide**
Ed Jones

**Managing with dBASE III®**
Michael J. Clifford

**Best Book of: dBASE II®/III®**
Ken Knecht

**Best Book of: Lotus® 1-2-3®, Second Edition**
Alan Simpson

**Macro Programming for 1-2-3®**
Daniel N. Shaffer

**Discovering MS-DOS®**
Kate O'Day, The Waite Group

**MS-DOS® Bible**
Steven Simrin, The Waite Group

**MS-DOS® Developer's Guide**
John Angermeyer and Kevin Jaeger, The Waite Group

**Tricks of the MS-DOS® Masters**
John Angermeyer, Kevin Jaeger, Rich Fahringer, and Dan Shafer, The Waite Group

**Microsoft® C Programming for the IBM®**
Robert Lafore, The Waite Group

**C Programmer's Guide to Serial Communications**
Joe Campbell

**C Primer Plus, Revised Edition**
Mitchell Waite, Stephen Prata, and Donald Martin, The Waite Group

**Advanced C Primer++**
Stephen Prata, The Waite Group

---

For the retailer nearest you, or to order directly from the publisher, call 800-428-SAMS. In Indiana, Alaska, and Hawaii call 317-298-5699.

# Personal Publishing with PC PageMaker®

*Terry Ulick*

**HOWARD W. SAMS & COMPANY**
*A Division of Macmillan, Inc.
4300 West 62nd Street
Indianapolis, Indiana 46268 USA*

© 1987 by Terry Ulick

FIRST EDITION
FIRST PRINTING—1987

All rights reserved. No part of this book shall be reproduced, stored in a retrieval system, or transmitted by any means, electronic, mechanical, photocopying, recording, or otherwise, without written permission from the publisher. No patent liability is assumed with respect to the use of the information contained herein. While every precaution has been taken in the preparation of this book, the publisher and author assume no responsibility for errors or omissions. Neither is any liability assumed for damages resulting from the use of the information contained herein.

International Standard Book Number: 0-672-22593-X
Library of Congress Catalog Card Number: 87-61481

Acquisitions Editor: James S. Hill
Manuscript Editor: Sara Bernhardt Black
Cover Artist: Tony Woodward
Indexer: Katherine Stuart Ewing

*Printed in the United States of America*

**Trademark Acknowledgments**

All terms mentioned in this book that are known to be trademarks or service marks are listed below. In addition, terms suspected of being trademarks or service marks have been appropriately capitalized. Howard W. Sams & Co. cannot attest to the accuracy of this information. Use of a term in this book should not be regarded as affecting the validity of any trademark or service mark.

Amdek is a trademark of Amdek Corportion

Canon is a registered trademark of Canon U.S.A.

CompuServe is a registered trademark of CompuServe Information Services, an H & R Block Company

IBM is a registered trademark of International Business Machines Corporation

IBM AT is a registered trademark of International Business Machines Corporation

LaserJet, LaserJet Plus, and LaserJet II are trademarks of Hewlett-Packard Company

LaserWriter and LaserWriter Plus are trademarks of Apple Computer, Inc.

Lotus 1-2-3 is a registered trademark of Lotus Development Corporation

Macintosh is a trademark of MacIntosh Laboratory, Inc., used by Apple Computer, Inc. with its express permission

MacLink is a trademark of Dataviz, Inc.

Microsoft, Microsoft Word, MS-DOS, and Multiplan are trademarks of Microsoft Corporation

MultiMate is a trademark of SoftWord Systems, Inc.

NEC is a registered trademark of NEC Information Systems

PageMaker is a registered trademark of Aldus Corporation

Palantir is a trademark of Palantir, Inc.

PostScript is a trademark of Adobe Systems, Inc.

SmartCom is a trademark of Hayes Microcomputer Products, Inc.

Symphony is a registered trademark of Lotus Development Corporation

The Source is a trademark of Source Telecomputing Corporation

Texas Instruments is a trademark of Texas Instruments, Inc.

Volkswriter is a registered trademark of Lifetree Software, Inc.

WordPerfect is a registered trademark of WordPerfect Corporation

# Contents

*Page ix*  *Acknowledgments*

*Page xi*  *Introduction*

**Part One**  *Assembling a Personal Publishing System*

1  Page 3  Assembling a Personal Publishing System
6  Hardware Switching
7  A Publishing System
8  The System Approach

2  Page 9  Selecting the Right Hardware
10  Upgrading Your PC
23  The Assembled System
24  Peripheral Hardware
31  Communication Links
32  A Turnkey System
33  The Final System

3  Page 35  Selecting the Right Software
35  A Natural System
36  Capturing Text
41  Creating Graphic Elements
47  Page Assembly Software
48  Downloadable Type Fonts
49  Electronic Page Assembly

## Part Two — The Nature of the Printed Page

**4**    Page 53   *The Page*
- 55   *Page Architecture*
- 55   *Page Elements*
- 62   *Other Page Elements*
- 63   *The Single Page*

**5**    Page 65   *More Than One Page*
- 65   *Multipage Environments*
- 68   *Designing Publications*

**6**    Page 71   *Pages on the AT*
- 71   *Formatting Choices*
- 78   *AT Advantages*

**7**    Page 79   *Electronic Page Assembly*
- 79   *Case Study*
- 81   *A Better Way*
- 82   *Computer-Aided Publishing*
- 84   *Conversion*

## Part Three — Page Design

**8**    Page 87   *The Grid*
- 87   *A Skeletal Structure*
- 89   *Defining the Live Area*
- 91   *Columns*
- 92   *Graphic Elements*
- 93   *Working with the Grid*

**9**    Page 95   *Working with Type*
- 96   *What Is Type?*
- 98   *Fonts*
- 98   *Identifying Type*
- 101   *Type Mechanics*
- 104   *Make Your Own Type Gauge*
- 105   *The Finer Points of Type*
- 106   *A Starting Point*

**10**    Page 107   *PostScript and LaserJet Plus Type Styles*

**11**    Page 121   *Formatting Type*
- 121   *Planning for PC PageMaker*
- 122   *Formatting Text into Type*
- 127   *Formatting from Various Word-Processing Programs*

## Part Four  Working with PC PageMaker

| 12 | Page 133 | Putting the Pieces Together |
|---|---|---|
|  | 133 | Page Assembly |
|  | 134 | Page Relationships |
|  | 136 | PC PageMaker |
| 13 | Page 137 | Working with PC PageMaker |
|  | 138 | Some Basics |
|  | 140 | PC PageMaker Tools |
|  | 140 | A Multilayered Page |
|  | 141 | Start Your Engines |
| 14 | Page 143 | Building Master Pages |
|  | 144 | Choosing a Printer |
|  | 148 | Creating a Master Page |
|  | 158 | Ready to Begin |
| 15 | Page 159 | Placing Elements on a Page |
|  | 159 | Placing a Headline |
|  | 163 | Sizing a Headline |
|  | 168 | Adding a Rule |
|  | 171 | On to the Next Page |
|  | 172 | Placing Graphics on a Page |
|  | 175 | Wrapping Type |
|  | 184 | Making a Page End Flush |
|  | 187 | Adding Type and Boxes |
|  | 190 | Publication Complete |
| 16 | Page 191 | Adding Graphic Elements |
|  | 191 | Using the Toolbox |
|  | 193 | Working with Graphics Files |
|  | 193 | Adding Shading to Areas |
|  | 194 | Covering Master Page Elements |
|  | 196 | TIFF and EPS Files |
|  | 199 | Experiment with All the Tools |
| 17 | Page 201 | Linking PC PageMaker Files |
|  | 201 | The First Options |
|  | 202 | Splitting Text Files |
|  | 203 | Shortcomings |

| 18 | Page 205 | *PC PageMaker Unleashed* |
|---|---|---|
| | 205 | *Stretching Text* |
| | 211 | *Odd-Sized Columns* |
| | 212 | *Changing Column Widths with Text Placed* |
| | 214 | *Changing Size and Leading of Type* |
| | 216 | *Hyphenation* |
| | 217 | *Tabs* |
| | 218 | *Kerning, Letterspacing, and Wordspacing* |
| | 219 | *Oversized Pages* |
| | 220 | *Reverse Type and Rules* |
| | 220 | *And It Keeps Coming* |
| 19 | Page 221 | *Printing Page Files* |
| | 221 | *Printing Pages and Files* |
| | 223 | *Using High-Resolution PostScript Services* |
| | 223 | *Top Quality* |
| 20 | Page 225 | *High-Volume Printing* |
| | 225 | *Large Print Runs* |
| | 226 | *When to Print Pages with a Printer* |
| | 226 | *Preparing Pages for Printing* |
| 21 | Page 229 | *Multicolored Pages* |
| | 229 | *Preparing Pages for Two-Color Printing* |
| | 230 | *Creating Color Separations* |
| | 233 | *Photocopier Printing* |
| | 234 | *Color Bonding* |
| 22 | Page 235 | *Grids and Page Samples* |

**Part Five**  *References*

| A | Page 261 | *Glossary of Graphic Arts Terms* |
|---|---|---|
| B | Page 265 | *Glossary of Special Terms Used in PC PageMaker* |
| C | Page 269 | *Product Reference* |
| | Page 275 | *Index* |

## Acknowledgments

I would like to thank: Bill Grout for starting the "Personal Publishing with..." series rolling; the many people at Aldus Corporation for their assistance; all the people at Howard W. Sams & Company, including Jim Hill, Greg Michael, Jennifer Ackley, Wendy Ford, Glenn Santner, and Sara Bernhardt Black; and finally my wife Linda for taking the pressures of publishing *Personal Publishing* Magazine to allow me time to complete this book.

# Introduction

What are you doing reading a book about publishing? That's for people who put together magazines, books, newspapers, and those high-priced newsletters. It's not for people who don't have hundreds of thousands of dollars and big staffs. That's the misconception most people, especially those in the publishing community, have always had.

If you look at publishing this way, it is a noun. For quite a while, publishing has been defined in terms of magazines, newspapers, and books. The cost of producing such publications has kept publishing in the hands of the rich (those who make money) or foolish (those who lose it).

Publishing, however, is not a noun. It is a verb. Most accurately, publishing is a process. *Webster's Seventh New Collegiate Dictionary* (I like student dictionaries; they fit on my desk) describes the word publish as:

1. to make generally known,
2. to make public announcement of.

It goes on to define a publisher as a noun—"one who publishes." With such definitions, it seems to me that publishing does not have to be limited to the high-end markets described above, although they are a small part of it. It has been estimated that in 1986 over 4 trillion sheets of paper were printed. Only 10% of that printing was done by professional publishers.

Where will all the rest of those sheets of paper come from? Just about everywhere. That's because publishing is a universal process. It occurs in every industry, at almost every level of profession, and is performed by individuals, groups, organizations, schools, government, large and small businesses, and, yes, even newspaper, book, magazine, and newsletter publishers.

The important consideration is that the majority of all publishing takes place as a nonprofessional activity. I'll illustrate what I mean by that.

Jane works for a small manufacturing company. The company makes cardboard boxes. These boxes come in hundreds of sizes and shapes, and the price varies based on how many are ordered. Jane has the wonderful job of keeping a price list of all the boxes and their volume order discounts.

She is lucky because up to two years ago this was done manually, but now, with the help of an IBM personal computer, she keeps a spreadsheet of the prices. When a base price changes, the formulas in the spreadsheet automatically adjust all the volume discounts. A database program helps keep track of inventory and availability and even invoices the customers.

She has even been able to take the prices from the spreadsheet, move them to a word-processing program, and create, on a dot-matrix printer, a pretty decent price list that could be sent to customers.

The computer has dramatically changed the way Jane manages information. But, being a very big cardboard box manufacturer, the boss doesn't want dot-matrix price lists going out to customers. He told Jane to give the price list to a typesetter and "Make it look professional." So every time there is a major change in prices, Jane sends off her list to a typesetter who charges the company about $2,100. The price is high since almost all the work is tabular in nature, something typesetting machines have difficulty with.

Once the typeset pages are back from the typesetter, Jane sends the pages to an instant printer who prints 500 copies (enough for the company's customers). The printing of the 16-page catalog/price list costs an additional $800.

Finally, a customer calls and asks for a price list. Jane tells him that she'll be publishing a new price list next week and will get one out to him then. She then turns him over to a salesperson who has a photocopy of the price list that is at the printer.

### Did She Say "Publish"?

That's right. She said in her phone conversation that the company would be "publishing" a new price list. And that's exactly what they will be doing since they are publishers. They publish a catalog every four months.

Now if you asked Jane what she did for a living, she would say she manages the price list for her company. But going back to the dictionary, she has "made public announcement of" her company's prices. That means she publishes information that makes her and her company publishers of catalogs, even though they have never thought of themselves as such.

So one day while picking up some diskettes at her computer dealer, she passes by a sign announcing a Desktop Publishing System. It consists of an IBM AT compatible and a strange square box with a sign calling it a laser printer. But she walks by. After all, she keeps price lists; she has nothing to do with publishing.

## A Chance Exchange

Being a regular customer, Jane has gotten to know her computer dealer quite well. He helped her set up her original system. He asks her how things are going, and she says that the typesetter is so late getting the type back to her that she has time to set up some new spreadsheets; hence, she needs some new diskettes.

The dealer, realizing why he set her up with her computer system in the first place, then takes her over to the Desktop Publishing System display and shows Jane how, with the system, she can bypass the typesetter and instant printer altogether. They work with some sample figures on a spreadsheet. In under an hour, the dealer has formatted some price lists, and they are being ejected from the laser printer with typeset quality. He explains how she can use the pages as the actual final art for printing or use the laser printer as the actual printing device to print the catalog and send customers who call a completely up-to-date price list.

In simple terms, Jane is blown away. She instantly begins realizing how much time and money can be saved by using such a system. There is no waiting for the typesetter, no outrageous typesetting charges, and no waiting for the printer. Even though she will still have the catalog printed, she will be able to get instant copies for those customers who need one before it's back from the printer. With the Desktop Publishing System, she will gain total control over the entire operation.

Jane gets all the facts on prices and software/hardware needed from the dealer and goes back to the office to prepare a cost analysis for her boss. After all, his bottomline is dollars. She has seen the benefits; now the tough part is to get her boss as excited about expanding their computer into a publishing system as she is.

She calculates that she will eliminate the typesetting costs, even though she will still print the catalog at the instant printer. Since the catalog is redone every four months at the cost of $2,100, in the first year they will save $6,300 in typesetting. With the laser printer costing under $5,000 and the software (PC PageMaker) costing $695, the system will essentially pay for itself by the savings from not using typesetting.

## The Bottomline

Jane goes to her boss and tells him that she wants to expand their personal computer into a publishing system. The boss looks at her, but, before he can get out a wisecrack about how they "ain't *Playboy*," she places the samples of the price sheets made at the computer store on his desk. She explains how they were made, then gives him the cost analysis she worked out.

He may be a tough cookie, but he knows that the computer has already been a real asset in the company. From what he can see, what Jane has shown him makes sense. It's a small investment for the company, so he agrees to give it a shot. Later that night he goes home and tells his wife that his company bought a publishing system today. She looks at him and says, "You bought a what?"

## A Publisher Is Born

Jane and her boss think they have gotten into something new: publishing. But they have always been publishers. They just never looked up the word in the dictionary or stopped to analyze what it was that they actually did when they created their catalog.

The exact same scenario is taking place all across the country. Hundreds of thousands of businesses, churches, universities, medical researchers, documentation directors, lawyers, architects, engineers, publishers, printers, artists, associations, writers, advertising agencies, and thousands of other occupations that produce information for sharing with others are discovering the benefits of something called desktop publishing. They are discovering that they are involved in the same publishing process as professional publishers and can take advantage of the new low- cost publishing systems that are available.

This book is for all of you who have realized that somehow you are involved in the publishing process. It is for those of you who are attempting to produce your own typeset-quality materials instead of sending them out to a typesetter, for those of you who want to take control over your publications and make them look better, and for those of you who suddenly realize that you are publishers.

For all of you, this book will teach you how to master personal publishing. I call it personal because, when all is said and done, it is you and your computer that make a page. It is a personal activity that requires personally developed skills and decisions.

## A System Approach

I have focused this book on creating an excellent publishing system using the an IBM PC AT or compatible. It consists of the computer, a laser printer, and, to control the page assembly process, the software PC PageMaker from Aldus Corporation.

With this software and hardware (and a few other helpful tools that I will detail for you), you will find yourself equipped with incredible publishing power for a remarkably low price (roughly $10,000 for a basic system). Best of all, as this book will demonstrate, the concepts are very easy to learn and use.

Although there are many computers and software packages available, I have decided to concentrate on one system and go into great detail using that system. If I were illustrating the advantages and disadvantages of several different systems, I would not be able to concentrate on the art of publishing, which is what all that equipment is for.

*Personal Publishing with PC PageMaker* is a guide to the use of a wonderfully configured publishing system for the art of publishing.

## Some Assumptions

This book assumes that you have worked with or are familiar with the IBM PC, XT, AT (or compatibles) and the MS-DOS operating system. PC PageMaker is intended for use with an AT-level machine or higher (such as an 80386-based MS-DOS computer). If you have a PC or XT (or compatible), you may find that you will want to upgrade to an AT-level machine or expand your current computer to AT performance levels with add-on boards.

Desktop publishing with MS-DOS also requires a bit more knowledge of DOS than usual, but this book will try to make learning how to deal with DOS as painless as possible.

Many people who will buy PC PageMaker have no doubt seen the original version of the product running on the Macintosh. The Macintosh is a beautiful computer where almost all the programs are designed to share data and almost all the hardware for it works fine just by plugging in a cable. The MS-DOS/IBM AT world is not as simple. PC PageMaker has made every attempt to bring that effortless user interface to you, but it's still more complicated than the Macintosh. If you have used a word- processing program or put your computer together (such as adding a memory board or graphics card and monitor), you should be ready for installing and using PC PageMaker. Even if you are just starting, don't worry I will show you how to make sense of the MS-DOS world.

*Terry Ulick*
*Itasca, Illinois*
*1987*

Part One    Assembling a Personal Publishing System

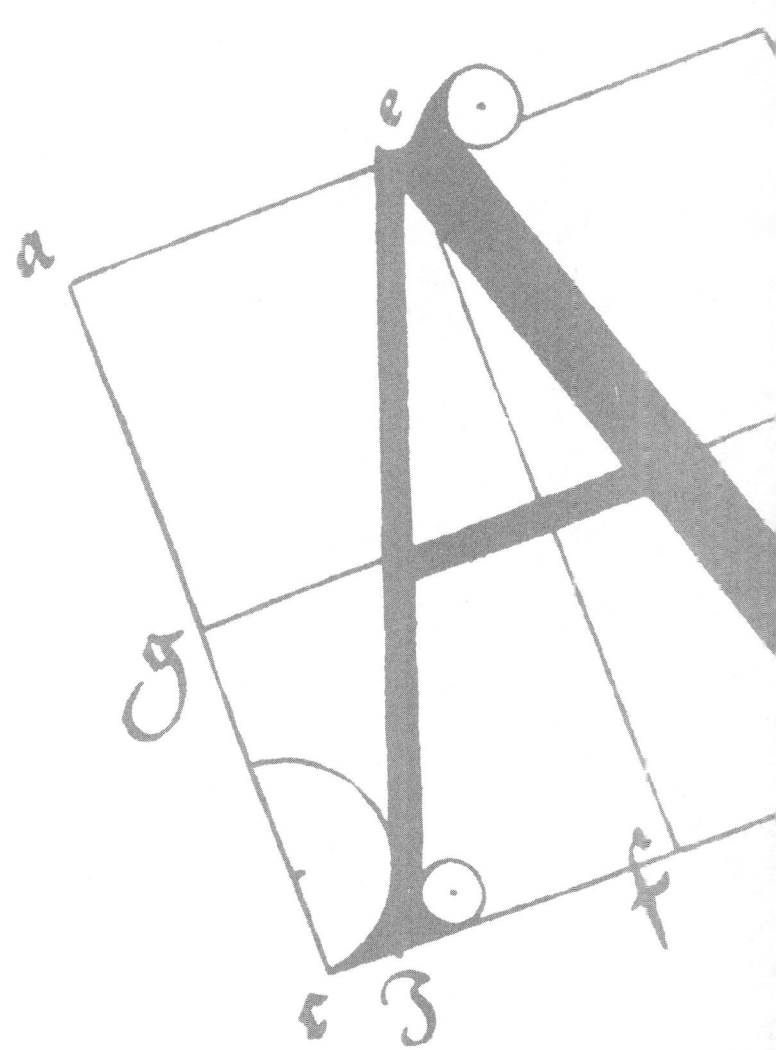

# Assembling a Personal Publishing System

*This* book looks at using an IBM AT or compatible (with compatibles to be considered as part of the term "IBM AT" from this point forward) to assemble a powerful desktop publishing system. If you have a standard PC, XT, or one of their compatibles, you can still use the system, but the operation of the programs used in the system will be painfully slow. There are ways to add cards to bring standard PCs and XTs up to AT speed, and I will cover that shortly.

The system this book covers uses an IBM AT, a laser printer, a high-resolution monitor, and a mouse. The software is made up of standard word-processing and graphics packages as well as PC PageMaker, the central page assembly tool for the system, and the Windows graphical environment. Windows is the program that allows you to work within a wysiwyg (what you see is what you get) display and lets you work with more than one program at a time. It is the program that integrates the programs in your system.

> **Helpful Hint**
>
> Windows is simple to use and is one of the most useful programs for the IBM PC family. If you are not familiar with Windows, it is a program that allows you to load more than one program into the memory of the computer at one time. Whenever you choose, you may switch from one program to another. For example, if you are working in Windows Write and find that you need to create a drawing for your text file, normally you would have to save your text file, quit the program, start a drawing program (such as Windows Paint), create your drawing, save it, quit Windows Paint, and return to Windows Write. Those are a lot of steps for such a simple task.
>
> By using Windows, you would start your session by first activating the Windows program. (See Fig. 1-1.) The screen displays a number of programs. In fact, the opening Windows screen, called MS-DOS Executive, is a visual representation of your MS DOS file directories. Windows allows you to start up a program, then at any time freeze the program and open up another program. You can open up as many programs as the memory of computer has room for and can not only switch between them but also have a number of program windows on screen at the same time. (See Fig. 1-2.) Only one program may be active, but you can create a drawing, bring up a word-processing program in a window next to it, and write a description of the drawing while looking at it. Simply put, Windows divides the memory of your computer and places your chosen programs in those memory areas.

When Windows-based programs are loaded into Windows, a black bar appears at the top of the screen. Moving the pointer icon up into the black bar and double clicking on the mouse will stop the program you are currently using, freeze it (keeping all your data intact without having to save it), and place an icon of the program at the bottom of the screen. (See Fig. 1-2.) Since the main menu, MS-DOS Executive, was frozen when you started a program, it too is now an icon at the bottom of the screen and is represented by a floppy disk. At this point, you can go to either program by double clicking the mouse button on the icon or by simply dragging the icon up into the top portion of the screen. The program will fill the screen and become the active window.

You can have more than one window on the screen. This is done by taking a program that has been loaded and placed as an icon on the bottom of the screen and dragging it up to fill the screen. If you have a number of such programs open, you can drag another program icon to the top, left, or right of the screen and that section of the screen will divide itself to show both programs. Only one program can be active at one time, but this allows you to view the active screens of a number of programs at one time.

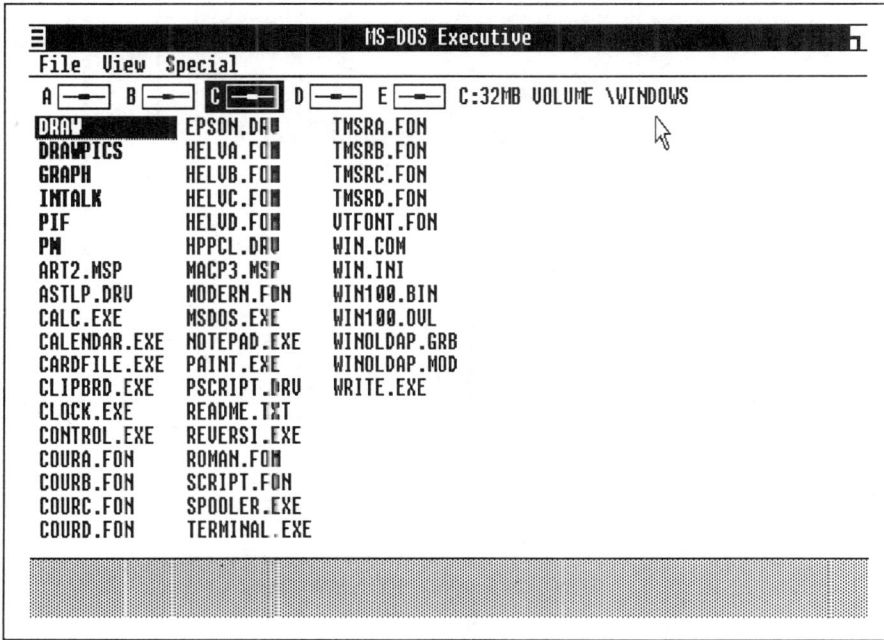

**Figure 1-1.** When you first enter Windows, you view the MS-DOS Executive program, which acts as an operating system manager. From here you can run programs; add, copy, or delete files; and even create or delete subdirectories.

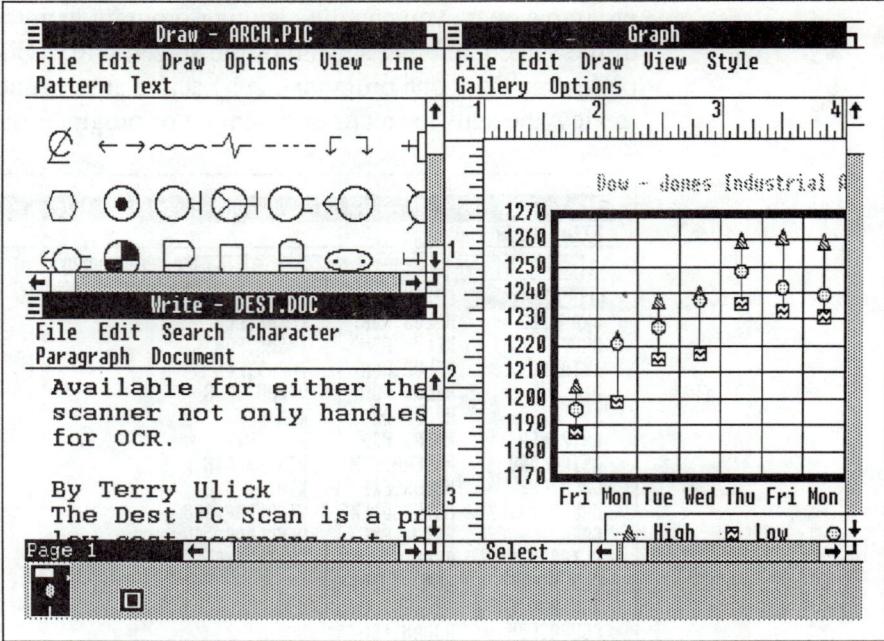

**Figure 1-2.** Windows in action with three windows open on the screen and two more program icons, which are located in the icon area and can be opened as windows at any time. Each time a window is put away as an icon, the program(s) on the screen will fill the area left vacant by the absent program.

With the power of Windows, you can assemble a group of programs that work together as a system. If you are writing text with illustrations, by using Windows you could load a word-processing program (such as Windows Write) and a paint program (such as Windows Paint) and switch between the two programs throughout the creation of a document. The same concept would apply if you were creating a financial document. You could load a word-processing program and a spreadsheet program and copy spreadsheet tables into your text file.

Windows transforms the IBM AT from a single-application computer into a multiapplication computer.

## Hardware Switching

Just as Windows allows you to assemble a combination of programs to create a larger software system configuration on your computer, you may also work with a variety of input and output devices. Hardware (such as a laser printer, dot-matrix printer, external floppy disk drives, hard disk drives, graphic input tablets, communication links to other computers, and digitizers) may all be connected to a single IBM PC or compatible to create a comprehensive publishing system. The system is capable of supporting a variety of devices, all with ease.

A typical publishing system can consist of an IBM AT, a hard disk drive, a laser printer, a mouse, a high-resolution graphics card and monitor, and a digitizer for scanning photographs or line art (graphics). The open architecture of the IBM allows you to have many different devices connected to the computer at one time. For example, a dot-matrix printer and two laser printers can be connected to a typical IBM AT at one time. For multiple input devices (such as a cable from another computer for data transfer or a digitizer), you can purchase inexpensive serial port or parallel port switchers and choose between the various devices you have connected to your computer if all available serial or parallel ports are occupied.

### Support Products
In addition to the basic programs (word-processing program, drawing/paint programs, page makeup software, and Windows), there are many supportive utility programs that will enhance and round out your publishing system. These programs often operate as memory-resident utilities. There are spelling checkers, keyboard macro programs, RAM disks, and even Window's own calculator, notepad, and clipboard, all of which will help complete your publishing system.

## A Publishing System

Fig. 1-3 illustrates the many hardware and software products that can be combined and used simultaneously to form an IBM-based publishing system. Each of the products will be detailed in following chapters, but for now we can see that as a publishing system the IBM AT is both powerful and flexible.

Each of the items in Fig. 1-3 performs a unique function. All can be used as stand-alone products. Together, they turn an IBM AT into a full-powered graphic arts workstation capable of creating professional-quality documents and publications.

> **Typical Publishing System**
>
> **Hardware:**
> IBM AT, 640k
> Floppy Disk Drive
> 20mb Hard Disk Drive
> High-Resolution Graphics Card
> High-Resolution Monitor
> Laser Printer
> Scanner
> Mouse
>
> **Software:**
> Windows
> Word-Processing Program
> Paint Program
> Draw Program
> Scanner Program
> PC PageMaker (page assembly program)
> Interactive Macro Program
> Interactive Spelling Checker

**Figure 1-3.** A small sampling of the hardware and software that can be assembled into one integrated publishing system on the IBM AT.

## The System Approach

As outlined above, creating documents and publications is best handled by assembling your hardware and software into a publishing system. The magical combination of hardware and software that makes up your publishing system will evolve and grow as your skills and resources grow.

Now is the time to stop thinking of preparing text as word processing, compiling line art and photographs as creating art, and putting pages together as making up pages. It is time to think of all of those functions as one and the same: publishing. And with your publishing system, you're ready to begin.

# Selecting the Right Hardware

# 2

*I*n creating your publishing system, you have many choices of hardware configurations. Whether you are about to purchase a computer or already own one, you must make these choices.

If your computer is a standard 8088 processor PC, XT, or clone, you will need to upgrade it to IBM PC AT standards if it is to work properly with PC PageMaker software. If you already own an AT, you're all set unless you do not have at least 512k of RAM and at least a 10mb hard disk.

The most important program in the publishing system is PC PageMaker, and it requires an AT-level computer, at least 512k RAM (although 640k is suggested), and a hard disk with at least 2mb for the program to be stored in and work in.

What will happen if you use your standard PC to run PC PageMaker even if you have 640k RAM and plenty of hard disk space? PC PageMaker will run, make pages, and print them out; it will just do so very slowly. Aldus, the maker of PC PageMaker, does not recommend running the program on any computer with less than the AT standards, and they are right. There is a major performance difference between an AT and a PC. The processor of the AT is much faster, the RAM chips used in an AT are faster, and the hard disk used in an AT has a much faster data access time than a standard PC. The AT and the PC are two very different machines, even though they can run the same software.

# Upgrading Your PC

If you have a standard PC, XT, or compatible, you have three different options: Keep your PC and endure painfully slow sessions of making pages; add an accelerator board to make your PC run faster; or purchase an IBM AT or clone.

The first choice is not recommended. You can run Windows and PC PageMaker on a standard PC, but you will not enjoy the true benefits and performance of PC PageMaker. Every menu call, screen refresh, file save, and action will make you feel that you are operating in slow motion. You can start off this way, but you will soon grow tired and frustrated, so do so at your own risk.

The second option, installing an accelerator board, is at best a stopgap measure. Accelerator boards can speed up the clock speed of the standard 8088 processor.

You could also add a new processor (such as the 80286, an AT processor). Such boards will make your computer run faster, but they do not bring your computer up to AT standards of performance. An AT not only has a faster processor, it also has faster acting RAM, and most importantly it has a hard disk that operates at 30- to 40-milliseconds (ms) access time, compared to the XT-level hard disk, which accesses data at about 80 ms. The AT hard disk is much faster. Put together, the 80286 processor, the faster RAM, and the much faster hard disk of the AT result in a configuration that cannot be matched by simply using an accelerator board in a PC.

The combined cost of an accelerator board (about $400 for a good one) and a faster hard disk is expensive. You will be spending quite a bit of money to bring your PC or XT up to date.

The final option is to purchase an AT or compatible. There are remarkably compatible units available for very low prices, so it is an option seriously worth considering. If you are starting from scratch, you will want to start right off with an AT or compatible.

## Mouse

Assuming you have assembled an AT-level computer system, the next piece of hardware you will need is a mouse. Many IBM PC users are new to using a mouse, and many do not think that it is a sensible device for any purpose. Nothing could be farther from the truth.

When working in the Windows environment and when using PC PageMaker, the mouse will be your primary input device. In fact, many sessions will go by without even touching the keyboard! The mouse is essential for making pages and creating graphics.

A mouse, is simply a cursor movement device with two or three buttons that act as an enter key and select items. It is connected to your computer through an RS-232 serial port or sometimes through its own bus expansion card (leaving your serial ports free).

Both Windows and PC PageMaker rely heavily on the use of a mouse for most actions, although true to the IBM world, both programs offer keyboard alternatives to mouse movements (such as using cursor keys). After about a day with a mouse, you will start to realize what a timesaver it is. For example, in Windows, the cursor takes the shape of an arrow, called a pointer. Either the mouse or the cursor keys move the pointer to select actions, such as starting a program. If you use the cursor keys, after hundreds of clicks, you can move the pointer to a program displayed on the screen and press the enter key twice to start the program. Or you could simply take the mouse and move it in the direction you wish the pointer to go; in less than a second, the pointer will be located above the program name. Press the mouse button twice, and the program starts. The mouse is intuitive, extremely fast, and much less work than using keystrokes.

Most importantly both Windows and PC PageMaker are designed to work most effectively with a mouse. You should take advantage of that fact.

There are three different types of mice for the IBM AT: optical, mechanical, and optical-mechanical.

A popular example of a mechanical mouse is the Microsoft mouse. It can be attached to your computer through a serial port, its own bus card, or with some newer expansion boards a special in-port socket that is built into the add-on board. It is a purely mechanical device: a rubber ball rolls freely on the bottom of the mouse. As you move the mouse, the movement of the ball on the work surface turns small wheels inside the mouse. The wheels sense the direction of movement and send that information to the computer. The mouse comes with software that interprets the movement information and is installed with Windows, so it is very easy to use.

The second option is an optical mouse. The advantage of the optical mouse (such as one made by Mouse Systems) is that there is no rubber ball or moving parts. Instead, the mouse has a light beam and a photocell. The mouse uses a small metal plate that has a grid painted on it. As the mouse is moved about the grid, the light reflects off its metal surface, and the light, when broken by the painted grid, allows the mouse to sense the direction of the mouse movement. Since there is no rubber ball, the mouse moves very smoothly over the metal plate. You are, however, stuck with a small metal plate on your desk, and you cannot move the mouse beyond its boundaries. It too is supported by Windows and PC PageMaker, so installation is quite simple.

The final option is a mouse that contains both systems; an optical-mechanical mouse. Logitech creates such a mouse. It includes software that emulates the Microsoft mouse and is inexpensive and easy to use. It uses a rubber ball, so it does not require a metal grid and can be used anywhere on the desktop. It does expand on the mechanical mouse since it interprets the movements of the rubber ball with an optical system, giving it less moving parts and a very fluid motion. Many stores now carry all three mice, so your best bet is to go to such a store and test them out. You will need a mouse, but which type is strictly a matter of preference.

**Graphics Card**

If you are an experienced PC user, you know that IBM PCs and ATs do not come with a monitor nor the required add-on graphics board to drive it. This means that you will have to decide which type of graphics board you will use with your publishing system.

If you already own a computer, chances are you may own a TTL monochrome monitor, the standard IBM-style green phosphor display that connects to the IBM Monochrome Display Adapter (MDA). The problem is that the monochrome adapter only handles text, not graphics, and all the images on the screen created by Windows or PC PageMaker are in the graphics mode. This means you will have to switch to a graphics card.

If you have an IBM Color Graphics Adapter (CGA) card and an IBM Color Graphics Monitor, you are also out of luck. Although Windows will support CGA, it is terrible for use in desktop publishing. The extremely low resolution (320 by 200 pixels—the smallest dot on the screen) makes text unreadable. Once again, you can use CGA, but it is not suggested.

What does work then? If you have an IBM TTL Monochrome monitor or compatible, you can keep your monitor but switch to a Hercules graphics card. In fact, Hercules offers the least expensive solution with a very high level of resolution (720 by 348 screen pixels). The advantage here is that it works fine with your existing TTL monitor, turns it into a high-resolution graphics display, and is excellent for use with Windows and PC PageMaker.

There are options even here. When you use Windows or PC PageMaker, the screen reverses, creating black type and art against a conceptually white background (much like the display of the Macintosh). If you use an amber or green phosphor monitor with a Hercules card, you will view a large screen of bright green or amber. This may be fine at first, but after a few hours you will realize that green or amber are not the best colors to spend hours looking at. The Macintosh has the best solution: a pleasant soft white.

There are now soft white phosphor TTL monitors that work perfectly with the Hercules card. The result is a screen that any Macintosh owner would envy. White phosphor monitors are available for under $250 from Amdek (the 410W) and Multitech (the White Monochrome Display).

PC PageMaker suggests the use of the IBM EGA (Enhanced Graphics Adapter) and the IBM Enhanced Color Monitor. The EGA standard is acceptable (640 by 350 screen pixels), and though not as high as the Hercules, it does offer color. There are now many EGA-compatible cards (most emulate EGA and offer higher levels of resolution) and many monitors that not only support EGA but also CGA and the higher resolutions offered by the newer EGA- compatible cards. A good example would be the Vega Deluxe card (which offers Hercules, CGA, EGA, and a higher-resolution EGA mode) and the NEC Multisync Monitor (which can work with any of the color modes at resolutions up to 800 by 480).

Color currently does not play an essential role in desktop publishing. Using the EGA standard, your display can show scroll bars, menu type, and backgrounds in a variety of colors, but the page you are creating is a black and white page. In this sense, the use of a color display is not essential to creating a page effectively. Since EGA cards cost more than monochrome boards ($400-$700) and EGA monitors also cost more than monochrome monitors ($600-$1,000), color is a very expensive luxury that does not offer any real benefit of higher resolution or a truly better display. Given the choice, the Hercules Card and a white phosphor TTL monitor give the best screen image for the lowest price.

Windows and PC PageMaker also support a new group of high-resolution monochrome display monitors (HRMs) (Fig. 2-1). These are large screen black on soft white displays with resolutions as high as 1664 by 1200 (LaserView Display System from Sigma Designs). Such HRMs as the Amdek 1280 or the Wyse WY-700 offer a very attractive blend of high resolution and attractive price. Both include the display adapter and monitor that offer 1280 by 800 screen resolutions and drivers for Windows and other programs. They retail for less than $1,000.

The advantage of HRMs is that their higher screen resolution allows you to view more of the page you are creating at one time and to work with a screen image that is close in size to the page you are actually creating. The result is a very good wysiwyg display at a price often less than the much lower resolution EGA standard.

Which card and monitor is right for you? As with everything in the IBM world, there are many options. The monochrome monitors, either Hercules or HRM, seem to offer the best solution in both price and screen resolution. Once again, shop around and take a look before you buy.

**Figure 2-1.** High-resolution monitor.

## Printers

Choosing the printer to use in your publishing operation is not simple because once again there are so many choices. If you need professional-quality type, you will need at least a quality laser printer. If you need very high quality output, you will need a typesetting device or access to time on one through a service bureau. If you are on a very tight budget and do not need a high-quality document, you can use a dot-matrix printer. About the only printer you can't use is a letter-quality printer.

To help you understand which of these devices will best suit your needs, it is important to note that each machine is very different in its approach to printing pages, as described next. (See Figs. 2-2, 2-3, and 2-4.)

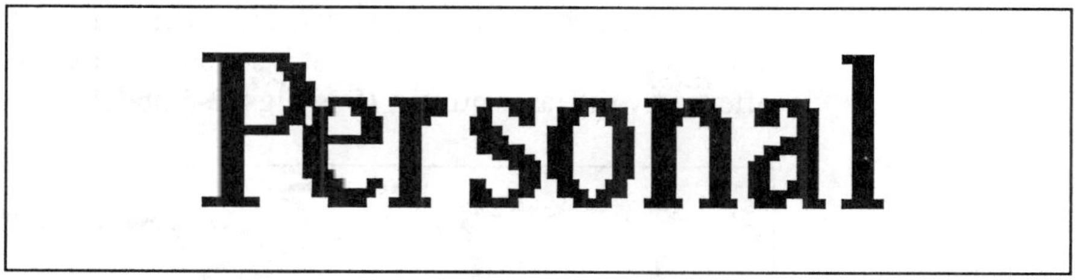

**15** Selecting the Right Hardware

**Figure 2-2.** Dot-matrix output.

**Figure 2-3.** Laser-printer output.

**Figure 2-4.** Typesetter output.

When comparing the power of the dot-matrix printer and the laser printer, the most obvious difference is that the dot-matrix printer is an impact printer, and the laser printer is a nonimpact printer that images a xerographic drum using a laser beam. One prints images by striking the paper with tiny hammers and an inked ribbon; the other, by imaging a xerographic drum, then transferring the image to a sheet of paper.

The dot-matrix printer is designed to reproduce exactly the image created on the screen of the computer, pixel by pixel. Additionally, the dot-matrix printer is a line printer. It can print only one line, 9, 18, or 24 pixels high, at a time. It has no on-board computer and cannot control what those lines will be. It is simply a reproduction tool for getting the images from the screen of the computer onto paper. This is great for data, mailing labels, and draft versions of publications, but it cannot approach the raw graphic power offered by the laser printer. (See Figs. 2-5 and 2-6.)

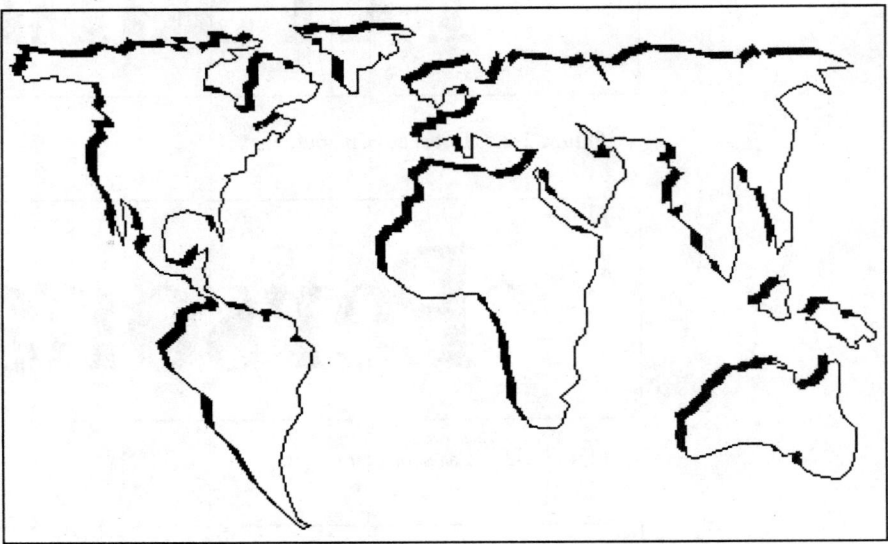

**Figure 2-5.** Images created by a dot-matrix printer. Although a great general-purpose printer, its low resolution will not meet the needs of many personal publishers.

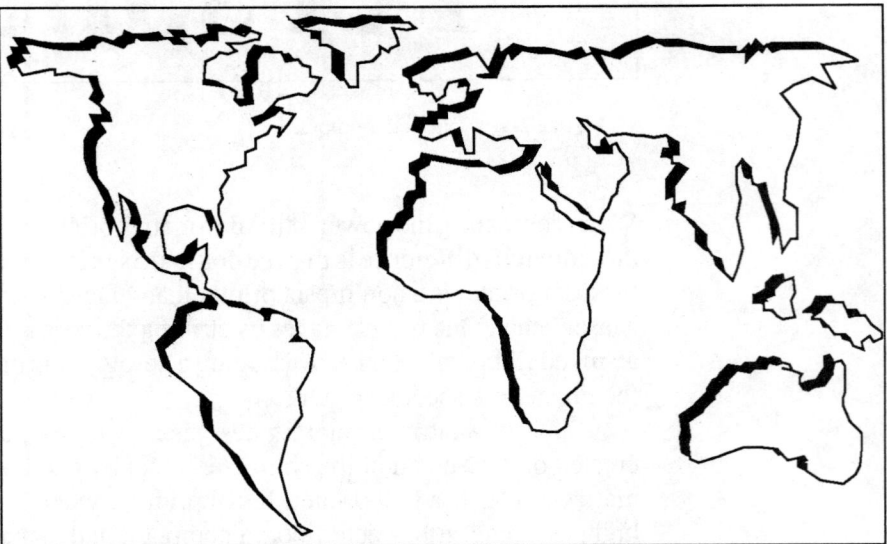

**Figure 2-6.** The same image created by a PostScript laser printer. With its 300dpi imaging, use of xerography instead of hammers striking an inked ribbon and of real typefaces with the PostScript page description language, this is a powerful tool for publishing.

## HOWARD W. SAMS & COMPANY
*Excellence In Publishing*

**Book Mark**

### DEAR VALUED CUSTOMER:

Howard W. Sams & Company is dedicated to bringing you timely and authoritative books for your personal and professional library. Our goal is to provide you with excellent technical books written by the most qualified authors. You can assist us in this endeavor by checking the box next to your particular areas of interest.

We appreciate your comments and will use the information to provide you with a more comprehensive selection of titles.

Thank you,

Vice President, Book Publishing
Howard W. Sams & Company

### SUBJECT AREAS:

Computer Titles:
- ☐ Apple/Macintosh
- ☐ Commodore
- ☐ IBM & Compatibles
- ☐ Business Applications
- ☐ Communications
- ☐ Operating Systems
- ☐ Programming Languages

Electronics Titles:
- ☐ Amateur Radio
- ☐ Audio
- ☐ Basic Electronics
- ☐ Electronic Design
- ☐ Electronic Projects
- ☐ Satellites
- ☐ Troubleshooting & Repair

Other interests or comments:
_____
_____

Name _____
Title _____
Company _____
Address _____
City _____
State/Zip _____
Daytime Telephone No. _____

HOWARD W. SAMS & COMPANY

*A Division of Macmillan, Inc.*
4300 West 62nd Street
Indianapolis, Indiana 46268 USA

22593

# Book Mark

**BUSINESS REPLY CARD**
FIRST CLASS    PERMIT NO. 1076    INDIANAPOLIS, IND.

POSTAGE WILL BE PAID BY ADDRESSEE

**HOWARD W. SAMS & CO.**
ATTN: Public Relations Department
P.O. BOX 7092
Indianapolis, IN 46206

NO POSTAGE
NECESSARY
IF MAILED
IN THE
UNITED STATES

*HOWARD W. SAMS & COMPANY*

Because laser printers are nonimpact printers, no hammers or pins strike the paper. Instead, laser printers employ a printing system exactly like the one found in a photocopier, commonly referred to as xerography. The current crop of laser printers are built around a Canon or Ricoh laser xerographic print engine. Just as a photocopier images a photosensitive drum with light reflected from a piece of paper on a platen and then transfers the image to a plain sheet of paper and bonds the image to the paper with heat, laser printers employ the same technique using a laser beam instead of the mirror and lenses found on photocopiers. (See Fig. 2-7.)

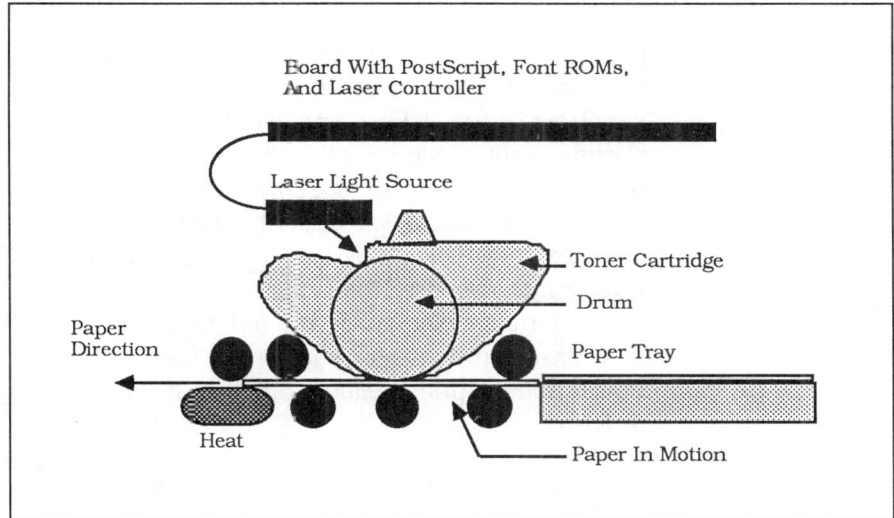

**Figure 2-7.** The laser images the surface of a xerographic drum, which is then transferred to the paper using a series of rollers and a heat-bonding process.

The laser beam images the xerographic drum as it rotates. Each line contains about 2400 pixels of information (8 inches by 300 dots per inch). The entire page is 10.9 inches long, resulting in 3270 pixels imaged vertically. The entire imaging surface (8 by 10.9 inches) contains 7,848,000 possible pixels that can be addressed. Since the printer sends a description of the entire page to the printer at one time, the printer obviously needs a great deal of memory and processing power to address those millions of possible dots.

There are two basic types of laser printers. The first type (such as a Hewlett-Packard LaserJet) uses cartridge or downloaded fonts for type and prints graphics as 300dpi bit-mapped graphics. The type resides in memory, so it does not have to be created as a bitmap like graphics. Graphics, however, are simply bit-mapped images that require a lot of memory to print. To image a full page at 300dpi, a minimum of 1mb of memory is required. Many laser printers are sold with only 128k of memory, so the number of graphics that can be printed on the page is very small. Most new laser printers entering the market are offering more than 1mb of memory for graphics. So if you are out shopping, be sure to get one that will image a whole page at 300dpi if you are planning to do almost anything in the way of graphics.

The second option, a page description language laser printer (such as one using the PostScript page descriptor language), is more expensive but much more flexible and powerful. Like dot-matrix printers in the bit-mapped graphics mode, the PostScript language does not need to define each possible pixel. For example, a horizontal rule 3 pixels high by 8 inches wide would not be described to the LaserWriter as "place a pixel at coordinate x1,y1; x1,y2; x1,y3, etc." Instead, PostScript would instruct the laser to start imaging at the starting point of the rule, keep the laser on until the beam has gone eight inches, go back, and do the same for two more pixel lines.

This efficient style of describing images allows the creation of intensely complex images such as type and art to be described to the printer by PostScript as opposed to having each bit on the page turned on or off in the classic bit-mapped manner. If a full page were to be described to the printer as a bit-mapped image, you would need 1mb of storage (RAM). With PostScript, the printer can accomplish imaging the page with only 1-1/2mb of RAM.

To do this, the information describing the page is stored in RAM, and the printer works with the native PostScript language to process those instructions into movements of the laser, turning it on and off to image the page.

Additionally, PostScript printers conserve memory and use true type fonts possible by holding the mathematically based descriptions of the type fonts in the printer's ROM (read only memory). A typical PostScript printer has 1/2mb of ROM, which holds the PostScript routines, three type families—Helvetica, Times, and Courier—and a symbol font. Each of the type styles features regular, bold, italic, and bold italic so the printer has thirteen type fonts located in its ROM. (See Fig. 2-8.)

A PostScript printer (such as the Apple LaserWriter Plus) offers the advantage of 1mb of ROM, which contains the PostScript routines, the Helvetica, Times, Courier, and symbol fonts, plus seven additional fonts—Palatino, ITC Avant Garde, ITC Bookman, Helvetica Narrow, New Century Schoolbook, ITC Zaph Chancery, and ITC Dingbats (a collection of cute symbols). Each of the additional fonts (except for ITC Zaph Chancery and ITC Dingbats) comes in regular, regular italic, bold, and bold italic. (See Fig. 2-9.)

Helvetica Regular
*Helvetica Italic*
**Helvetica Bold**
***Helvetica Bold Italic***

Times Regular
*Time Italic*
**Times Bold**
***Times Bold Italic***

Courier Regular
*Courier Italic*
**Courier Bold**
***Courier Bold Italic***

Symbols:
θωερτψυιοπασδφγη
jκλ;ζξχϖβνμ,.

**Figure 2-8.** Fonts available on a standard PostScript laser printer.

Helvetica Narrow Regular
*Helvetica Narrow Regular Oblique*
**Helvetica Narrow Bold**
***Helvetica Narrow Bold Oblique***

ITC Avant Garde Gothic Book
*ITC Avant Garde Gothic Book Oblique*
**ITC Avant Garde Gothic Book Demi**
***ITC Avant Garde Gothic Book Demi Oblique***

ITC Bookman Light
*ITC Bookman Light Italic*
**ITC Bookman Demi**
***ITC Bookman Demi Italic***

Palitino Regular
*Palitino Italic*
**Palitino Bold**
***Palitino Bold Italic***

New Century Schoolbook Regular
*New Century Schoolbook Italic*
**New Century Schoolbook Bold**
***New Century Schoolbook Bold Italic***

*ITC Zapf Chancery Medium Italic*

ITC Zapf Dingbats: ●▲✿✳✴✺✶✹●▼I▼□✺

**Figure 2-9.** Fonts available exclusively on the LaserWriter Plus.

**Hot Tip**

The Apple LaserWriter Plus costs about $800 more than a standard Apple LaserWriter, and a standard LaserWriter may be updated to a LaserWriter Plus at any time for that amount. Because Adobe—the manufacturer of the PostScript language, controller cards, and fonts—charges $185 for a typical family such as Palatino Regular, Palatino Regular Italic, Palatino Bold, and Palatino Bold Italic, the cost of buying downloadable versions of these fonts on disk (discussed in Chapter 3) would result in a cost of over $1200 to get the typographic resources of the LaserWriter Plus. As a result, if you like the type styles on the LaserWriter Plus, it is more economical to purchase it than use a standard LaserWriter with the same fonts in downloadable form. (See Fig. 2-10.)

**Figure 2-10.** The LaserWriter and the LaserWriter Plus are identical in appearance. Neither contain any complex controls, just simple lights to indicate the condition of the unit (such as a yellow light for when the unit is out of paper).

An RS-232C serial port allows such printers to work with virtually any computer. Any computer using a communications program and talking to a PostScript printer will let PostScript files be printed. There is often an additional special setting that allows the PostScript to emulate the Diablo 630 command set. This allows the units to act as letter-quality printers using the Courier monospaced font, controlled by any word-processing program that drives the Diablo 630 printer. The printers can, once a page is described to the printer (anywhere from a few seconds to a few minutes, depending on the complexity of the page), output pages at up to 8 per minute (although some new printers such as the Texas Instruments 2115 can output at up to 15 pages a minute). A wide variety of papers (even transparency materials) can be used, as can odd-size sheets and envelopes if the manual feed slot is employed.

Obviously, there is a lot that can be said about page description language printers, and there are books devoted exclusively to their workings. This discussion will give you a working knowledge of the units, their power, and why they are so important as part of your publishing system. The combination of the 300dpi imaging power, the PostScript language and controller, the excellent resident typefaces, and the ability to use with ease the printer from almost any computer makes page description language devices (such as PostScript printers) premiere personal publishing tools.

PC PageMaker comes with a set of advanced PostScript and Hewlett-Packard LaserJet printer drivers. These drivers are installed as Windows printers and can then be used by any Windows program. Printer support includes dot-matrix printers, bit-mapped laser printers, PostScript laser printers and typesetters, and in the near future (as of the time of this writing) the DDL (Document Description Language) printer language, which will initially be available from Imagen. Fig. 2-11 contains a list of printers currently supported by PC PageMaker.

## Hardware Supported by PC PageMaker

**Display Cards and Monitors**
EGA
Hercules
Conographic ConoVision 2800
Micro Display Systems Genius Display
Moniterm Viking 1
Wyse WY-700
(Other high-resolution displays that provide their own Windows drivers.)

**Scanners**
Canon IX-12
Datacopy 730, JetReader
Dest PC Scan
Microtek MS-300A
Ricoh IS-30

**Laser Printers**
Apple LaserWriter/LaserWriter Plus
Dataproducts LZR 2665
DEC PrintServer 40
HP LaserJet/LaserJet Plus
IBM Pageprinter 3812
Laser Connection PS Jet
QMS PS800, PS2400
TI OmniLaser 2108, 2115

**Typesetters**
Linotype 100, 300

**Dot-Matrix Printers**
C-Itoh 851
Epson FX-80, LQ 1500, MX-80 Graftrax
HP ThinkJet
IBM Pro Printer
NEC P2, P3
Okidata 92/93, 192/193
TI 850, 855
Toshiba P1351

Figure 2-11. Assorted hardware supported by Windows and PC PageMaker. Even more devices will be supported by the time this book is printed, so check with your dealer on updates to this list.

### Hard Disks

From the description of the laser printers, you can see that the imaging of a page in the highly graphic form used with a publishing system requires large data files. A typical PostScript file describing a 16-page document can take up to 270k of disk space. If you put enough pages together, you will quickly realize that you will need more storage space than any floppy disk can hold. A 10 or 20mb hard disk will do fine, but if you are just assembling your computer system, you may wish to opt for more storage space, such as with a 40mb hard disk.

### Hot Tip

An attractive storage system for your files is an internal 40mb hard disk. The current low prices of hard disks make it possible to have lots of extra storage space by using such a hard disk. That storage will be used more rapidly than you can imagine when doing desktop publishing. A disk this size will not only allow you to hold all of your word-processing, graphics, Windows, and PageMaker files and programs, but it will also allow you to not worry about running out of space. In building a serious publishing system, the mass storage offered by a hard disk will benefit you both by making available vast amounts of data and numerous programs and by providing a faster-working system.

## The Assembled System

The ideal publishing system as shown in Fig. 2-12 includes the speed and performance of the AT, the wonderful library of resident type families of the LaserWriter Plus or the large downloadable font library for the Hewlett-Packard LaserJet Plus, and the mass storage of a hard disk. In addition, the system should include a second disk drive (for easy duplication of disks, holding master disks for copy-protected software).

**Figure 2-12.** A simple publishing system: IBM AT, Hewlett-Packard LaserJet Plus, and PC PageMaker complete with Windows.

# Peripheral Hardware

Beyond your base publishing system, you will find that you can make your system even more powerful by adding a few key peripherals. Most are inexpensive yet will prove to be worth far more than their price.

The basic peripherals to your system fall into three categories: graphic input devices, mouse alternatives, and communication links.

Graphic input devices, quite simply, allow you to take real objects or images and convert them into a picture on the screen of your computer and print them on the final page. This process is called digitizing.

You no doubt have an opinion on the mouse. People either love it or hate it. I have come to truly appreciate the speed and simplicity of the mouse. However, there are definitely some activities (such as tracing a line drawing with great detail or writing or drawing as if I were holding a pen or pencil) I cannot perform with it. For these situations there are graphic input tablets. As described later, such tablets act as an electronic sheet of paper where you can write on the surface, replacing the mouse with a pencil-shaped stylus.

Finally, there will be times when not all the information in your publication will be created on your computer. You may wish to get information from an electronic bulletin board, on-line information service, or another computer. For such situations, you will need a modem, a cable for connecting to the modem or another computer, as well as the software to control the communications between your computer and the outside world.

## Scanners and Digitizers

Microcomputers are at a halfway point in the capture of real- world images for reproduction. The low resolution of computer screens and the vast amount of storage it takes to hold a high- resolution image electronically makes digitized images possible, but currently only for casual art.

Digitizers are great for reproducing line art, and are capable of creating a low-quality halftone of a photograph. Even though this may indicate that there are limitations on what can be digitized, it does not mean that digitizers are not truly useful devices.

Line art (such as drawings, type, and such unique items as company logos or signatures) can be digitized. Since the images are generally saved in paint file format, you may go in and clean up the images using the paint program's fatbits feature and eraser, as well as any of the drawing tools to enhance the digitized image. The ability to clean up line art makes it possible to incorporate company logos, technical drawings, and art that would be difficult to create from scratch using paint or draw programs. (See Fig. 2-13.)

**Figure 2-13.** Sample of a logo captured by a digitizer and then enhanced and cleaned up using the fatbits editing feature of a paint program.

Although line art reproduces well enough to be cleaned up, digitizing photographs presents a different set of conditions. Unlike line art, photography includes a full spectrum of grays. There is no way for a computer, working in a bit-mapped mode (pixels that are either black or white), to represent the color gray. It can only show black or white. The reproductions of photographs you see in magazines and newspapers face the same problem. A newspaper, for example, is printed only with black ink. To reproduce a photograph, a halftone must be made. This process may be a bit difficult to comprehend. In fact, a halftone is really an illusion. The photography you see is really a collection of black "dots" that are made larger or smaller. These dots are very small. When side by side, an illusion of the photographic original is created by the smaller dots giving the impression of light grays or no dot at all for white, and larger dots giving the impression of darker tones, including full-size dots side by side to represent black. All the dots are capable of being the same size (a full dot creates black), but instead the dots shrink in size to create a matrix of different sizes that give the impression of gray tones found in a photo. The easiest way to understand this is to examine a halftone from a newspaper. (See Fig. 2-14.)

**Figure 2-14.** A photograph that has been converted to a halftone using a screen placed in front of a piece of film that can create only black or white images. The screen converts the gray values into large or small dots.

If you look closely, you can see that this photo is made up of thousands of tiny dots. The more dots per inch, the finer the appearance of the halftone. Most newspapers use halftones that are made up of 65 lines of dots per inch. Most magazines use 133 lines per inch. Higher-quality printing allows halftone screens of up to 300 lines per inch, resulting in a halftone image with dots so small it is hard to tell that they are there at all! (See Fig. 2-15.)

**27** Selecting the Right Hardware

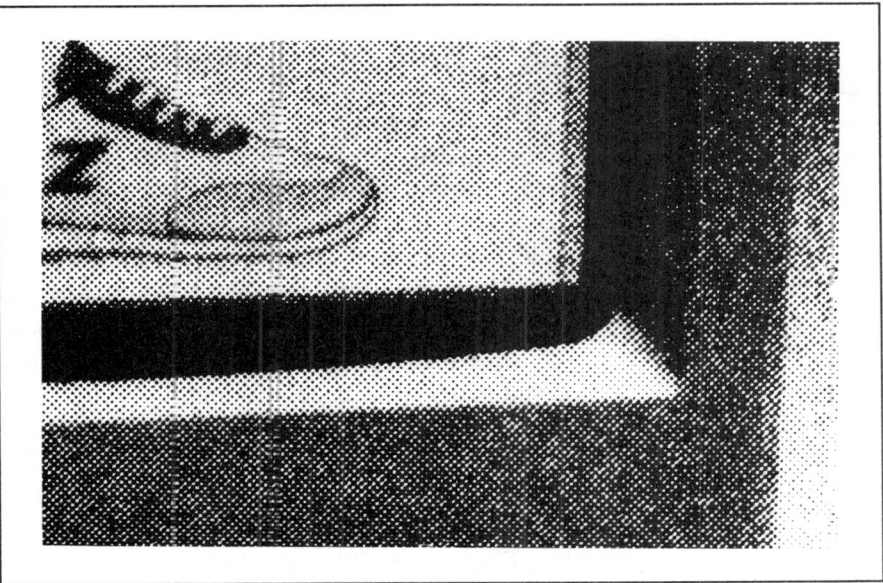

**Figure 2-15.** When magnified, the dot pattern and the various sizes of dots that make up a halftone can be seen. Note that all the dots are part of a grid that allows them to be the same size, but they are made larger and smaller to simulate gray.

The reproduction of photographs uses a process not unlike that of the computer screen—a matrix of dots. However, unlike the dots in a halftone, computer dots (pixels) can be only one size. They cannot shrink to create an illusion of gray value information. Pixels on a computer can be either black or white, and all are the same size. As you can see, this creates a real dilemma when it comes to creating an electronic halftone. There are ways for a halftone to be created, but as of now, the results are not of a quality equal to the film halftones used in conventional printing.

For example, using a laser printer with a resolution of 300dpi, it is conceivable that you could create a halftone dot matrix of 5 by 5 pixels, or 60dpi (in 5-pixel matrix dots). Each matrix contains a 25-dot grid that can be filled with varying numbers of pixels to create a gray tone. For example, a very light gray would have only one pixel made black in the very center of the matrix, and a black would be made of turning all 25 pixels in the matrix to black pixels. The various combinations in between would, conceptually, give you a workable set of gray-scale information from which to create a halftone.

>  **Helpful Hint**
>
> This works great conceptually, but it cannot be executed very well. The devices that can work out this complex system are very expensive, and the resulting electronic halftones take a long time to create and require an enormous amount of storage space on your disk drives. For all practical purposes, if your publication needs a good halftone and is going to be reproduced using conventional offset printing, the best way to get it is to have a professional printer create a film halftone for you and place it in your publication as a film negative or as a positive version that you add to your page.

This does not mean that photographs and digitizers cannot work well together. Far from it. The current scanner can create pretty good halftones, but they just cannot equal the quality that we are used to in other printed matter.

There are a number of scanners available for digitizing line art and halftones for the AT that are inexpensive and create impressive, high-quality images.

**Scanners**

There are many flat art scanners available in the $1,000 to $5,000 price range that can not only digitize line art and photography (Fig. 2-16) but act as optical character recognition device (OCR) as well. With an OCR, you can scan a typed or typeset page and read the text on the page into your computer as a text file. This is very practical when you have to reenter the text of documents that were not supplied to you in electronic form. There are a number of models of scanners in various configurations from Canon, Datacopy, Microtek, Abaton, Princeton Graphic Systems, Hewlett-Packard, Ricoh, AST, and a growing list of new companies.

Flat art scanners come in two varieties: flatbed and sheetfed. Each serves a special purpose and should be considered.

When scanning line art, such as a company logo or precision art work, a flatbed scanner is best. The flatbed scanner has a flat glass platen where you place the art and a cover that holds the art in place, much like a photocopier. The advantage here is that you can move the original on the platen for precise adjustment. Since the image is being scanned at 300 lines per inch, a straight line on the original art, if not perfectly parallel to the scanning element, will result in a line that runs up or downhill, having a ragged effect from the pixels attempting to create this slanted line. With a flatbed scanner, you can lift the cover, and nudge the art to correct the placement to be parallel and thus scanned correctly.

If you were to use a sheetfed scanner, where the art is pulled across the imaging element with rollers, it is hard, and sometimes impossible, to align the art with any degree of accuracy. The sheetfed scanner does have real advantages in other areas.

Sheetfed scanners are perfect for scanning a large number of casual art originals where alignment is not crucial and are especially useful when using OCR features to scan a large number of pages. If you had a 20-page document that you were performing an OCR scan on, the sheetfed device allows you to load up the document and let the scanner feed the sheets for you, freeing you from the chore.

**Figure 2-16.** Halftone created with a Datacopy JetReader.

### Graphic Input Tablets

Even though a mouse is an intuitive and deceptively powerful movement device, there are times where an alternative to the mouse can be more effective. A classic example is creating your signature. No matter how hard you may try, it is very difficult to create your signature accurately using the mouse. It just isn't good for that type of cursor movement.

**Hot Tip**

A practical and attractive alternative to the mouse is a graphic input tablet. Like a sheet of paper, a graphic input tablet is a flat surface where, using a penlike stylus, you may write or draw just as you would on paper. The movements are captured on screen with a paint program. With a bit of practice, the device will help you with creating freehand art but will not replace the mouse as a pointing and cursor-movement device.

Graphic tablets, as indicated in the preceding Hot Tip, will help you with art and freehand sketching that would be difficult with a mouse. The tablets are large, often about a foot square, and have an electronic stylus, a pen-shaped pointer that has a button on it that acts in the same way as the mouse button. When you place the stylus on the pad, moving the stylus will move the cursor. If you are using a pencil or brush drawing tool, for example, when you press the button, the drawing tool will start and continue until you release the button. The stylus must act both as the pointing device and the drawing tool, and the button allows you to control which action it performs. (See Fig. 2-17.)

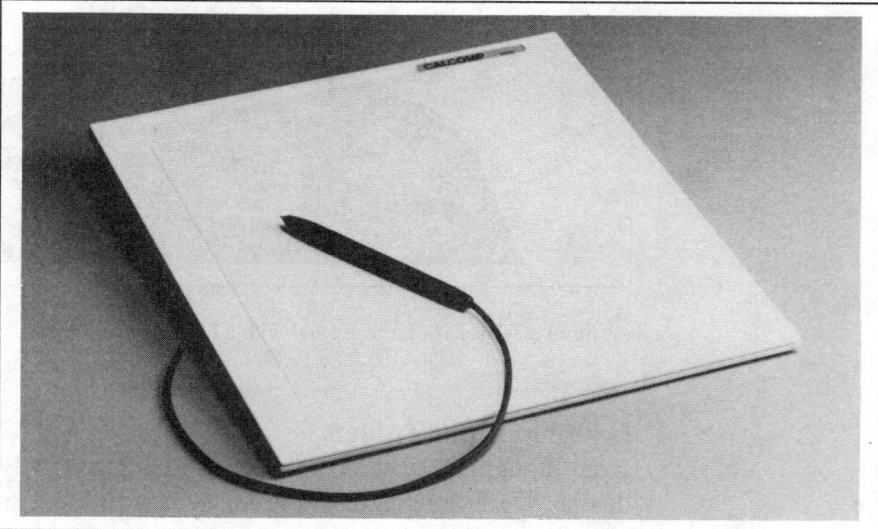

**Figure 2-17.** A graphic input tablet.

## Communication Links

Your publishing system will be lacking if it cannot communicate with the outside world. This is done with a modem and, if you have another computer (such as a Macintosh or an IBM PC or clone), a null modem cable.

Why do you need a modem? For many purposes. It will allow you to communicate with other computer owners, transfer text files from an author or field office computer, and access the wonderful world of on-line information services (such as CompuServe and The Source). Also, and this is perhaps the most important reason, it will allow you to transfer your PC PageMaker files to a professional typographer who can output your files on a typesetting machine at a resolution of up to 2,540dpi. Using such a typesetting service allows you to get the ultimate in quality from your documents. Output on a typesetter, they are of a quality equal to that found in any book or magazine. Of course, this service is an additional cost. You can proof your page on the laser printer, send it via your modem to a typesetter, and get back an exact duplicate of the laser-printed page except that the resolution will be much higher than that of the 300dpi the LaserWriter is capable of.

This option is for special documents. A good case study would be a company who produces financial reports. The monthly reports it produces are perfect for printing on the LaserWriter, but once a year it creates Annual Reports for shareholders and wants the type in the Annual Reports to be of the highest quality. A modem allows them to send their pages for output on an Allied 300P typesetter at 2,540dpi. This way they have the best of both worlds: inexpensive laser-printer-produced type for day-to-day activity and top-quality typesetter output when needed.

The AT is connected to a modem by a cable connected to a serial port of the computer. If you use another computer, either a Macintosh or an IBM PC, you will find it desirable to connect the two computers with a cable. The cable connects to the serial ports of the computers but requires a special cable called a null modem cable. The cable is the same as the one used to connect a modem, except that it switches two of the wires used inside the cable. It is a small distinction, but without it the two computers would never be able to talk to one another.

With the correct software (covered in Chapter 3), you will be able to transfer files directly between the two computers without using a modem. This is essential if you have only one phone line If you connected your two computers, each to its own modem, each would need its own phone line to call the other. Obviously, a direct link (such as the null modem cable) is much more practical.

>
> 
> **Hot Tip**
> 
> Communication is becoming an increasingly important part of personal publishing and computer use in general, making a modem purchase a wise decision. One word of advice: Purchase a modem that is either a Hayes or adheres completely to the Hayes protocols. Others will not work with all software and will result in trouble in the communication process. Hayes is the standard, and why buck the system on something as terribly tedious as telecommunications?

## A Turnkey System

As you can tell from all the possible product combinations, putting together a desktop publishing system takes careful thought and planning. It is your responsibility to assemble the right hardware and software—and make sure it all works together. An easier solution is a turnkey system—one where all components have been assembled for you. With such a system, you simply unpack the components, attach a few cables to connect them and, in essence, turn the key to start the system by turning on the power. In such a system, all the software is installed on a hard disk. The system has been configured so that you start work immediately and do not have to try and set up all the components yourself. If you are attracted to this approach, a perfect system for you may be the IBM Solution Pac Personal Publishing System. As described above, the system comes with everything you need, from software to a mouse, and all the configuration problems have been taken care of for you.

The Personal Publishing System from IBM (Fig. 2-18) comes with the following: An IBM Personal Computer Model 30, 20mb hard disk, graphics monitor, mouse, IBM Personal PagePrinter, PostScript expansion card (which allows the Personal PagePrinter to function as a PostScript printer), PC PageMaker, Windows, and MS DOS. The list price of the system is $8,533.

If you already own an IBM computer such as an AT or a Model 30, IBM offers an upgrade kit to bring your system up to the Personal Publishing System level. This includes the PostScript card, the Personal PagePrinter, and the software already mentioned for the price of $5,795.

33  Selecting the Right Hardware

**Figure 2-18.** The IBM Solution Pac Personal Publishing System features the IBM Model 30 personal computer (shown) and the IBM Personal PagePrinter.

## The Final System

So there you have all the hardware you will need to have a complete publishing system on your table or desktop. You are probably asking yourself: "That's a lot of equipment—what's it all going to cost me?"

Assuming that you own none of the equipment and that you go to a store and work with list prices and have not yet begun negotiating the price, I have computed the prices of a minimum and maximum system at current prices (March 1987, but, remember, they keep dropping). Please note that the prices do not include software.

| Hardware | Cost |
|---|---|
| **Minimum System** | |
| AT Compatible | $1,900 |
| 40mb Hard Drive | $900 |
| Hercules Card | $299 |
| White Phosphor Monitor | $250 |
| Mouse | $125 |
| HP LaserJet II | $2,495 |
| Modem | $399 |
| **Total:** | **$6,368** |
| **Maximum System** | |
| IBM AT | $3,995 |
| 40mb Hard Disk | $900 |
| 360k Floppy Disk Drive | $299 |
| Mouse | $125 |
| Wyse WY-700 HRM Display System | $995 |
| TI OmniLaser 2115 PostScript Laser Printer | $7,995 |
| Modem | $399 |
| Graphic Input Tablet | $499 |
| Digitizer | $2,999 |
| Serial Port Switcher | $49 |
| Null Modem Cable | $39 |
| **Total:** | **$18,294** |

Start off small, or if you have the need and financial resources, take full advantage of the amazing power of the maximum system. If you already own an IBM AT, the upgrade to a personal publishing system will be a reasonable investment. Either way, if you purchase any sort of professional typesetting services or graphic arts services, such a system should be able to pay for itself in a short period of time.

Dollar savings may at first be the most attractive reason to purchase a publishing system, but as a user myself, it is the power the system affords me that has been the most beneficial, not the money it has saved me.

# Selecting the Right Software 3

*I*n the beginning of Chapter 2, I called hardware the heart of the publishing system. This chapter will introduce you to its soul, the software needed to drive all that hardware.

In writing this chapter, I am especially impressed by the power and abilities of the software covered here. It will allow you to do amazing things. You will start with a blank screen, and in a very short time be able to convert that blank page into a page full of type and graphics.

Since the beginning of the book, I have stressed that you must build a system. This rule is very evident in the selection of software. All the programs you will use in your publishing system, when assembled and under the control of Windows, will act as one complete publishing program.

## A Natural System

If you examine the path you follow in producing your publication, or almost any other publication, you will discover that there is a well-defined process involved in publishing. The steps are remarkably simple, but often look complex when you are doing them, simply because you are in the middle of doing detailed work.

The functions that your personal publishing system software should allow you to perform are:

> **Capturing text**
>
> **Formatting text**
>
> **Creating graphic elements**
>
> **Integrating type and graphics into page form**

It's that simple. Now stop and think about what you do when you create a document or publication. You write it, perhaps have it typeset or print it out on a letter-quality printer, get photographs or line art that will be included, then finally paste those elements together page by page so that they may be reproduced. This is the "publishing process."

The goal in gathering software for your publishing system is to duplicate those tasks, only in an electronic fashion. Ideally, all of the functions detailed above should take place directly from your system and never involve manual assistance of any kind.

The following discussion examines which software will allow you to convert your manual efforts to electronic activity in each of the publishing functions previously listed.

## Capturing Text

Most of your time in producing any publication is spent writing, editing, or rekeying text. If you currently own a computer, you are most likely already doing this on your PC.

The choice of word-processing programs to use with PC PageMaker is quite large; chances are you may already be using one of the supported word-processing programs. If not, you can still work with PC PageMaker if your word-processing program can create clean ASCII text files.

PC PageMaker keeps as much formatting information in your word-processing program as it can. For example, it will keep boldface or underline, justification commands, and some indent information from WordStar. Word-processing programs that use true typographic conventions (such as Microsoft Word) allow you to set type size and style, line spacing in points, paragraph indents, and many other such conventions. PC PageMaker uses these features when placing type on a page, so there is very little formatting to do on the page if you have done it in such a word-processing program. (See Figs. 3-1 and 3-2.)

At the other end of the spectrum, a straight ASCII text file will allow virtually no formatting. All formatting will take place in PC PageMaker. Don't worry; it's easy to do within the program.

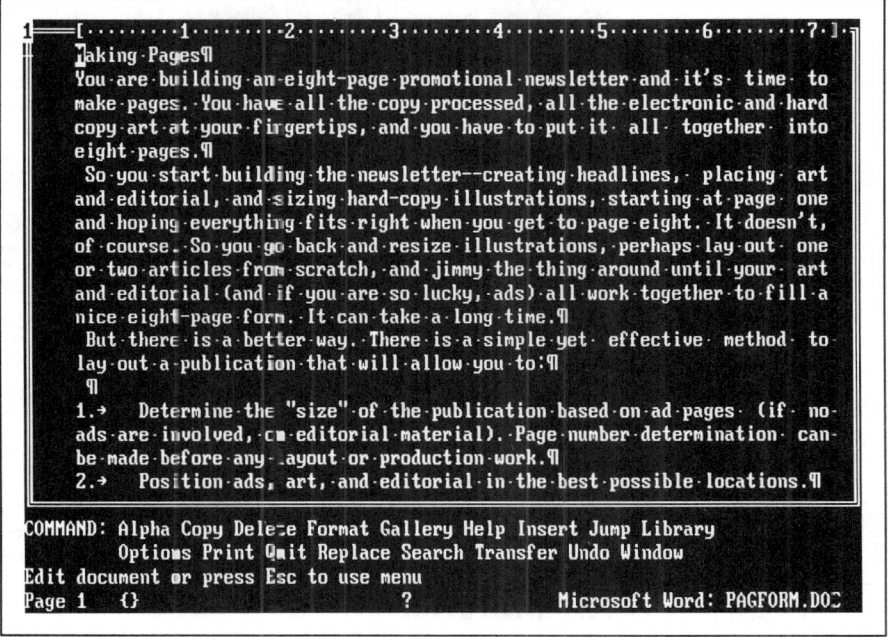

Figure 3-1. An unformatted text file from an ASCII word-processing program.

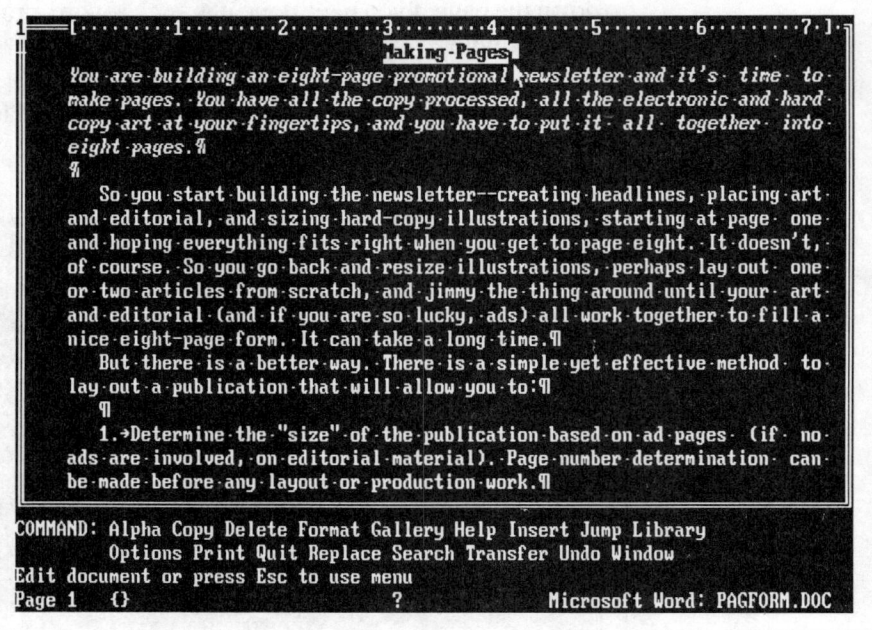

**Figure 3-2.** The same file formatted as type directly in Microsoft Word.

### Helpful Hint

It is best to format text files as completely as possible in the word-processing program. Although PageMaker does have text-editing features and the ability to format type, it is slower and not as fully featured as the word-processing programs. It also lacks features such as search and replace.

### PC PageMaker Conversions

Type is quite different from word-processed text. Many characters used in typesetting are simply not available with word processors. Such characters include open and close quotes instead of the simple standard quote; long dashes, called em dashes, instead of two hyphens; possessive apostrophies instead of the single quote used for both apostrophies and foot marks. Special indents for the beginning line in a paragraph and special spacing between paragraphs are also available from typesetting.

Fortunately, rather than having you place special ASCII characters or codes for these characters, PC PageMaker allows you to keep using standard quotes, hyphens, and apostrophies and converts them for you automatically when you place word-processor files in PC PageMaker. Taking a word or words in quotes, it will change the first quote mark into an open quote and the second quote into a close quote. When only one quote is preceded by a number (such as used for indicating inches), it remains an inch mark character. Double hyphens convert to an em dash, and apostrophies convert to typographic possessive apostrophies unless they follow numbers indicating the foot mark character. From a paragraph menu, you can also define first line paragraph indents and the amount of space between paragraphs.

PC PageMaker saves you a lot of time and trouble with such automatic formatting.

**File Transfer Programs**

As mentioned in Chapter 2, your system should include such hardware as a modem and a null modem adapter cable to allow for file transfers. You will need software to control the transfer of files between your computers, either by modem or by direct link between two computers.

For telecommunications with a modem, you will need a telecommunication program (such as SmartCom II from Hayes or inTalk from Palantir), both of which are available for both the IBM and the Macintosh and allow modem communications or direct file transfers between computers. (See Fig. 3-3.) Telecommunication programs allow you to transfer files from computer to computer and access information services (such as CompuServe or The Source) and electronic bulletin boards. The programs handle the sending and saving of files and other such disk-based activities for you.

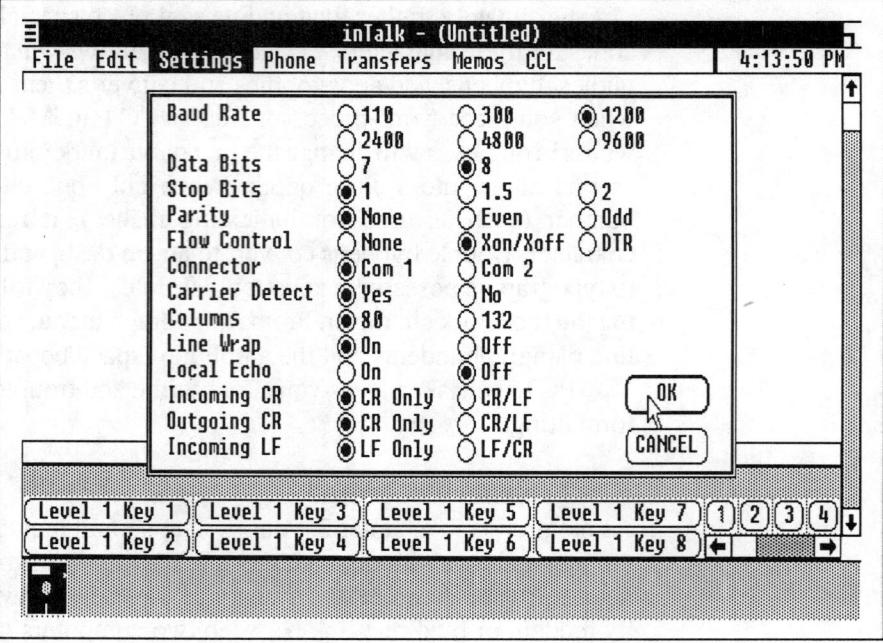

**Figure 3-3.** The screen from Palantir inTalk, a Windows-based telecommunications program. Everything you need to telecommunicate easily is contained on menus or icons, making it one of the easier telecommunication programs to use.

In addition to telecommunication programs, if you connect two computers to transfer files, you could use the telecommunication programs in a terminal mode (simply waiting for data from whatever it is connected to). There is a better answer; it will make the process much less difficult.

Such Programs as MacLink (DataViz, Inc.) and The Missing Link (PC QuikArt) are designed expressly for the purpose of file transfer, primarily between the Macintosh and the IBM PC. They allow a quick, simple file transfer process with a null modem cable.

Of the two, MacLink is especially useful in that it not only transfers text and data but also keeps the formatting from many of the data files of programs such as WordStar, MultiMate, Multiplan, and Word. When these files are transferred, attributes such as margins, boldface, underline, and other such formatting is kept intact. This saves a lot of formatting time. (See Fig. 3-4.)

The Missing Link is a graphics transfer utility between Macintosh and IBM paint files and between various IBM paint program formats (such as PC Paintbrush to Windows Paint). The big advantage here is that the huge library of electronic clip-art for the Macintosh can be transfered over to the IBM for use in PageMaker.

Both programs have error-checking protocols, so data transfer is next to flawless. If you are going to be using data from IBM PCs, either one of these programs is essential.

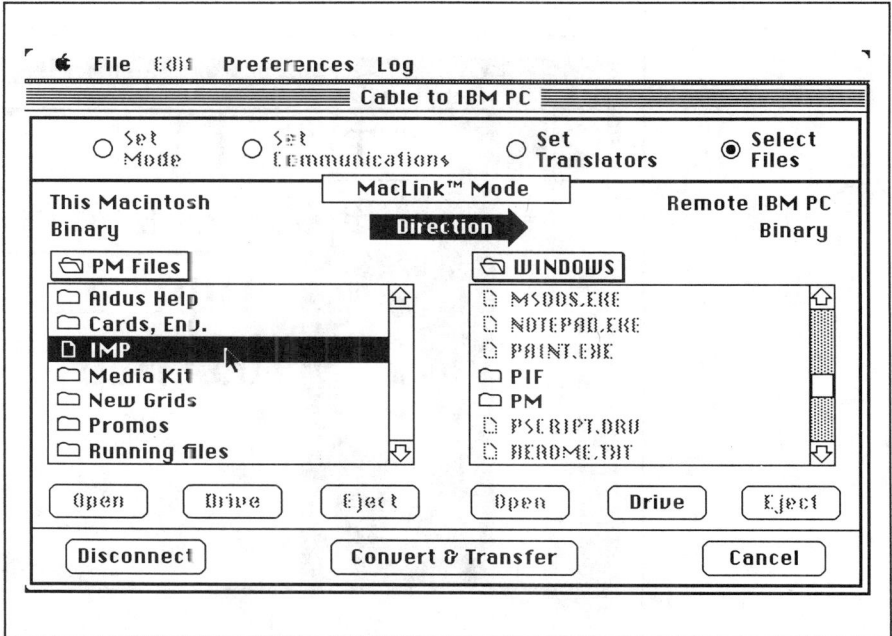

**Figure 3-4.** Macintosh screen from MacLink indicating the conversion of files between the Macintosh and the IBM PC. Note that it indicates file formats, which allows you to retain the formatting attributes in the file during the file transfer.

## Creating Graphic Elements

For too long, if you had to prepare a document, report, newsletter, or publication, the creation of illustrations was time consuming, expensive, and usually required the use of an artist or design service. As a result, many publications ended up as pages and pages of type, with very few illustrations to enhance or articulate the information in the text.

The good news is that the door has opened for the creation of professional-looking graphics in personal publishing. With the availability of very easy-to-use drawing programs, charting programs, and even clip-art (files of predrawn graphics to be used as needed), you can now produce graphics quickly, inexpensively, and without sending out for help.

Graphics programs for the IBM PC world come in three varieties. The first is the free-form paint package (such as Windows Paint or PC Paintbrush) where you create graphics and drawings from scratch. These programs allow you to create a wide range of bit-mapped drawings, from abstract renderings all the way to highly structured presentation graphics complete with type. (See Fig. 3-5.)

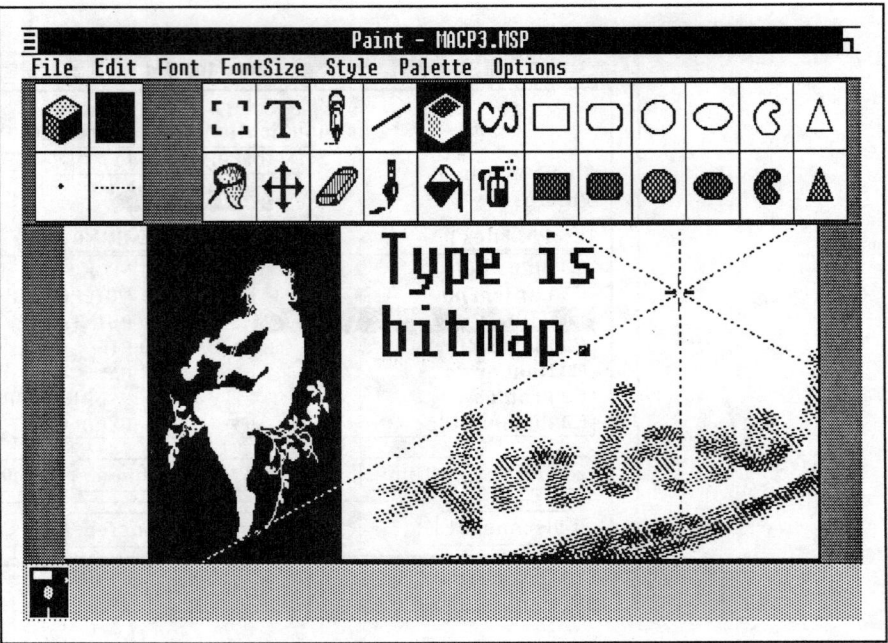

**Figure 3-5.** The Windows Paint screen. Here, just about any image you can imagine can be created using the simple drawing tools represented on the menu.

## Paint Programs

Paint programs use a drawing system called bit-mapped graphics, which allows you to control each addressable pixel on the screen (a pixel is the smallest point on a screen that can be presented as either black or white). Bit-mapped graphics can be modified, stretched, condensed, inverted, rotated, and outlined. You may even magnify the screen to a fatbits mode where you may edit your drawing pixel by pixel.

For these reasons, paint programs prove to be an effective, multipurpose drawing tool. If you are creative, a paint program will allow you to create drawings quickly and precisely.

Paint programs, even when printed on a PostScript printer, are still bit-mapped images. They are usually limited to the screen resolution they were created at, so they will not allow smooth circles or slanted lines, and type will be bit-mapped, not actual type. This can be used to an advantage in some cases, but many times you will want a drawing with real type, perfectly smooth arcs, circle, and slanted lines. For this, you should use draw packages.

## Draw Programs

For more complex drawings and drawings that will print at the actual resolution of your output device, you will need to use a structured drawing program. It uses many of the same principles and techniques of a paint program, but it is intended for more advanced uses such as drafting, charting, making drawings that may be enlarged or reduced dramatically, and working in pages larger than standard 8-1/2 by 11 inches. Unlike paint programs, object-oriented drawing programs work with a coordinate system, remembering where lines, circles, and shapes start and stop. It connects those shapes with the width and texture of line you desire and will fill those shapes with patterns or solids if indicated. What makes draw programs special is that when you enlarge or reduce a drawing, it actually redraws the shape to the new size. It connects the shapes with the same rule width as the original drawing and refills the drawing with a desired texture if chosen.

This procedure is quite different from paint programs, which enlarge or reduce drawings much like a magnifying glass. To illustrate this, examine the simple triangles in Fig. 3-6, which are created with a paint program (PC Paint) and a draw program (Windows Draw). Each is then enlarged to 200 percent of its original size.

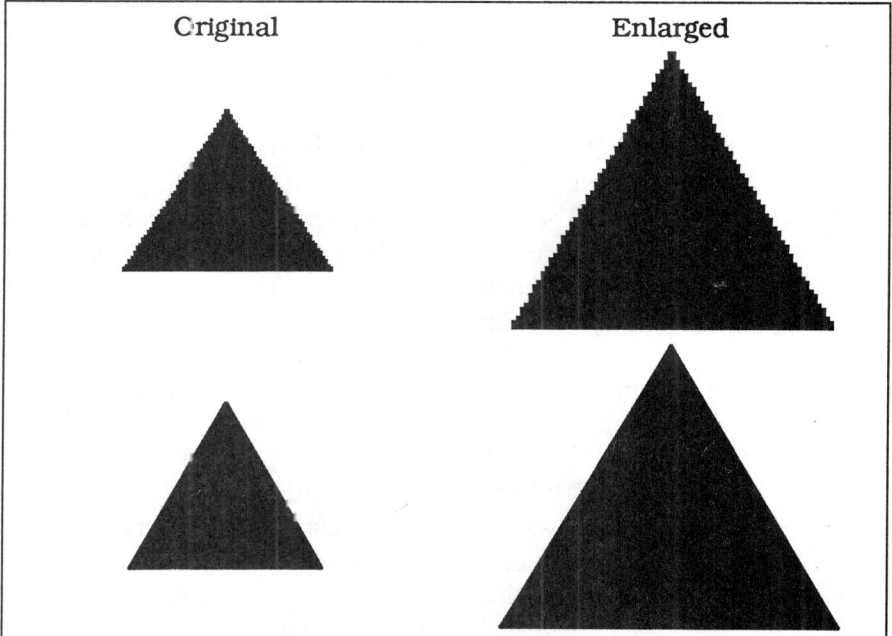

**Figure 3-6.** Two triangles. The ones on the top are created in PC Paint; the ones on the bottom in Windows Draw. Note that when enlarged, the bit-mapped paint drawing becomes distorted, but the draw triangle, being plotted by coordinates, is redrawn smoothly. All were printed on an Apple LaserWriter.

Note that by using bit-mapped graphics, the paint program's enlarged drawing simply magnifies the ragged slopes of the triangle sides. Also, the pattern inside the triangle is enlarged, making a visible, exaggerated dot pattern.

The Windows Draw enlargement holds up much better. The rules that make up the triangle have been completely redrawn at the new size, keeping the weight of the rule the same, and there is no ragged quality to the line. Additionally, it refills the pattern inside the triangle, keeping the same pattern as in the original drawing.

This quality makes it possible to create very complex drawings at a large size, then reduce them, keeping all the quality of the larger original. It also allows small drawings to be made larger without distortion and enables you to change the proportions of a drawing without changing the quality.

Object-oriented graphics are also created by programs such as AutoCAD, PostScript, and even from Lotus 1-2-3 PIC files when imported into a draw-based program for modification.

## Clip Art

Not everyone can sit down and create drawings from scratch, especially when it comes to drawing people, buildings, cars, fancy borders, and banners and using special type fonts and other such artistic enhancements. Fortunately, there are now a number of clip-art packages that contain ready-to-use drawings for your publications.

Clip-art programs are usually created in the paint format and can be used by PC PageMaker by placing them on a page like any other paint file. The drawings may be modified with paint programs.

The drawings range from outright bad to exceptionally good, so you will want to preview all of the drawings in a clip-art package before purchasing it. Most good computer stores keep a clip-art sample book of the packages they sell. Each of the drawings has been printed out for you to examine. Choosing the right set of drawings can be difficult, but, fortunately, many packages have been grouped in a sensible fashion, such as borders, letters, or drawings of people. Figs. 3-7 and 3-8 show the variety of clip-art images available.

There are also clip-art files of draw art, such as clip-art collections for Windows Draw (Micrografx). Such a library is quite useful since the art may be modified in dozens of ways. The rule widths can be changed, patterns can be made different, and the drawing can be stretched in various directions, enlarged and reduced, with no loss of quality. Draw-based clip-art is often more stiff and structured, but as the Windows Draw clip art shows, it doesn't have to be.

**Figure 3-7.** Samples of electronic clip-art from PC Quik-Art in a paint format, although these drawings are paint files using a 300dpi resolution.

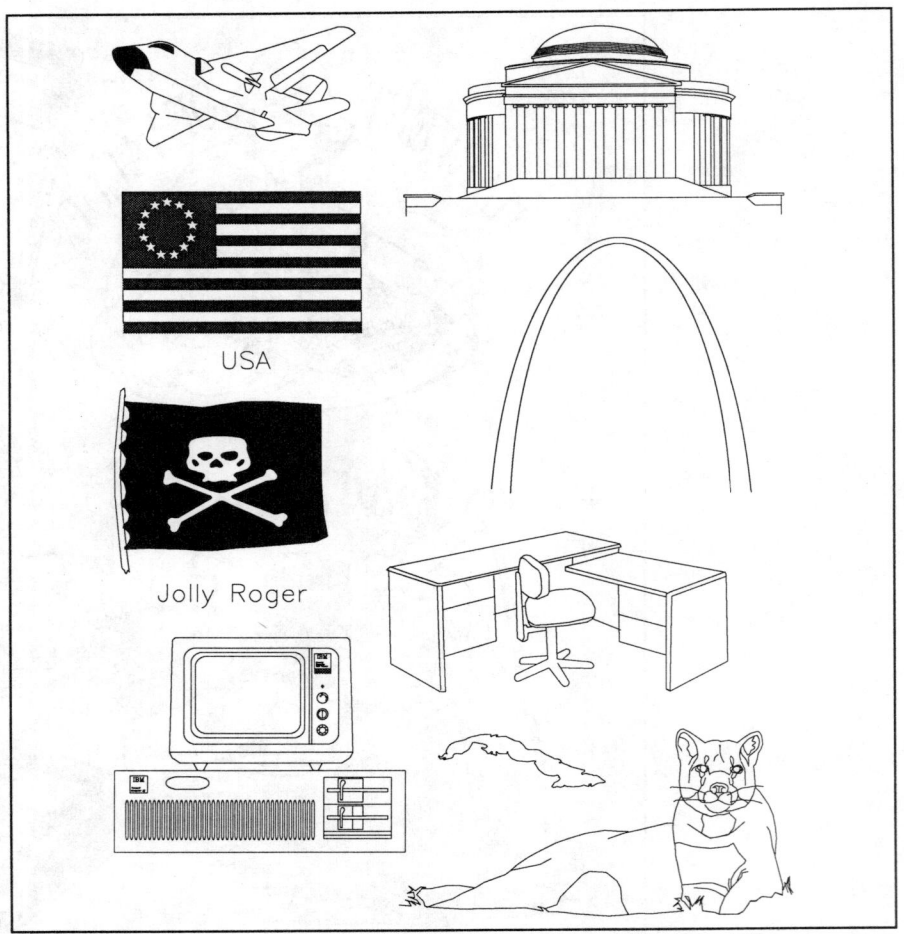

**Figure 3-8.** Samples of electronic clip art from Micrografx Windows Draw, which are all draw-based object-oriented graphics that can be modified and resized without loss of quality.

## Charts

One of the most difficult and time-consuming tasks is producing charts and graphs. It requires taking statistical data and converting it into accurate graphic representations that not only inform but are also attractive. Charts and graphs are some of the most commonly used publication and presentation graphics, and creating them requires a special type of program. A few determined souls could produce charts and graphs from scratch using paint or draw programs, but this would be pointless since there are excellent charting programs available.

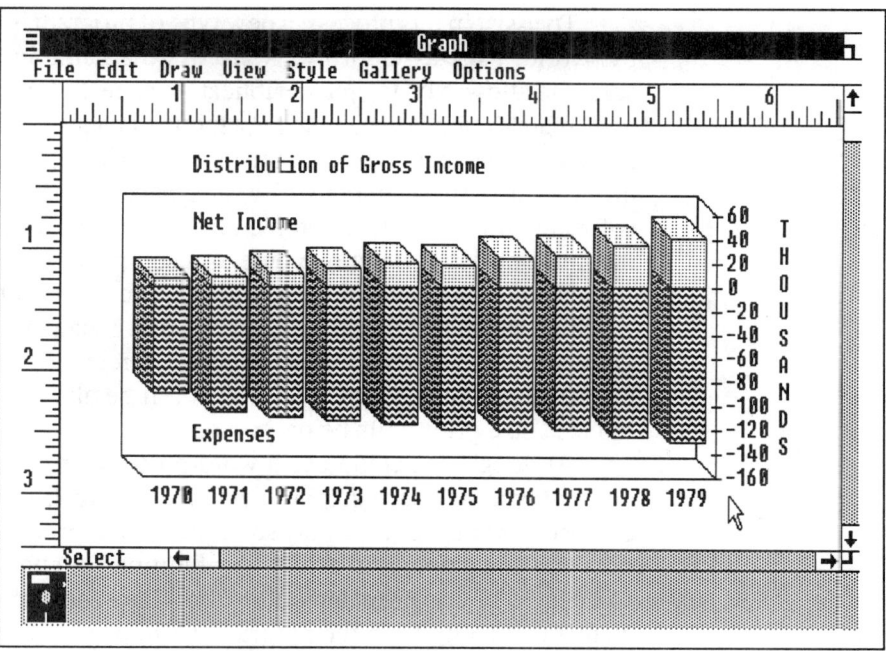

**Figure 3-9.** A sample of Windows Graph in action, creating a bar chart, and adding dimension to the chart to achieve an attractive three-dimensional quality.

Charting packages (such as Micrografx Windows Graph shown in Fig. 3-9) offer a combination spreadsheet/statistical analysis program and graphics package all in one. They allow you to enter all the values needed for your chart or graph at one time into a spreadsheet-style grid. They then take that information and draw line charts, bar charts, pie charts, scatter charts, and combinations of those styles. Once the data has been entered, you may redraw the chart as many times as you wish, in as many styles as you wish. Labels, headlines, and additional graphic elements may be added to the drawing, allowing you to customize it to your most demanding specifications.

## Page Assembly Software

At this point you have been introduced to software packages that allow you to create text files using a word-processing program and a variety of illustrations using paint and draw packages, charting programs, and clip-art. The final step in preparing your publication is to put all those elements together in publication form.

To assist in this process, a new type of program is available for the IBM PC world: page assembly software. As the name implies, page assembly software allows you to create publication pages. Working with this program, you create a publication, which is a group of pages that is usually in a column format (more than one column of type per page) and contains several different text files, graphic files, and page elements. The page assembly software allows you to assemble all of these pieces quickly and then print them in finished form at one time as a complete publication.

Using this type of program allows you to assemble pieces of text and graphics, much like a keyline-pasteup artist assembles them on an art board. Only you'll be assembling them on the screen of the computer, using the mouse to move pieces of type, and you'll be able to preview the page at a reduced size prior to its being printed.

Although you could use a word-processing program to assemble columns of type and place graphic elements, it is much easier to work in the page environment of page assembly software. Word-processing programs display only text and graphics in actual size, limiting your ability to study the design of a page. They do not offer tools to draw lines, boxes, and other such graphic elements directly from the program, as do page assembly packages.

The purpose of page assembly software is to allow you to assemble your publication much in the same manner as if you were to do it with galleys of type, graphics, and photostats, using rulers, T-squares, and paste. They allow you to move elements about on a page with little difficulty, enabling you to pursue a what-if attitude toward the page being created. Since the page is presented to you at a reduced size on the screen, you are constantly aware of its appearance, much as an artist uses a reduced-size photostat of a page to study its design.

Page assembly software provides a special set of features that will make producing your publications much more efficient. Page assembly programs are the great integrators. They are the only programs that allow you to take data files from a wide range of programs and bring them together in one common environment: the page.

## Downloadable Type Fonts

The last software you will aquire will be new typefaces for use in your publications. These are type fonts that use the full resolution of the printing device you are using, but rather than residing in the printer's ROM, they come on disk for downloading to the printer.

Laser printers, typesetters, and even many dot-matrix printers are capable of using such fonts by storing them in the machine's RAM and using them just as they would a resident type font. In addition, you must install screen versions of the fonts so that you can place them on a page and your program will know how to instruct the printer to access them.

Downloading the fonts is a simple matter. You can use either a special download program that comes with the fonts or the automatic downloading routine in PC PageMaker, which will call the fonts from the disk for you. Either way, it is quite easy.

Laser resolution fonts come from a variety of suppliers, and the variety of fonts entering the market should allow you to find the type style you need for your publication if you have to match one that you are currently using.

## Electronic Page Assembly

The remainder of this book will examine how to combine text and graphics files using a page assembly program called PC PageMaker (Aldus Corporation). The result is a publication created electronically. Once you work with such a system, you will experience control and flexibility in your publication work. The age of electronic page assembly has arrived!

The many file formats this great integrator supports is illustrated in Fig. 3-10. Study the list before you go out and buy any programs. It may contain programs you already have and use.

**Software Supported by PC PageMaker**

**Word-Processing Programs**
Microsoft Word
WordStar 3.3
MultiMate
XyWrite III
WordPerfect
Windows Write
IBM DCA Format (includes Samna Word, DisplayWrite 3, WordStar 2000, Office Writer, and Volkswriter 3)
ASCII Text

**Graphics Programs**
Windows Paint
Windows Draw
Windows Graph
In*a*Vision
PC Paint
PC Paintbrush
PublisherUs Paintbrush
AutoCAD (ADI format)
Lotus 1-2-3 (PIC format)
Symphony (PIC format)
Windows GDI Metafiles
TIFF Files
Encapsulated PostScript Files

**Figure 3-10.** The many word-processing and graphics file formats that can be opened directly by PC PageMaker.

Part Two    The Nature
            of the
            Printed
            Page

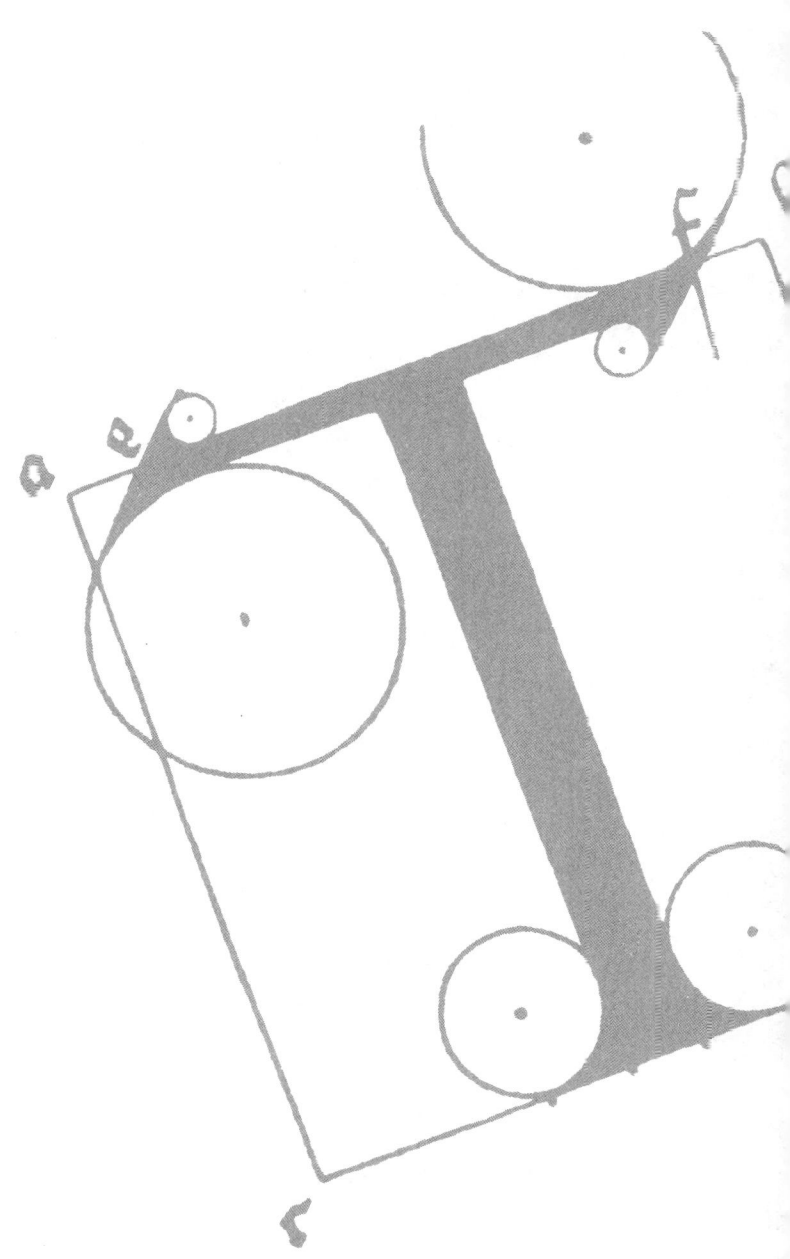

# The Page    4

*T*he page is similar to the trees in the forest. Imagine how hard it would be to envision the forest you are standing in when you can see only the trees that surround you. The trees are beautiful. They all are. It gets dark, and soon you are lost.

Imagine being a forest ranger high above the trees. From that height, you can see not only the beauty of the trees but also the grandeur of the forest. You are above the forest and in control. The forest ranger has the best of all possible situations. He or she can climb down and walk through the woods or climb the tower and view the trees as a whole, examining the intricate patterns and colors they create.

No, I'm not rambling, I'm simply stating an obvious trait that most people have when they start creating documents and publications. They are wrapped up in words and letters. They get hung up on the most minute detail (such as the absolute right word), yet they do not look at the page. Beautiful words on an ugly page make beautiful words look ugly.

Like the forest ranger, you have to be in command and be able to climb the tower and view the page as a landscape, as a whole. You must also, like the ranger, be able to go down and examine your words from their roots up.

If this all sounds philosophical, it is. Page assembly is not simply a mechanical or electronic activity; it is a way of looking at pages. If you are going to be the one who puts the page together, that means that you are responsible for everything on it. It means that you must be in control of the page and have the power to make it look the way you want it to. To achieve this level of skill involves a philosophical approach. Before you can attempt to assemble a page with any authority or skill, you must first understand what a page is, what its role is, and how it relates to those who read it.

## Many Hats

Page assembly requires that you wear many hats. You must be a writer, editor, proofreader, artist, and critic. Putting a publication, newsletter, or document together is an art. We now have technology that allows us to perform that art ourselves. In the past, we often relied on artists, typesetters, or printers to control the appearance of our works. With personal publishing technology, that responsibility now rests on your shoulders.

I am not going to concentrate on the words that go into your publication—just their value and how to place them. To understand the nature of a page, you must first examine what a page is and what goes on it.

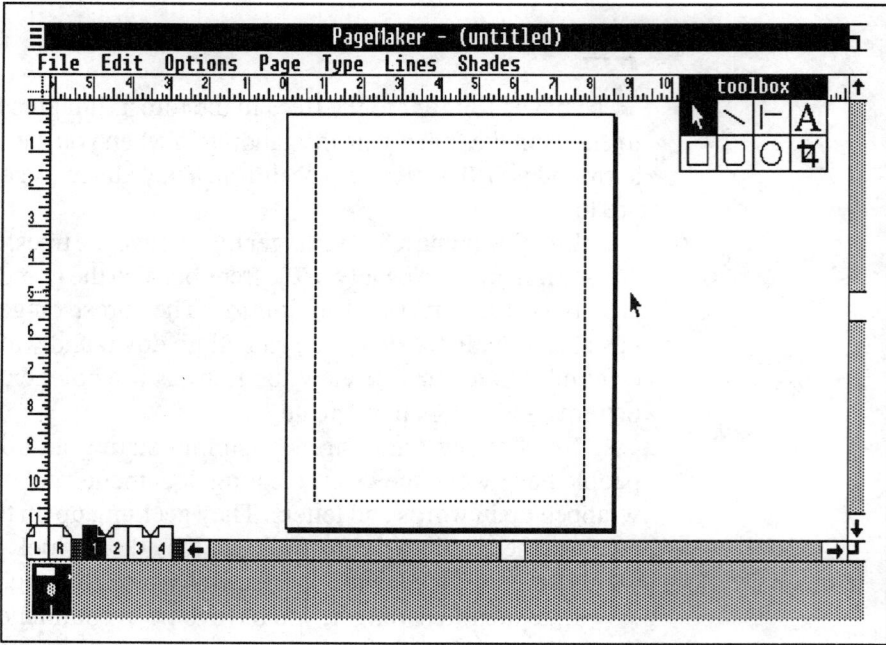

**Figure 4-1.** The page. All pages start off the same: blank. It is up to you to decide what will go on it.

## Page Architecture

Fig. 4-1 shows the bare essence of a page. A rectangle, usually vertical in nature, with nothing on it.

The rectangle is what most people have come to expect a page to be. Publications that deviate from this shape are often attention getting, but somehow the reader will always react to the fact that the page is sideways, square, or whatever shape you have made it.

Many people, especially when they are trying to promote an idea or want to get attention, will try to change the shape of a page. Yes, they get attention, but not always results. A very simple principle on the shape of a page comes from looking around you. Pick up a piece of paper, a magazine, a sales brochure, or a phone book; almost all adhere to the standard vertical rectangle. For good reason, it works.

The vertical rectangle is the de facto standard page shape. It is what people expect and anticipate a page to be. This is not to say that your pages have to follow this rule. It simply says that if you wish to communicate effectively, use the standard page shape as your first attempt.

Odd-shaped pages are for special situations or documents that need a special shape. The vertical rectangle is the standard for one reason: It is the most pleasing shape for a page or publication. If it wasn't, paper would not be 8-1/2 by 11 inches, and neither would most publications.

It is the shape, not the size, that matters. For example, software documentation, paperback books, pamphlets, and other such off-sized publications all adhere to the basic vertical rectangle. Even though their size differs from the standard, they all adhere to the proportions.

The nature of a vertical rectangle creates a subtle set of rules of what looks good on it and what doesn't.

## Page Elements

Starting with the blank page, you must make decisions of what you will put on it. Most likely, it will be text, and in many cases there will be additional elements such as headlines, subheads, illustrations, and photographs. Each of these elements will affect how the page looks. Blending all those elements and making them look good together is an art. This can be evidenced by examining the difference between a simple report (single column of type, set full width, with no graphic elements) vs. a magazine page (multiple columns of type, heads, subheads, captions, photography, rules, page numbers, and other such elements).

The report is simple in nature. There is little chance of creating a bad-looking report as long as the type is the right size and margins are sized in proportion to the type. It is a simple concept, carried out in a simple and effective manner, and there is little that can hurt the design or distract the reader.

The magazine, working with the same amount of space, has much more to deal with. There are dozens of elements on the page, all of which must strike a balance or the page will look bad and readability will suffer. The rule here is that the more elements there are on the page, the more chance there is of disrupting the value of the page or distracting the reader.

No matter what type of page you are producing, there are simple rules that should be followed to make page elements work in harmony and make a page more readable.

These rules apply to most published works, but not all. They are intended to make the page more readable. If you are producing a scientific document, the subject matter may not allow you the luxury of putting all of the following design concepts in place, but you can try. I will explain the major elements on a page one by one and discuss how they work best.

## Headlines

Not every page should have a headline, but almost every document or publication should. Simply put, a headline is the identifying element that tells readers what it is that they are about to read. For this reason, the headline should be clear and readable, both in the content of the words used and the way it is presented graphically. Headlines should, in all cases, identify the subject matter of the document or publication without confusion.

The type used for the headline can be any size or style and placed almost anywhere on a page. The main thing is that it identifies itself as the headline.

If the page your headline is on has a lot of text on it, the headline should be larger than the text and stand out clearly from the text. If there is only a headline and no text on a page, you are free to create a headline from virtually any readable size of type and position it freely on the page. The concept here is simple. The headline is the identifying element. What it must compete with determines its nature. (See Fig. 4-2.)

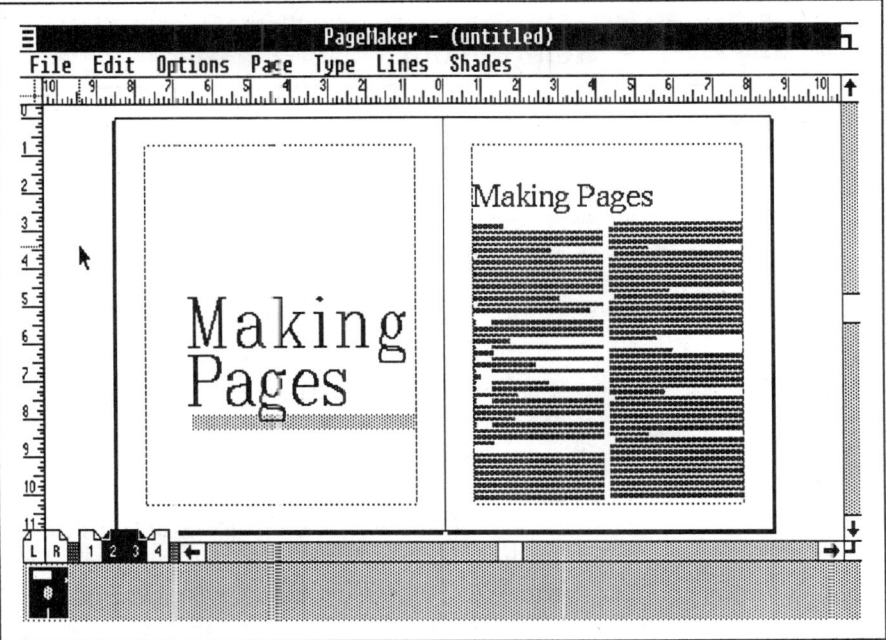

**Figure 4-2.** Two headlines on two very different pages. The page without text has the freedom to be aesthetic, but the headline on the page with columns of text must be large and wider than the columns to identify itself as a headline.

Headlines are used throughout publications. In books, they start sections; in magazines, they start articles; in reports, they act as title pages. Wherever you use the headline element, follow the simple rule of looking at the page and making sure the headline is the first thing that captures your attention.

### Text

The bulk of most pages is made up of words that have been typeset and are in a column format. This is usually called the text of a page. Since it will occupy the majority of pages and will be the main information environment for your readers, text should be easy to read. Text on standard-size pages works best when broken into more that one column on a page. For most documents or reports, two columns are preferred. Magazines look best with three columns. Books, which tend to have smaller pages (even though they follow the vertical rectangle rule), look best with one single column.

There are additional differences among books, magazines, and reports. The size of the type in each is different. Reports are often typewritten or use larger type. Magazines use a lot of text and small type. Books, having smaller pages, tend to use larger type than magazines.

> **Helpful Hint**
>
> A rule starts to emerge. A column is determined not by the nature of the document but by the size of type used. Maximum readability is at 50 characters per column. That means a typewritten page looks best with a single column, since with a 10-pitch you can fit about 50 characters on a line on a standard 8-1/2 by 11 inch page with 1-1/2 inch margins.

The same goes for books. Their pages are smaller, but, in general, the type is sized to contain about 45-50 characters per line. Magazines, with their small type, can fit between 35-45 characters per line. So the rule is that the number of characters in the line establishes the column width. There is another way of looking at it. If you want to design a page that uses two columns, how large should you make the type? Simple! It should be large enough to fit 50 or so characters across each column. Modern typesetting has allowed such tight spacing of type that 65 characters is common. A good example of this is a typewritten page. Using a standard 10-pitch type, 50 characters would look good. If you changed your typewriter element to a proportional- spaced type style, you would most likely end up with over 60 characters in the same space, with the same readability.

Fig. 4-3 illustrates how various type styles and sizes are used in different column widths. Note how each different type size results in a different-size column width. Readability is the main concern. Never force your type just to fit a layout. Let the layout evolve from the readability of the type.

> Modern typesetting has allowed such tight
>
> ## Modern typesetting has allowed such tight
>
> Modern typesetting has allowed such tight spacing of
>
> Modern typesetting has allowed such tight spacing of type
>
> Modern typesetting has allowed such tight spacing of type

**Figure 4-3.** Samples of various typefaces in different sizes and column widths, all set to be easy to read.

## Subheads

A page full of text, except in very specific scientific, medical, and financial publications or literary works, can become very tedious. Further, column after column of text makes it hard for readers to go back and find certain sections for reference or to scan through a document or publication and find subjects that interest them. To solve this problem, use subheads to break up columns of text and, more importantly, identify changes of subject matter within the text. The chapter you are reading, for example, contains many subheads. This section of text was identified by the bold type "Subheads."

Imagine reading this entire book without subheads. If I did not place subheads in the text, the result would be pages and pages of type. Not only would the book look uninteresting as you flip through the pages in a store trying to see what type of information is held within, but it would fail to help you locate the subjects in the book. The secret of developing effective subhead is to use them not to stimulate your readers visually but to provide reference points for them. Just as you must divide your thoughts into sentences and group sentences into paragraphs, you must group paragraphs with like subject matter and identify them with a subhead.

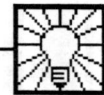

**Helpful Hint**

Graphically, a subhead can take on a variety of sizes and styles. There are some basic rules to follow:

Do not make subheads larger than headlines.

Do not use subheads simply as a graphic element.

Use subheads to define blocks of related subject matter.

Make subheads bolder than text. Be sure they are easy to see.

Keep subheads short, to the point, and easy to understand.

Subheads should have a line of space preceding them.

Text can start on the line after a subhead, or you can skip a line.

As already described, subheads play a very specific role on a page. They add color and definition to a page, as well as serve as reference points for readers. If your publication lends itself to subheads, use them to your advantage. Keep the style tasteful, usually flush left, and in a typestyle that compliments the text (such as in the same style except in bold).

**Graphic Elements**
Adding line art and photography to a page creates a more complex page environment. Not only must you choose the line art or photograph to be used but also size it and locate it on the page.

Later in this book, in the chapters on designing pages, I will explore various layouts when using line art or photography. At this point, it is important to consider that using either will greatly enhance the page for the reader. The page will be more interesting graphically, and the photographs and line art should help illustrate concepts within the text.

Art for art's sake is not a good practice in building a page. Certainly, a piece of text that has no break in subject matter, with few subheads, can become boring. A solution is often to add a graphic to a page. The page will be attractive only if the graphic compliments or enhances the text in some fashion. I have seen stories on people in industry illustrated with abstract graphics, pictures of trees, silhouettes of what appear to be the person, and other similar attempts. Sometimes they work, but many times they don't.

If you are stuck with a page that is just downright boring, you must come up with either a fantastic graphic idea (the role of an art director at a magazine or book publisher) or run the text as is, not making matters worse with a poor illustration or—even worse—an exaggerated use of type as a graphic element.

### Captions

If you use line art or photos on your page, another element that will be used is the caption. A simple element, the caption's role is to elaborate or explain the illustration. Never make the caption type larger or more expressive than the text. The goal is to stay within the style of the text, since a caption is actually an extension of the text.

Use the same (or a complimentary) typeface and a size slightly smaller than you are using for your text. Often, captions are made italic to set them apart from text. The same rule applies when numbers or names such as "Illustration One" are used. Keep them the same size as the text; with shorter statements such as these, often a bold version of the type works better than italic.

### Page Numbers

Multiple-page documents need a numbering system. The location and style of page numbers is also an important page element.

Traditionally, page numbers are called folios. The running head includes the name of the publication, the issue date, or other header- or footer-style material.

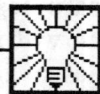

**Helpful Hint**

As with every page element, there are rules that will help make folio lines more effective.

The page numbers look best when they are on the outside of the page. For example, on a left-hand page, the page number is easiest for the reader to find if it is to the outside left corner of the page. The same principle applies to the right-hand page.

There are no specific rules on where page numbers work best vertically. They can be on the top, the bottom, or about one-third down from the top of the page on the outside. This location is called a visual reference. Studies have shown that when a person first looks at a page, his or her eyes tend to go to that location; hence, folios are placed in such a location.

Often, page numbers are centered. This works well if the folio is at the bottom of the page. Page numbers centered on the top of the page are often hard to find.

## Other Page Elements

There are several other page elements that will end up on your pages: charts and graphics, author photographs, and deck copy (a long subhead that simply describes the text in greater detail than the headline to draw the reader into the text).

All these elements should follow the basic concepts expressed in this chapter. They should all have a relationship to one another and work together to make an attractive page. (See Fig. 4-4.)

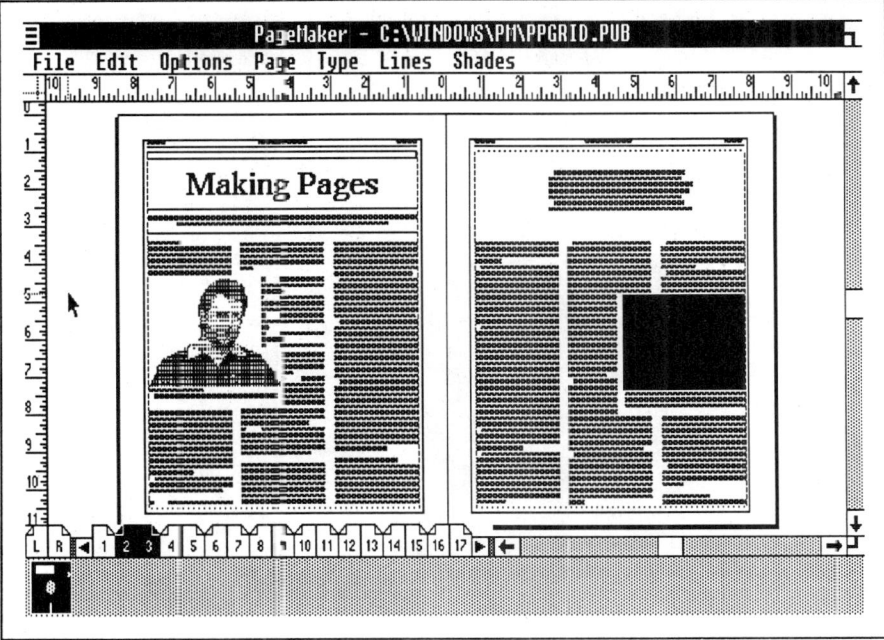

**Figure 4-4.** A magazine spread incorporating a number of graphic elements including headline, subhead, deck copy, captions, folio, photographs, illustrations, and rules. All these elements make the page more interesting and informative. The secret is to get all of the elements to work in harmony.

# The Single Page

All the concepts discussed in this chapter relate to a single, isolated page. But in producing a publication or document, pages do not stand alone; they must exist with other pages. Chapter 5 discusses how to create relationships between pages

It is essential to make a single page look good and to understand the nature and balance of elements upon it before you start building multipage environments.

# More Than One Page 5

*I*f a page is a singularly unique entity, as discussed in Chapter 4, then what happens when you put a number of pages together? The very nature of a publication or document is that it contains more than one page. And, of course, all of the pages must work together to form a whole, a unified effort. This complicates matters greatly because now not only does the single page you were working on have to look good—they all do!

## Multipage Environments

A publication is difficult to put together for many reasons, mainly because there is so much going on. Each page can contain dozens of elements: headlines, photos, subheads, captions, artwork, color, text, and folios. Further, each page faces another page. Sometimes a page will face a blank page, but mostly pages full of multiple elements face pages full of multiple elements. When pages face each other, the two pages are called a spread.

Spreads are the first tier in a multipage environment. When people look at your publication, they do not view just a single page; they also view the page across from it. For this reason, when designing a publication, you must stop thinking in terms of single-page units. You must, at a minimum, think of designing pages as spreads.

Since two pages face each other, you have to ensure that elements on one page do not interfere with elements on the other. The goal is to create a symmetry of shapes and a balance of typographic design. For example, if you are working on a spread that contains two photographs and each is a different size and shape, the two facing photographs might create a visual conflict. If you are able to make each photo have the same size and shape, you may then create an attractive spread, with the photos not only illustrating ideas but also creating a sense of order on the pages. They would then build a relationship with each other and bring order to the visual impact of the pages.

You will not always be able to have the correct elements on every spread to create a perfect balance, but there are a number of conditions to avoid. The goal is always to have pages that work together and do not fight each other.

Why is this so essential? Let's take a look in Figs. 5-1 and 5-2 at a good spread and a bad spread from a report.

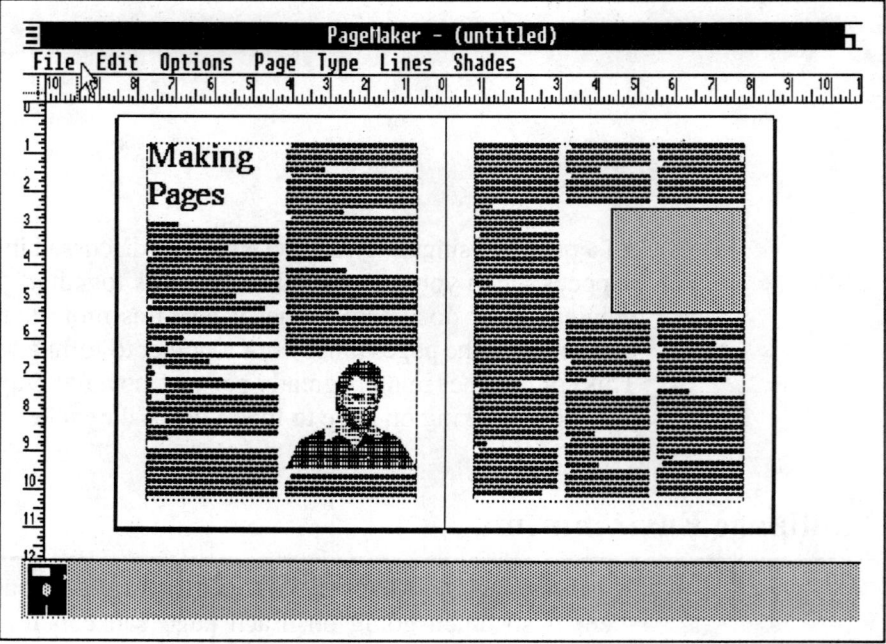

**Figure 5-1.** Example of a bad spread. The pages have columns of different widths, the graphic elements are placed without concern for balance, and it creates confusion in the mind of the reader.

**67** More Than One Page

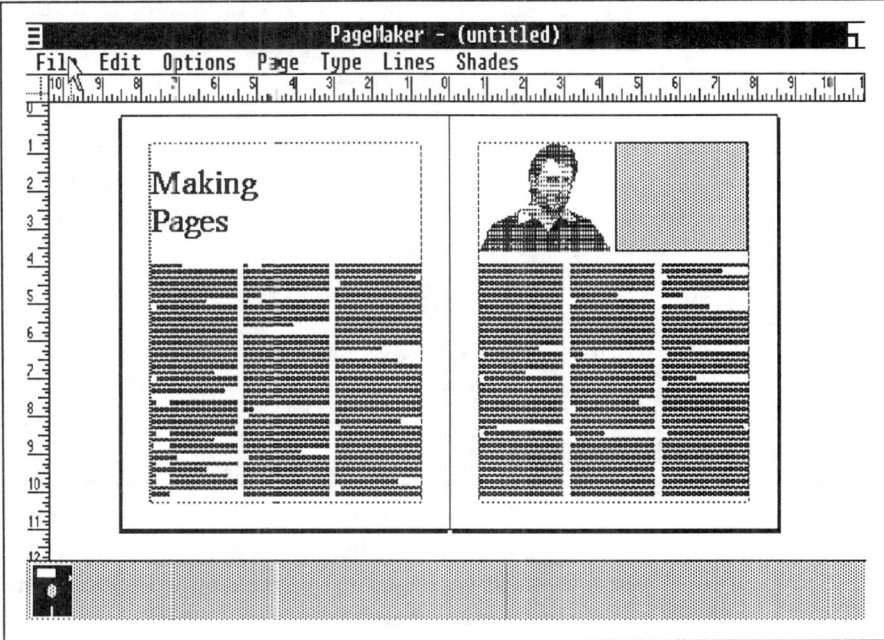

**Figure 5-2.** The same pages from Fig. 5-1 reassembled to have balance and order. Columns are now of equal width, and the graphic elements have at least some unity by starting at the same horizontal point on the two pages.

As you can see, a bad spread can be made into a good spread if you plan properly. This requires some advanced planning, taking into consideration that spreads are the lowest common denominator in publication design. Keeping elements consistent will help with the design process, but there is more to it than that.

### Expectations

When you design a publication of any type, your reader begins to relate to it in a subconscious manner. If you have done a great job on a collection of short stories, with the first five stories all starting on the right-hand page with a pleasant illustration on the left-hand page of the spread, you would disrupt the flow your publication has established if suddenly you were to change the format and start the sixth story on the left-hand page and put the illustration on the right-hand page.

First, it would defy logic to use this practice. Obviously, the pages should be kept consistent with the first five stories. But such things do happen. Pick up books or magazines and you will see this type of layout practice all the time. The reason for this is that the person who was placing the elements on the pages was not thinking of the publication as an entity, a single unified work. And a publication is a single unified work.

When a reader picks up a publication, all the pages—not just the spreads—have an impact upon the reader since they are all part of a whole. The reader is looking at a publication. The individual stories and pages are all single elements inside the publication. If the publication lacks an overall design and if there are no relationships developed throughout the pages, the design is not good.

Being a multipage environment, your publication must be designed so that all pages compliment each other. In well-designed publications, you can tear out any two pages, and they will look good together.

## Designing Publications

Once you have mastered the art of making spreads look good, the next step is to try to make the entire publication look good, having a cohesive structure just as the two pages of a spread must. Soon you will start looking at magazines and seeing beautiful spreads; however, farther back in the magazine you will see spreads full of odd-sized ads and poorly placed text. You will start noticing that perhaps an art director did the opening spread but did not do the pages later in the book. Those were left to a nonartist. Such conditions will show whether the publication was designed as a publication or as a series of spreads. Most publications, especially magazines, that we see use the spread design level. It is easier to create a publication this way. It is much more work to design an entire publication than it is to design two pages. With tight deadlines, it is easy to see why magazines take this route, but there is little excuse for it in any publication. (See Fig. 5-3.)

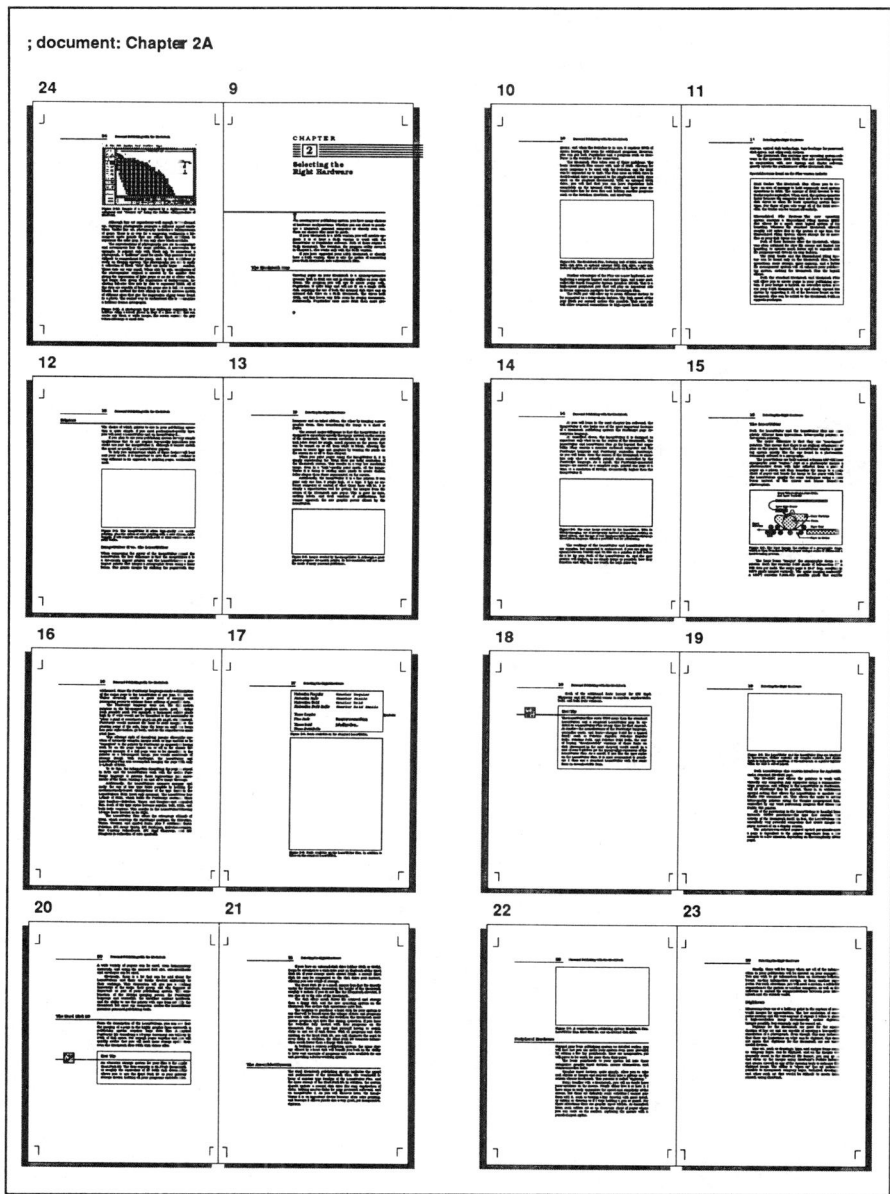

**Figure 5-3.** A 16-page publication examined as a single unit. Each page has a relationship to another page in its spread, and every spread and page have a relationship in the entire publication. This is best understood when you are able to view all of the pages at one time.

# 6

Pages
on
the
AT

When you use the AT to create pages, you are creating a page that is conceptually the same as described in the previous two chapters. It still has all the elements of text, heads, graphics, folios, etc. It still creates pages one at a time, and you must be sure that those pages abide in harmony with the rest of the pages in your document or publication. The main difference is that the AT simply allows you to make pages faster and better. It also allows you to modify and change elements easily.

Chapter 4 describes all the elements on a page. Using manual methods of page assembly, you would create these elements in an abstract manner. Text would be written on a typewriter or word processor. Examining a type book, you would pick out an appropriate type style size and column width and send these specifications and the text to a typesetter.

When the type is set, you may find that it does not look as good as you would like. But after considering the time it took to set and the cost of setting it over, you end up using the type that you have, even though you are not completely satisfied..

## Formatting Choices

Using the AT for creating type from your text offers you the option of resetting that type quickly. If you set the type in 10-point Helvetica and find you are not happy, all it takes is to select the type and, from pull-down menus, change the selected type to 10-point Times Regular, as shown in Figs. 6-1 through 6-4.

```
1═══[·········1·········2·········]·········4·········5·········6·········7···
    Making·Pages¶
    You·are·building·an·eight-page·
    promotional·  newsletter·  and·
    it's·time·to·make·pages.··You·
    have·all·the·  copy·  processed,·
    all·the·  electronic·  and·  hard·
    copy·art·at·your·  fingertips,·
    and·you·have·  to·  put·  it·  all·
    together·into·eight·pages.¶
     So· you· start· building· the·
    newsletter--creating·
    headlines,·  placing·  art·  and·
    editorial,·  and·  sizing·  hard-
    copy·  illustrations,·  starting·
    at·  page·  one·  and·  hoping·
    everything·fits·right·when·you·
    get·to·page·eight.·It·doesn't,·

FORMAT CHARACTER bold: Yes(No)      italic: Yes(No)           underline: Yes(No)
               strikethrough: Yes(No)    uppercase: Yes(No)      small caps: Yes(No)
             double underline: Yes(No)  position:(Normal)Superscript Subscript
                   font name: Helvetica    font size: 10            hidden: Yes(No)
Enter font name or select from list
Page 1   {}                              ?           Microsoft Word: PAGFORM.DOC
```

**Figure 6-1.** Text has been entered into Microsoft Word using 10-point Helvetica. The column width is 3 inches. After examining the type, you decide that it is not what you really wanted.

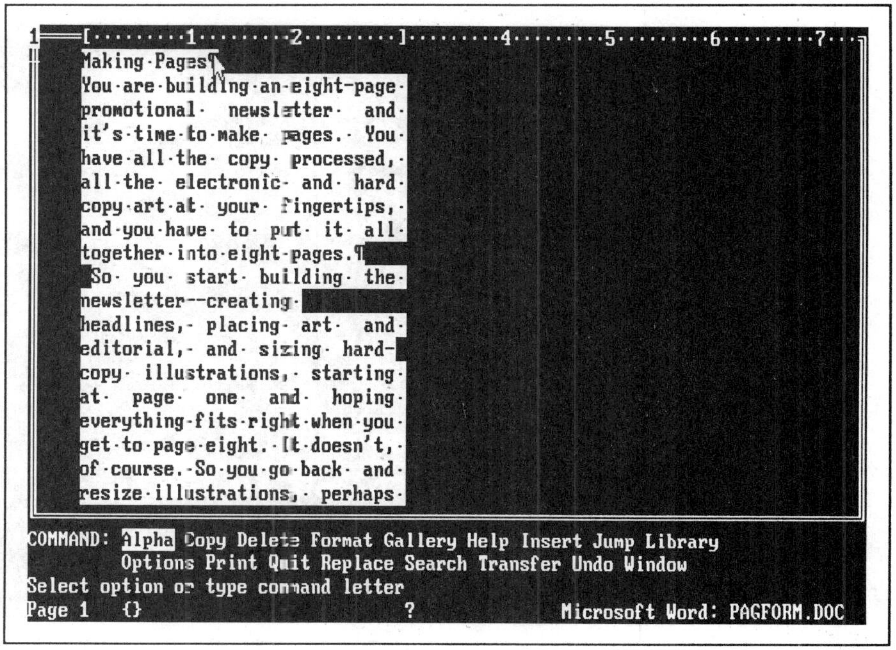

**Figure 6-2.** The entire text file is selected and ready to accept a type size, style, or font change.

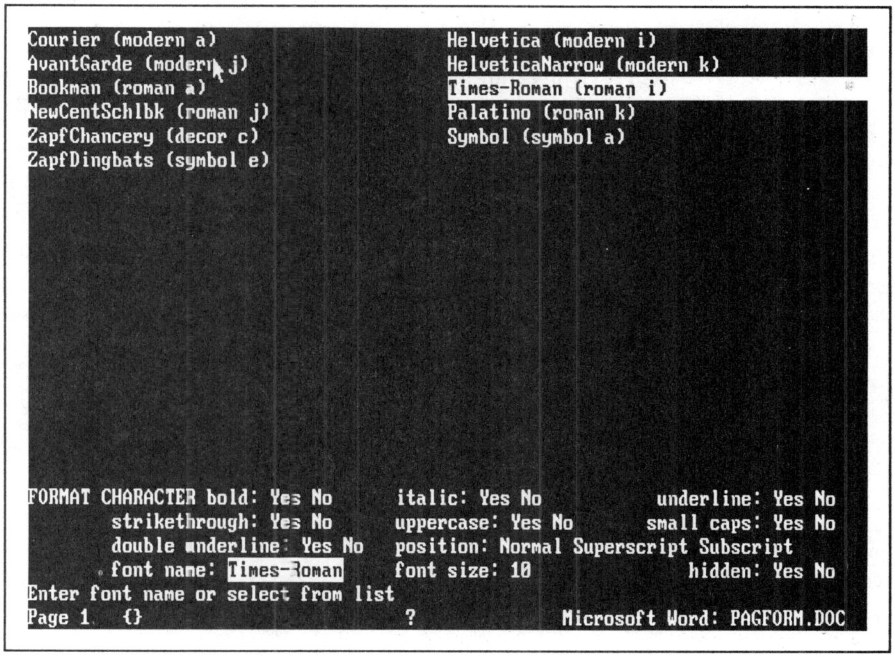

**Figure 6-3.** From the type menu, Times is chosen. The entire text file is changed in a matter of seconds from Helvetica to Times.

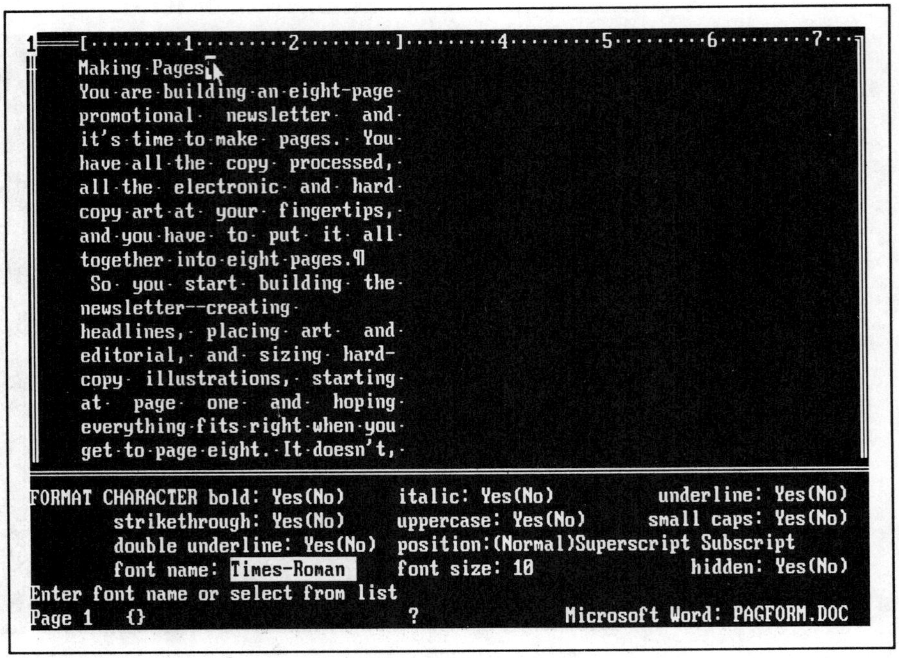

**Figure 6-4.** The final type in Times Regular. The whole process took less than a minute. When changes can be made that easily, you have the ability to modify page elements until they are just the way you want them without incurring added expense.

The rules that apply to type also apply to other page elements (for example, photographs). Chapter 2 detailed devices such as scanners, which allow you to create digitized images of type and photographs. Using the AT and images created with such scanners, you can also preview the size of your line art or photographs and view them prior to printing in a page environment. Figs. 6-5 through 6-9 show a digitized for-position-only photo being placed on a page in the page assembly program PC PageMaker. This example will show how, working electronically, you can make changes before the work is done or the publication is printed.

**75** Pages on the AT

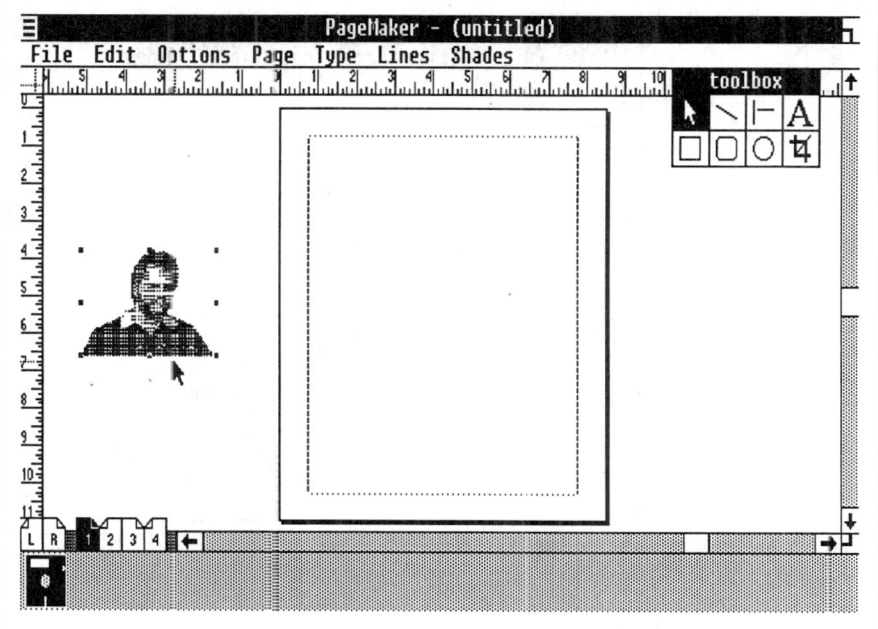

**Figure 6-5.** The small box represents a page. A digitized photo is off to the side of the page.

**Figure 6-6.** The digitized photo is moved onto the page. It looks a bit small, so you decide to see if it would be more effective at a larger size.

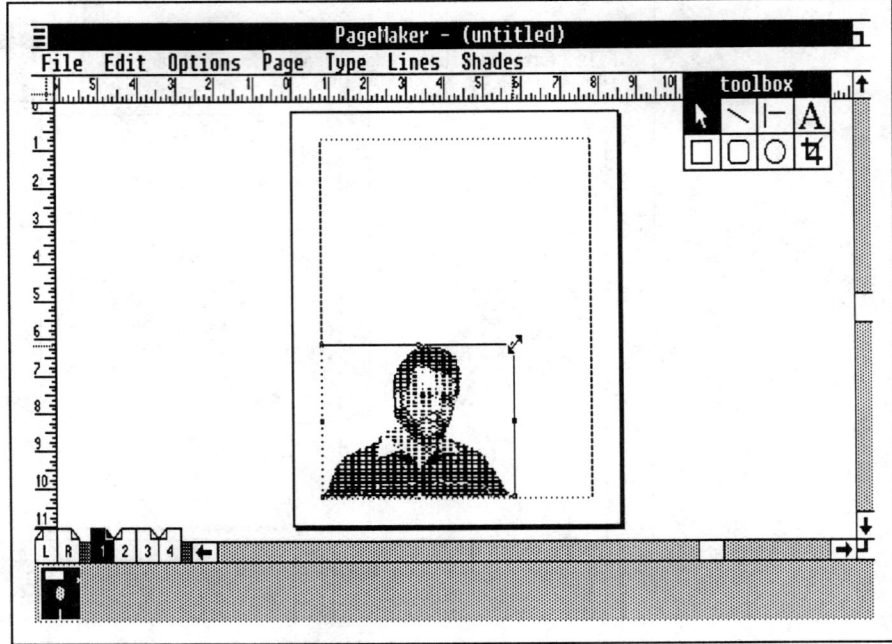

**Figure 6-7.** By clicking on the photo, a set of handles that allows the photo to be stretched and pulled are made available. Using the upper corner handle, the photo is pulled out to fill the width of the page.

**Figure 6-8.** The photo at full width is much more pleasing. Now, the actual photo will be sized to match this digital representation.

**Figure 6-9.** Finally, type is added to the page, giving a real feel of how the photo works on the page.

## AT Advantages

The examples in this chapter illustrate how the AT helps you explore the page concept fully. You can, as described in the beginning of Chapter 4, see the forest for the trees. You can examine type with incredible detail and flexibility. You can size and scale line art and photographs on the page and mingle text and graphics freely from the word-processing program on through to the page assembly software.

The AT, assembled as a publishing system, allows you to view the creation of your publications with both perspective and detail. From a single headline to the page to spreads to entire publications, the screen of the AT allows you to examine your page and romance it.

Fig. 6-10 shows PC PageMaker once more, this time with the spread the photo is on. This is the way to make pages, with the ability to preview them and understand them.

**Figure 6-10.** PC PageMaker allows you to examine a spread at a reduced size on the AT screen at any time, allowing you to view relationships between pages.

# 7

Electronic Page Assembly

*C*hapters 5 and 6 stressed the nature of the page and how single pages bound together in publication form must work together as a single entity. This is not an easy task. It takes a good understanding of what a page is and what a publication is (Chapters 4 and 5). Furthermore, it takes a working knowledge of typography and page design. These will be covered in upcoming chapters.

For many people, the thought of putting words, pictures, and the dozens of other elements together is an overwhelming task. For example, say that I handed you a pile of typewritten text, photographs, and a list of elements that have to be placed at specific locations in the text and told you it all had to fit in a 32-page publication. And that's all. Could you deal with it? Could you work out all the details such as how large to make the type and column width, crop the photos, make sure that the special graphics elements end up in the right spots, and, finally, fill the 32 pages completely, with the last line ending at the bottom of the last page? It's easy.

## Case Study

That may sound like a mean example, but every day thousands of publication designers are faced with this problem. When I was an art director for a magazine, the editor and publisher would each come in with a stack of goodies for me. The editor would have all the text that was to be sent to the typesetter, as well as line art, photographs, headlines, captions, and other such elements. The publisher would have all the ads that were to go in the magazine. The ads were especially fun, since some were color and had to go only on the pages of the magazine that had color. Many of the ads had to be on certain pages, such as color ads that had to be on black and white printing forms. The publisher would also tell me that, based on the number of ads sold, the magazine would be X number of pages long. The magazine had to be printed on forms that would be 8 or 16 pages, so if things didn't work out right, there was no room to compensate. When the publisher said 96 pages, that was how large the magazine would be, and that was it.

So there I sat with text, art, ads, position requests, and the job of making it all fit perfectly in the size the publisher wanted. Not only that, I could not have columns or stories end abstractly. They had to end flush. On top of all that, it all had to go in, and it all had to look good. After all, I was the art director. That was what I was paid for.

How did I do it? The hard way. I sat there and counted everything. I would estimate how long the type would be, spec it, and send it to the typesetter. I would add up all the ads and begin a plan of what ads would go on what pages. I would place all the color and special-position ads first and leave the rest for placement to balance out pages when I did the actual layout.

When the type got back, I would measure it precisely and add all the type and all the ad page values together. If they came within 4 to 6 pages under the page count the publisher wanted, I knew I was all right. If they went over, I would meet with the publisher and editor and tell them that there was not enough room for everything they wanted in. Something would have to change. The magazine would need to be made bigger or we would have to cut out editorial. (We always cut editorial.)

Then, when I was only a few pages off the mark, I would begin laying out the magazine one article at a time. I would take one article, for example, and count its page value (type, heads, photos, captions, etc.). I would take the value (for example, 3-1/2 pages) and say that the minimum number of pages this article would fit in will be 4 pages. On my layout, I would mark the next 4 pages for that article. So what about the 1/2 page that was short of filling 4 pages? Simple. I would go to the ads, pick out a 1/2-page ad, and place it on the last page of the article. This way I would have an opening spread that I could do something nice with graphically and then follow it by a clean type layout of the text sharing the page with a simple 1/2-page ad.

I would continue this method throughout the magazine, keeping a closer watch as I approached the end of the magazine. If all went well, I would have an attractive magazine by using a principle of estimating, working with real values, knowing that all the elements would fit tightly into the defined space, and then laying each element in one by one, making all articles end flush by compensating with fractional-sized ads. If there were no ads, I would adjust with the size of the photos.

It was pretty simple, and I got to do it every month!

# A Better Way

The above example is a perfect argument for a better way of handling the page assembly process. While I was sitting there with stacks of text waiting for typesetting, art, and illustrations that needed to be sized and working with ads that the publisher gave me, I spent most of my time wading through it all just trying to make heads or tails out of it. Today, there is a better case study. For example, let's say that I was at the same publishing company, but instead of typewriters and legal pads with notes on them, the publisher, editor, and art director (yours truly) all had ATs, computers, and a laser printer.

Starting with the editor, instead of typing his or her text and having me mark it up with typesetting codes and sending it to a typographer, the editor would enter the text on the computer and format it at the same time. I, as art director, would set up different formats in Microsoft Word, in which the editor would start an article (a department format, a feature format, etc.). The column widths would be there, and the editor would know whether the story was too long or too short. Best of all, when it came time to give the magazine to me, I would have all the actual editorial values available. I would know exactly how much space the editorial would occupy. Using a scanner to digitize art and halftones, I would create scaled-to-size position stats for the pages. Those editorial values and the photo values would give me a perfect estimate of the editorial for the issue.

The next benefit is that the type is set. The editor entered all the text as formatted type, so there is no further proofreading of the type when it comes back from a typesetter. Additionally, I do not have to spend time putting typesetting specifications in the text.

That gives me my editorial budget. Yes, budget! Publishers equate type and ad values and create a budget based on how much there is to work with.

Next, the publisher keeps track of all of the advertisers, but rather than handing me a handwritten list, advertisers are tracked with a spreadsheet program. All the ads are marked in columns for size, shape, color, and position. This is much easier for me to work with. I can take the spreadsheet and sort the ads by color, size, or alphabetically (when I need to find materials).

Working with an AT of my own, I have created an electronic budget that simulates my old paper version. This time a spreadsheet takes all the measures of type and the value of ads and tells me exactly how many pages the material will require. From there on out, it is still a battle of working things out between the publisher and the editor if anything needs to be cut.

The savings in time is incredible. What used to take at least a week is now done in a day. And once all of us agree on the final layout and budget, I could start putting the magazine together. The type is set, I have a computer equipped with page assembly software, and the magazine will be ready for the printer in a matter of days.

As a result, the time we have saved creating these complex pages electronically has given the sales staff more time to sell ad space for the magazine. Using this system, the sales staff gains at least a week.

## Computer-Aided Publishing

The concepts just discussed can apply to any publishing situation. Computer-aided publishing can give a newsletter more time to gather the latest-breaking stories. It allows fund-raising groups to cut their cost on typesetting and hiring an artist every time they need to send out fund-raising brochures. It gives almost everyone in the publishing process an advantage by allowing them to create type, put it into page form easily, and, most of all, stop to look at the publication as a whole. If it doesn't look right, it's easy to change.

When you compare the manual process with the computer-aided process, there is no way the manual process can compete with the benefits of computer-aided publishing.

On a time-savings basis alone, the publishing system wins hands down, as Fig. 7-1 illustrates.

**Typical Newsletter Production Cycle**

*Activity* *Hours*

**Manual System**
Text Entry .................................................................................. 10
Type Specification ....................................................................... 2
Typesetting ................................................................................ 14
Proofing Galleys .......................................................................... 4
Layout ........................................................................................ 3
Pasteup ...................................................................................... 8

Total: ........................................................................................ 41

**AT-based Publishing System**
Text Entry .................................................................................. 10
Proofing Galleys ....................................................................... 1.5
Layout ........................................................................................ 3

Total: ..................................................................................... 14.5

**Figure 7-1.** Time-saving comparison between manual production of a newsletter and electronic production of a newsletter done on a Macintosh publishing system.

As Fig. 7-1 shows, the publishing system saves a great deal of time. The text still takes the same amount of time to enter. There is no typesetting, so that cost and time are saved. Since the galleys are created directly on the AT, the editor has already proofed them, but the files are passed through an electronic spelling checker again and reread, resulting in 1.5 hours of final proofing time. The layout of the newsletter is still a process of experimentation and thought, so the amount of time is the same as in traditional typesetting. But, since the artist is working on the screen of the computer using actual electronic type rather than photocopies of galleys, once the layout is complete, it is done. There is no need for a pasteup, since the type and art are made up as pages in the computer.

Finally, before being printed, the art director can print out a thumbnail-sized version of the newsletter ("thumbnail" is a term used for very small drawings of layouts, often real pages reduced photographically to only 1 or 2 inches tall) and view the newsletter as a whole, examining the layout one more time and getting approval from the publisher.

Such a system allows the production of publications to take place in a more sane manner. The electronic environment the computer uses is much easier to manipulate than galleys of text and pieces of paper. The publication is produced as a whole, not in single pages. Clearly, there is an advantage here.

## Conversion

Once you understand the benefits of electronic page assembly, you may begin assembling your IBM AT publishing system. From there, you can take over the jobs you may have traditionally sent out. This will offer you savings in production time and cost. However, if you are to be successful, you will need to master the skills you have relied upon others for. You will need to master type usage, layout, and graphics.

If you are ready, this book now makes the jump from why to how.

| Part | Page |
|---|---|
| Three | Design |

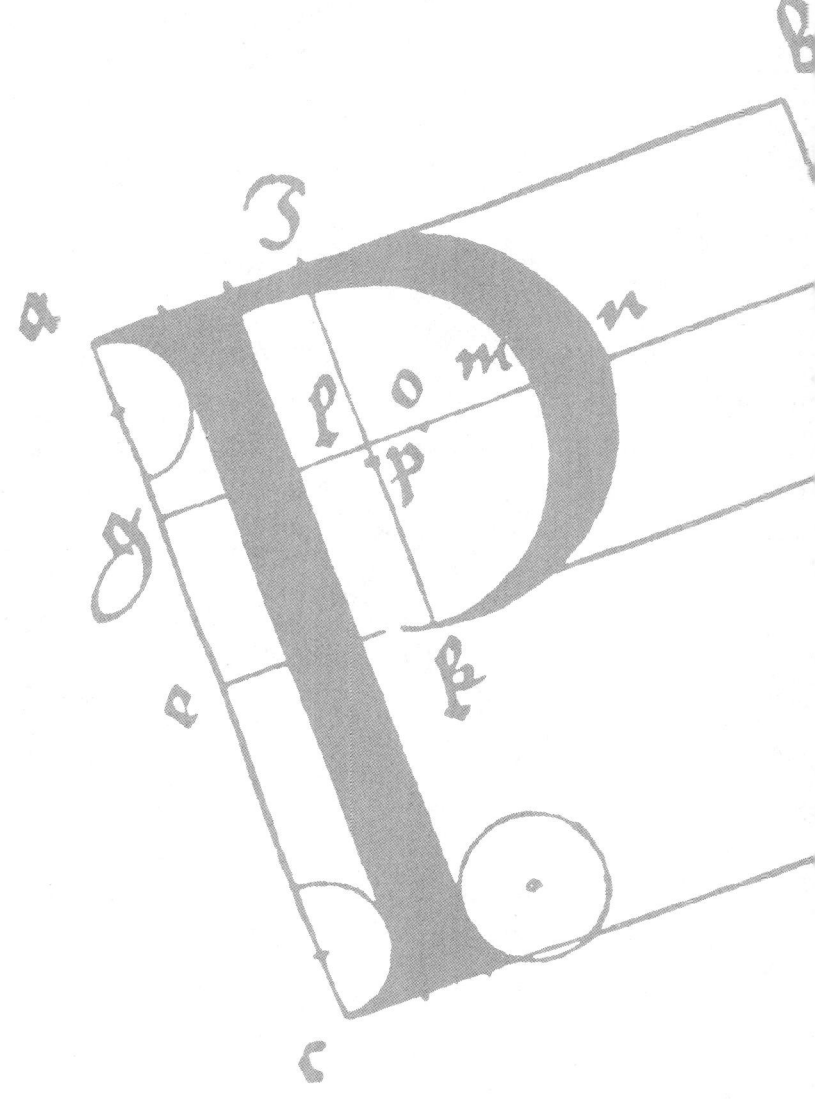

# The Grid 8

*F*inally, we begin to make pages. But even before we get into page assembly using PC PageMaker, there is more to learn. We have identified that a page is an individual element that must coexist in a publication environment with other pages, but that is all we have learned.

Before we can jump in and start making pages, we have to learn the structure of a page, the dynamics of type, and how to choose the elements that will go on the page. It boils down to the question: Now that we know that the page is the lowest common denominator in a publication, what is the lowest common denominator of the page? The answer is: the grid.

## A Skeletal Structure

OK, to indulge in more imagery, if the final page is the completed animal that we are out to capture, then under the skin and the flesh must lie a skeleton—something that gives form to all those columns of type and graphic elements.

Every page does have such a structure, even though the creator of the page may not realize it. In publication creation, the framework of a page is the page grid.

The grid does pretty much what its name implies. It establishes a structure to build upon. Fig. 8-1 shows the most basic example of a page grid. It is a standard-size page (8-1/2 by 11 inches), with a grid defining the live area (the area that will be occupied by type and graphic elements) as 5 inches wide and 9 inches tall. The live area is centered on the page, with equal margins on the top, bottom, and sides.

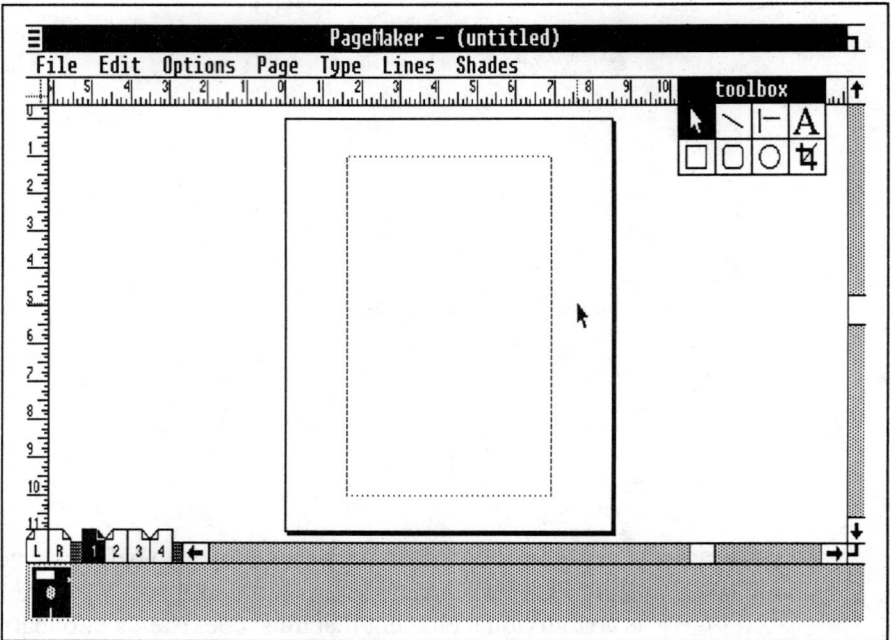

**Figure 8-1.** A simple page grid. The solid line is the 8-1/2 by 11 inch page, the dotted line the 5 by 9 inch live area that will become a column of type.

Looking at the grid, it appears to be pretty basic. You might ask why bother to create one. There are many good reasons to create a grid for even the most simple of pages. First, in a multipage document, you will want the type, or live area, to fall in exactly the same location on every page. If you were to go and just start putting type on a page, the type would jump from page to page. The grid establishes the exact location of the live area on every page.

When done manually, most newsletter, book, and magazine publishers print actual grid sheets with a light blue ink (the light blue ink, called nonrepro blue, will not show up when printed). The pasteup artists use the grid to ensure that type and graphic elements are positioned at the same locations on every page, and the printed grid also allows them to save a lot of time since they do not have to draw a grid for every page they must paste up.

PC PageMaker, the page assembly program we will use, allows us to create a grid, called a master page. This grid is shown on the screen (and in the examples created in this chapter) but, just like the nonrepro blue ink, does not print when your page is printed. Creating master pages will be explained in Chapter 14, Building Master Pages.

# Defining the Live Area

In creating a grid of any type, you will need to establish your page size (often called the trim size), the margins, and the live area. The live area is where active elements such as type will go. The margins can contain elements as well, some of which may bleed off the page, For example, a header, footer, or folio can reside in the margin instead of the live area. These are elements that will remain constant from page to page, so they do not need to be part of the live area.

The first step in creating your grid is to determine the actual size of the physical page. For our example, it is 8-1/2 by 11 inches. Once this parameter is established, you must determine whether the pages will be printed on both sides of the page (double sided) or just on one side (single sided). The reason for this is that double-sided pages will require both folio and margin adjustments. The actual trim area is identified by crop marks, simple rules in each corner that say where the page starts and stops.

### Working in the Gutter

Most publications are bound. Whether spiral, three-ring notebook, saddle-stitched, or perfect bound, the result of binding is that the area of the page that is bound is not visible. With very thick books, the part of the page that is bound can have up to 1/4 inch that you cannot see.

The part of the page that rests in the bound area is called the gutter. On a spread, the right side of the left-hand page is the gutter, and the left side of the right-hand page is the gutter.

If you center the live area on a page and it is bound, the loss of space in the gutter area will result in the live area not being centered on the visible page. To solve this, it is best to put a wider margin on the gutter of your page.

Publications bound in three-ring notebooks are difficult to plan for. The holes come in almost a 1/2 inch, but when the page is viewed, the reader still views the entire page. Here, you could leave the page centered accurately, just as long as it has enough of a margin in the gutter area so that there is no chance that type or live matter will end with holes in it.

### Helpful Hint

In planning either single- or double-sided pages, examine the binding process your publication will use and allow enough room for the gutter. Single-sided pages need a gutter margin only on their left side; double-sided pages need gutter margins on the right side of the left-hand page and on the left side of the right-hand page.

We will now make our sample page in Fig. 8-1 a single-sided page, but we will adjust our live area to accommodate the gutter. We will add 1/2 inch to the gutter. The live area was 5 inches wide centered on the 8-1/2 inch page, leaving a left and right margin of 1-3/4 inches. Being a single-sided page, the gutter falls on the left, so we must make this margin wider and the outside right-hand margin smaller. This results in the gutter margin being 2 inches and the outside margin being 1-1/2 inches, as shown in Fig. 8-2.

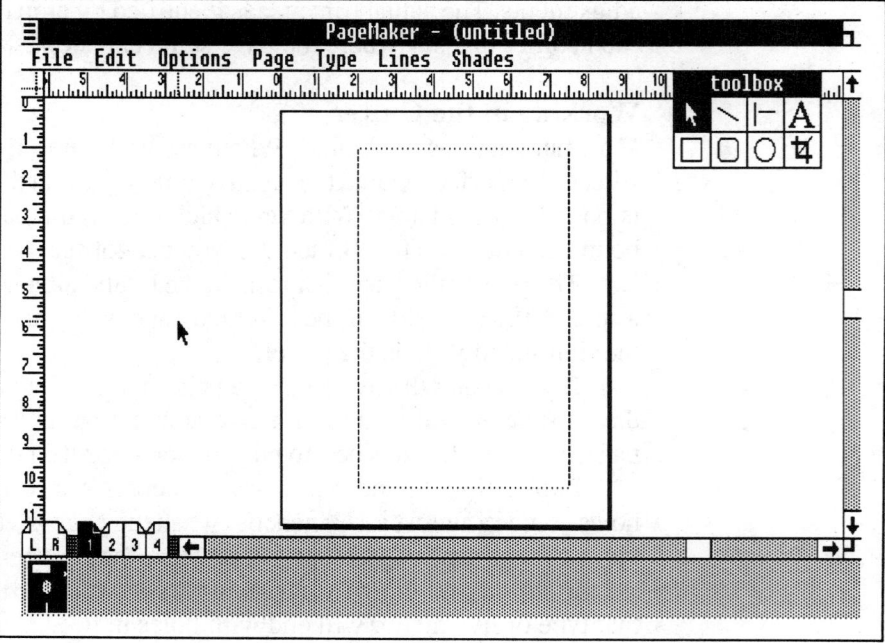

**Figure 8-2.** The page grid, now reflecting the gutter margin. The live area has been shifted away from the gutter, creating a wider margin to accommodate the binding process.

This same principle will apply to any bound publication. The first step in establishing the value to add to the gutter margin is to talk to the person who will bind the publication for you and discuss how much room should be allowed for that binding process. Try to keep the gutter allowance as small as possible. If you overcompensate, you will have a page with a live area that looks off-center.

# Columns

Now that your live area and margins have been firmly established, the next areas a grid should define are columns. If your column will be the same width as the live area, then you have already defined your column. If you are working with multiple columns, you must decide how many and what their widths are to be.

On our sample page, we are going to create a simple two-column format. Each column will be 2-1/4 inches wide, with 1/2 inch of space between the columns. These columns are indicated on the grid in Fig. 8-3.

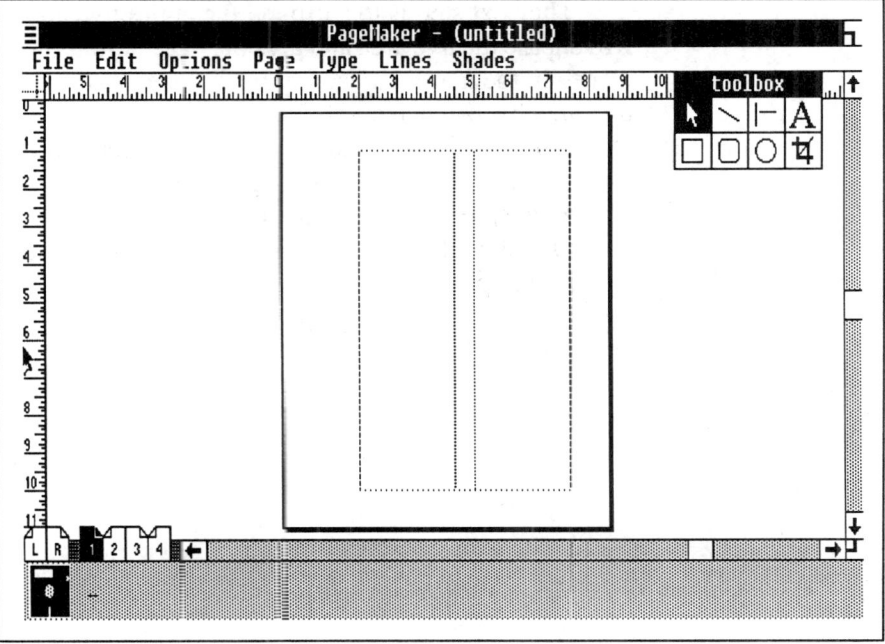

**Figure 8-3.** A two-column format has been established. Each column is 2-1/4 inches wide and touches the outside live area, leaving a 1/2-inch margin between the columns filling the 5-inch live area.

## Graphic Elements

Now that the columns have been placed, we can enhance the page with grid locations for graphic elements that will appear on every page. We are going to complete our page with a vertical rule between the columns, a box around the live area, and a folio line for the page number. All the graphic elements we will be adding are printing elements, simply meaning that we want them to be black on our grid instead of nonrepro blue. We want them to reproduce when printed, so they will be printed along with the type when added to the page.

Printing elements are drawn the same way as nonprinting elements. If you're printing grid sheets, the sheets would be printed in black and nonrepro blue. In printing the sheets, you would instruct the printer which items are printed in blue and which are printed in black. When creating an electronic master page in PC PageMaker, the same concepts will apply. We will learn how that is done in Chapter 14, Building Master Pages.

Back to our grid. We first draw a rule that is centered between the two columns, or 1/4 inch from either column since the space is 1/2 inch wide. The rule runs the same height as the type columns.

The next step is to surround the entire live area with a ruled box. This will encase the live area and give the page definition. This boxed rule will be placed in the margin area, not the live area of the page. It will surround the live area by 1/4 inch on all four sides.

Finally, a folio is added. The folio will contain only the page number and will be centered at the bottom of the page. A simple baseline rule will indicate where the type will be placed. The baseline will be 1/4 inch down from the bottom of the ruled box, centered. Fig. 8-4 shows the completed grid with all elements in place.

**93** The Grid

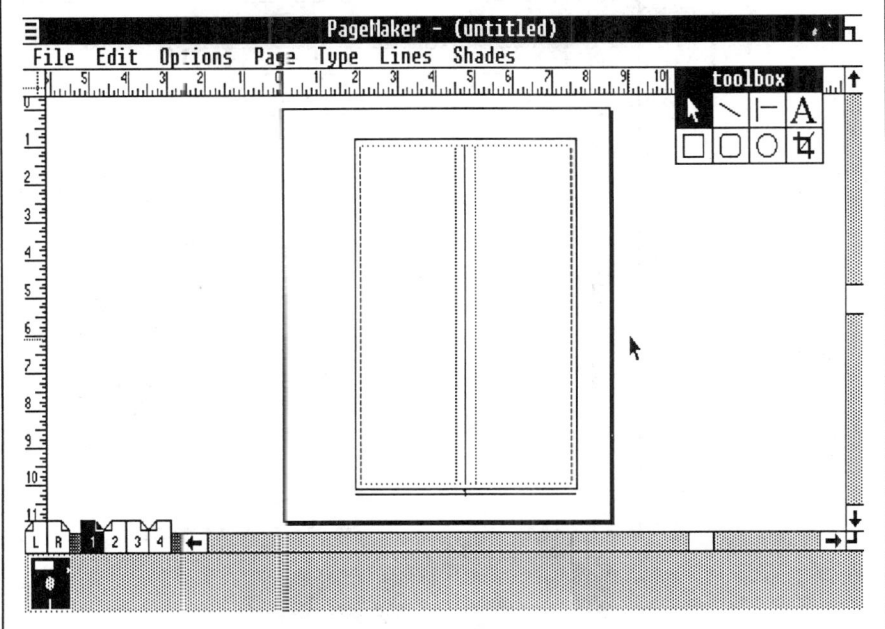

**Figure 8-4.** The completed page grid.

## Working with the Grid

Once your grid is complete, you will have a defined set of sizes to work with. Type will be set at 2-1/4 inches wide and break into 9-inch columns. The rules that remain the same from page to page are already printed for you, saving you the tedious task of adding them to every page.

But just because you have a grid does not mean there is no flexibility. Far from it. You may run type full width, blocking out the vertical rule when space is needed for headlines or captions for full-width photographs.

Elements do not have to remain inside the box, either. A photo can start inside the box and bleed off the page, knocking out the outside rule as it does so.

The grid is simply the structure for the majority of elements that are on your page, and allows for consistent placement of those elements. Furthermore, since each page uses the same box, rules, and graphic elements, every page will be consistent. The grid is a foundation but not a boundary. (See Fig. 8-5.)

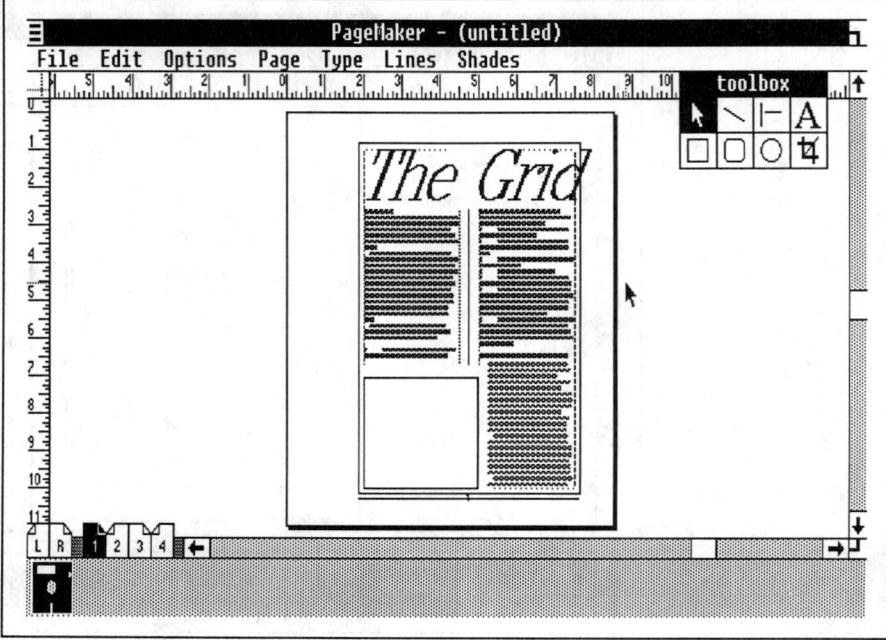

**Figure 8-5.** An actual page created using the page grid. Note how the grid has acted as a guide but has not restricted the creative use of graphic and typographic elements.

# 9

# Working with Type

*T*ype is so abstract that it is almost impossible to make definitive statements about it.

What is good typography and what is bad typography? What is type? What's the difference between the type from a professional typographer and the type produced by a laser printer? Such questions are hard to answer.

Different people have different typographic needs. A publisher of fine art prints would need to have the ultimate in quality type. A small businessman needing sales order forms would not need such quality.

For a very long time, typesetting has been in the hands of professional typographers and professional publishers. This is a very small market, and, as such, they have had to pay a high price for their typesetting devices. A professional typographer, for example, may have customers ranging from very demanding advertising agencies to small companies needing only price lists and forms typeset. The problem is that because the typographer has those advertising agencies demanding ultra-high-quality type, they must purchase equipment and staff to meet those demands. They charge a good price for the service, and the ad agencies are willing to pay it. Unfortunately, the smaller company that has type set ends up paying that large price because the typographer has set his type on equipment that far exceeds his typographic needs.

The reason for personal publishing's incredible popularity is that, for the first time in history, typography is out of the hands of the typographer and in the hands of the person who has bought type. Type can now be created in house, on devices (such as laser printers) that are appropriate for the typographic needs of most people.

Simply put, people with medium-resolution typographic needs can use a laser printer instead of a typesetter.

### Responsibility

It may sound as if I am knocking typographers. I'm not. Typographers are first and foremost a service organization. They specialize in producing high-quality type on high-priced, high-resolution typesetting devices. They are needed and have a place in the publishing process. It is just that now you have the option of using typography that matches your real needs.

You also must not fool yourself into thinking that all your typesetting needs can be handled by a laser printer. The laser printer produces a resolution of 300dpi. In the professional typesetting community, the lowest-resolution type is generally about 1000dpi. That is quite a difference. If you need to produce your documents at a higher resolution, you can still produce them and proof them on the laser printer. But you would send them out to a professional typographer that has a typesetting device capable of outputting your files at a higher resolution (such as 1,100dpi or 2,540dpi).

You must know when you can work with the 300dpi output of the laser printer or when you need to send out for higher-resolution output.

## What Is Type?

This is a tough question, but the answer is quite interesting. Type is commonly known as letters and numbers that are created on machines such as typewriters and typesetters. The characters are well formed and consistent in their size and style. Unlike handwritten text, type is most often created by machines or devices rather than by our own hands. But there is more to it than that.

For example, the type you are now reading is not actually type at all. It is an impression, created on a printing press, of an image created by a laser printer, of a digitized photograph of an impression of an actual piece of type.

Sound complicated? Well, a history lesson will help. The most accurate definition of type is the old wooden or metal casts of letterforms that were used prior to the 1950s. At that time type was a physical entity—you could pick it up and hold it in your hand. The various pieces of type were put together by typographers and locked up into forms. The type was then coated with ink, and a piece of paper was placed on the type, pressed with a roller, and removed. The paper would then contain an impression made from the real type. So what a reader actually read was not type, but an image of the type.

This was the standard method of creating printed documents for centuries, until about 30 years ago. Someone figured out a great system to replace the wood or metal type. The process involved taking photographs of type impressions, putting them on a strip of film, and photographically reproducing the type images. This was the start of phototypesetting. This beginning process was very crude, but, eventually, it ended up being controlled by computer devices from a keyboard and became the standard for typesetting. The old process of using physical letterforms was replaced by a system that used photographs of the letters' images.

The next step came when lasers entered the scene. Using a laser beam to image a sheet of photosensitive paper, type could be digitized (at a much higher level than discussed in Chapter 2) and then imaged by moving the laser on the paper to create the letterforms. Today, digital typography is becoming the standard imaging device used by typographers to create images of type.

Laser printers employ the same concept and technology to image type. They use a digital image of type that is stored in the memory of the machine, image the photosensitive drum inside, and make an impression of that image on a piece of paper passing through the laser printers.

Many typographers will try to tell you that what you get from a laser printer is not real type. This could not be further from the truth. Laser printers employ the same imaging process and many of the same type originals as the most expensive typesetting device. The only difference is that laser printers do so at a lower resolution and, to the typographers' dismay, in your place of operation, not theirs.

### Once Again, What Is Type?
Now we can examine the nature of the letterforms that we have come to call type. Type comes in a variety of styles. Each style creates a different feel when you look at it. For example, script brings to mind wedding invitations and flowing images. Serif type, which is the style of type you are viewing right now, is what we have come to expect in books and information. It has authority and makes a definite statement. Sans serif type (such as Helvetica) is clean and modern. It is easy to read, so it works well for headlines, road signs, or wherever words need to be communicated quickly.

Type is a series of letterforms, forming the alphabet and numbers, in upper- and lowercase, in a consistent manner. Handwriting, for example, could not be called type because you could not repeat two letterforms in the exact same way.

Furthermore, type has an individual style: serif, sans serif, scripts, outline, block, and cursive.

So type is a set of letterforms of a unique style that can be repeated as many times as needed to form words, sentences, paragraphs, and pages.

# Fonts

You will see the name "font" used in connection with type. It is simply the name of the specific typeface that you have chosen, such as Times or Helvetica. The many programs used in desktop publishing use the term font in a liberal manner, allowing you to make a font bold, italic, outlined, or shadowed. A true font is only one of those versions, but the digital nature of the type allows you to modify one font into many different fonts by electronically altering the type.

Laser printers, however, do contain different fonts for regular, bold, regular italic, and bold italic. This is because each of these is a different font. The user interface of the AT, however, groups all these versions as styles of a font, so they have continued with that form of user interface, even though it is technically inaccurate.

# Identifying Type

To begin to decide which typeface you will use, it is important to be able to identify the different fonts available for your laser printer. Let's take a look at the most commonly used font, Times, which is a serif typeface. (See Fig. 9-1.)

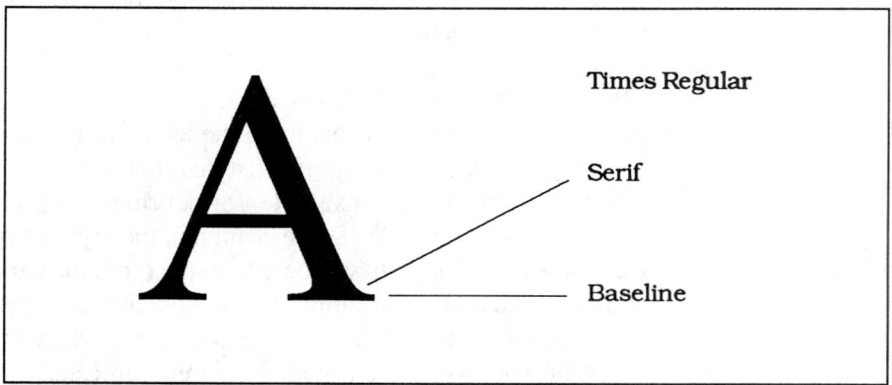

**Figure 9-1.** The letter "A" in Times Regular. This is a serif typeface and is one of the most popular typefaces of all times. The additional strokes on the bottom of the letter are serifs.

Times is distinguishable as a serif typeface. It has thick and thin strokes and perpendicular strokes at the ends of the strokes. Almost all serif faces share this trait.

The differences between serif and sans serif faces (typefaces that do not contain serifs and most often have even weight in their lines) from this point on are more subtle. For example, Fig. 9-2 shows the same letter in Bookman Regular.

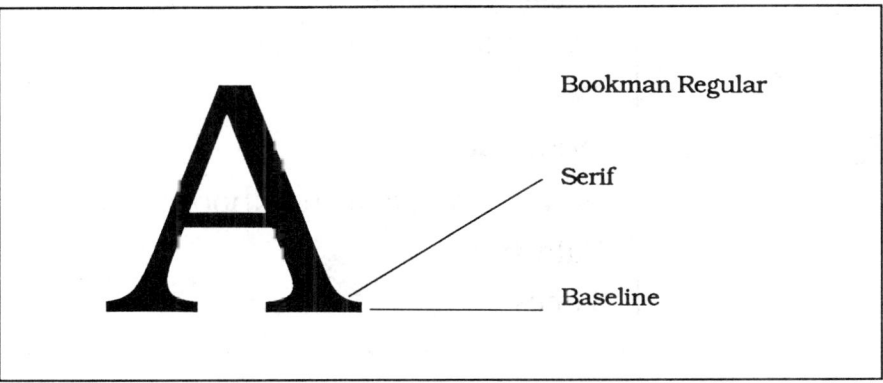

**Figure 9-2.** A Bookman Regular capital "A". Note that it shares many of the characteristics of the Times Regular "A", but the differences are now subtle. Different widths, line thickness, and other subtle traits make it different from Times.

As you can see in Fig. 9-2, the differences between many typestyles are subtle. Learning to identify typefaces by sight is a learned art. You must simply work with them enough to learn those subtle differences.

The typefaces resident on laser printers are fairly distinct, but the serif faces are similar enough to one another that it may take some time before you can quickly identify one from another. Let's take a look at some typefaces:

> Helvetica
> Helvetica Narrow
> Avant Garde
> Courier
> *Zapf Chancery*
> Bookman
> New Century Schoolbook
> Palatino
> Times

As you can see, they are all attractive, but some are similar. I placed the serif typefaces last. Right now they may seem easy to identify because they are large and are associated with their names. Let's take a more difficult test. Examine the next four blocks.

> The differences in typestyles are subtle. They can be identified by looking for classic traits, such as the
>
> The differences in typestyles are subtle. They can be identified by looking for classic traits,
>
> The differences in typestyles are subtle. They can be identified by looking for classic traits, such as the
>
> The differences in typestyles are subtle. They can be identified by looking for classic traits, such as the shape of the lowercase

Now, without names and the large sizes, could you quickly identify each of these four typefaces? As you can tell, each is quite different but still similar enough that you may confuse one with another. The answer, by the way, is, from the top: Palatino, Bookman, New Century Schoolbook, and Times.

This example does more than illustrate that type must be learned; it shows how the subtleties and differences can affect the look and feel of a document. For example, Palatino is more condensed than Bookman, which is the widest of the typefaces above.

There are many type styles from which you may choose. The one that is right is a purely selective process. But once you find a typeface that you want to use, you will need to learn the mechanics of type.

## Type Mechanics

Type is available not only as a style but also in many sizes, weights, and line spacings. The size and line spacing of a typeface make changes in its overall appearance. To use type, you must learn the sizing system as well as how to select the line spacing for it.

The first consideration is how big the type is or should be.

### Helpful Hint

Type is not measured in inches but in points, a unit of measurement used in the graphic arts industry. A point is simply a very small unit of measurement. It measures 0.0138 inch, with 72 points to an inch. Both type size and line spacing are generally measured in points. This is a convention that you will have to learn to live with. Type comes in so many sizes that, realistically, it needs a very small unit of measure to identify its size. It would be difficult to measure the difference between 24-point type and 28-point type in inches.

Fig. 9-3 shows the range of one typeface in a variety of point sizes.

> Helvetica 10 Point
> Helvetica 11 Point
> Helvetica 12 Point
> Helvetica 13 Point
> Helvetica 14 Point
> Helvetica 15 Point
> Helvetica 16 Point
> Helvetica 17 Point
> Helvetica 18 Point
> Helvetica 19 Point
> Helvetica 20 Point

**Figure 9-3.**   Helvetica in a range of point sizes.

OK, now for more confusion. Just because a typeface is identified by a point size does not mean that it is actually the exact height of the identifying point size.

Type is identified by three main characteristics. Fig. 9-4 illustrates the identifying traits.

**103** Working with Type

**Figure 9-4.** The body of the type is the x height, or the size of most lowercase letters. The upper strokes (such as the upward line in the letter "h") is called an ascender. The strokes below the baseline are descenders.

What is interesting is that even though a typeface may be identified as 36 points, it is not actually 36 points tall. Believe it or not, there is a reason for this. As described in Fig. 9-4, type is made up of ascenders and descenders: basically, the tops of letters such as h, l, or k and the bottoms of letters such as g or y. If the type were set so that the tops of the ascenders and the bottoms of the decenders went to the full height of the point size, then there would be times that when the type was set solid (no extra spacing between lines), where the bottom of a y would touch the top of an h. To avoid this, type is designed to fit aesthetically within its point size, so that when type is set solid—for example, 24-point type on 24-point line spacing—no characters will touch one another.

So, the question arises, if you cannot measure type by its actual size, how do you know what size it is? Refer once again to Fig. 9-4. Note that type has a baseline. When set solid, the measurement from baseline to baseline will tell you the size of the type, as long as it has been set solid with no extra space between lines.

Identifying the size is not difficult. Most 24-point type, for example, matches pretty much in height. Most professionals use a clear plastic type gauge (available at art supply stores), which are simply different sizes of type printed in black on a clear background. You lay this gauge over your type, and it will indicate the type size of your sample is. It will also contain a leading guide. Leading is the graphic arts term for line spacing. It is used in the program PC PageMaker, so remember that the term "lead" or "leading" simply means the number of points between each line.

## Make Your Own Type Gauge

I have found that one useful trick is to make a type gauge right off of a laser printer, using a clear transparency sheet instead of a piece of paper. Simply set all the different sizes of type in this fashion:

---

9 Point

10 Point

12 Point

14 Point

18 Point

## 24 Point

---

The same method can be used for line spacing. Set baseline rules using the underline key, and then set the line spacing (in PC PageMaker) to various line spacings, as follows:

---

_____
_____
_____
_____

10 point spacing

_____
_____
_____

12 point spacing

## The Finer Points of Type

Beyond identifying and sizing type, there are a few more essentials that will assist you in working with type.

**Picas.** A unit of linear measurement used by typesetters and printers. You will often see this as a standard for measuring the width of type. There are 12 points to a pica or 6 picas to 1 inch.

**em Space and em Dash.** A unit of width in typesetting that is equal to the height of the typeface's size. For example, an em Dash in 12-point Times is a dash that is 12 points wide. The em space is commonly used for paragraph indentation. The em dash is used as the wide dash, the equivalent of the double hyphen used in typing to represent a dash.

**Letterspacing.** The amount of space between letters. On sophisticated typesetting machines, this can be controlled. Using PC PageMaker, you can control the maximum and minimum amounts of letterspacing. If you study the type in this book, you will see that the amount of space between letters in each line will vary. This is the result of justifying lines.

**Wordspacing.** The same concept as letterspacing, except that space is controlled between words. The rule of thumb in typography is to add wordspacing first, and then if the space between words becomes too excessive, add letterspacing to fill the line out using the maximum allowable word spacing. Word spacing is preferred over letterspacing. Once again, you can control the maximum and minimum amounts of word spacing in PC PageMaker.

**Justification.** Justification makes the right- and left-hand margins flush. Space is added between the words and/or letters to fill out the width of the line to create an even right margin. You may be familiar with this concept from using word-processing programs.

**Kerning.** Kerning, an important feature, is the process of removing space between specific pairs of characters. For example, when a capital "T" and a capital "A" are set without kerning, there is too much space between the "T" and the "A". The reason for this space is that the "A" has a slanted shape and the "T" has empty space on the bottom. When the two characters are next to each other, the space between the letters is exaggerated. Fig. 9-5 shows this effect, and how by using a kerning pair the "A" is moved slightly to the left to create the correct visual spacing between the letters.

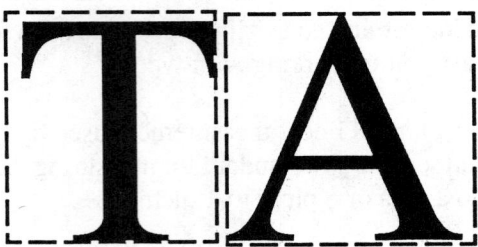

Without kerning, widths butt together.

With kerning, selected pairs overlap, avoiding excessive space between various letter pairs, such as "TA" or "YA."

**Figure 9-5.** Kerning overlaps the two characters "T" and "A" to create the correct visual spacing between the letters. This particular kerning instruction would work only with the "TA" pair, not when a "T" or an "A" is next to any other letter.

## A Starting Point

Working with type is a learning experience. Handled properly, type can make your page look great. Bad typography can ruin a page. The next two chapters take a look at choosing a type style and how to format your text consistently to give your pages a slick, finished look.

# 10
# PostScript and LaserJet Plus Type Styles

*T*his chapter details the typefaces available to you from the LaserWriter and the LaserWriter Plus. It will show each PostScript typeface in detail, at 14-point size, and all the variations of each face.

If you have not yet purchased a LaserWriter or LaserWriter Plus, this will help you decide which model has the typefaces you will want. If you already own a LaserWriter or LaserWriter Plus, this chapter will act as a quick reference to the typefaces available to you.

All typestyles shown are laser fonts. When you buy a LaserWriter or LaserWriter Plus, a disk comes with the unit with screen fonts for a Macintosh, but there will be none for Windows or any IBM PC program. PC PageMaker provides its own set of fonts to represent the PostScript type shown here. Although the program can use all the fonts, it represents them on the screen of the computer with generic representations. For example, one serif typeface will represent all the different serif faces shown in this chapter, including those for the Hewlett-Packard LaserJet.

A sampling of fonts available as downloadable fonts for the Hewlett-Packard LaserJet Plus and LaserJet II follows the PostScript fonts found on the Apple LaserWriters (and other PostScript printers as well). Unlike PostScript fonts, which can be made any point size, the fonts for the LaserJet Plus and LaserJet II are discreetly sized. For example, 14-point Times can only be 14-point Times. It cannot be made bold or italic or have its size changed. The LaserJet fonts are true fonts in the sense that each font is a single size and style.

The following pages will identify the name of the type font and which Laser printer it works with.

Name of font: Helvetica 14 point
Available on: LaserWriter, LaserWriter Plus

Regular:
abcdefghijklmnopqrstuvwxyz
ABCDEFGHIJKLMNOPQRSTUVWXYZ

Regular Italic:
*abcdefghijklmnopqrstuvwxyz*
*ABCDEFGHIJKLMNOPQRSTUVWXYZ*

Bold:
**abcdefghijklmnopqrstuvwxyz**
**ABCDEFGHIJKLMNOPQRSTUVWXYZ**

Bold Italic:
***abcdefghijklmnopqrstuvwxyz***
***ABCDEFGHIJKLMNOPQRSTUVWXYZ***

Outline:
abcdefghijklmnopqrstuvwxyz
ABCDEFGHIJKLMNOPQRSTUVWXYZ

Bold Outline:
abcdefghijklmnopqrstuvwxyz
ABCDEFGHIJKLMNOPQRSTUVWXYZ

Shadow:
abcdefghijklmnopqrstuvwxyz
ABCDEFGHIJKLMNOPQRSTUVWXYZ

Bold Shadow:
abcdefghijklmnopqrstuvwxyz
ABCDEFGHIJKLMNOPQRSTUVWXYZ

Name of font: Helvetica Narrow 14 point
Available on: LaserWriter Plus

Regular:
abcdefghijklmnopqrstuvwxyz
ABCDEFGHIJKLMNOPQRSTUVWXYZ

Regular Italic:
*abcdefghijklmnopqrstuvwxyz*
*ABCDEFGHIJKLMNOPQRSTUVWXYZ*

Bold:
**abcdefghijklmnopqrstuvwxyz**
**ABCDEFGHIJKLMNOPQRSTUVWXYZ**

Bold Italic:
***abcdefghijklmnopqrstuvwxyz***
***ABCDEFGHIJKLMNOPQRSTUVWXYZ***

Outline:
abcdefghijklmnopqrstuvwxyz
ABCDEFGHIJKLMNOPQRSTUVWXYZ

Bold Outline:
abcdefghijklmnopqrstuvwxyz
ABCDEFGHIJKLMNOPQRSTUVWXYZ

Shadow:
abcdefghijklmnopqrstuvwxyz
ABCDEFGHIJKLMNOPQRSTUVWXYZ

Bold Shadow:
abcdefghijklmnopqrstuvwxyz
ABCDEFGHIJKLMNOPQRSTUVWXYZ

Name of font: Times 14 point
Available on: LaserWriter, LaserWriter Plus

Regular:
abcdefghijklmnopqrstuvwxyz
ABCDEFGHIJKLMNOPQRSTUVWXYZ

Regular Italic:
*abcdefghijklmnopqrstuvwxyz*
*ABCDEFGHIJKLMNOPQRSTUVWXYZ*

Bold:
**abcdefghijklmnopqrstuvwxyz**
**ABCDEFGHIJKLMNOPQRSTUVWXYZ**

Bold Italic:
***abcdefghijklmnopqrstuvwxyz***
***ABCDEFGHIJKLMNOPQRSTUVWXYZ***

Outline:
abcdefghijklmnopqrstuvwxyz
ABCDEFGHIJKLMNOPQRSTUVWXYZ

Bold Outline:
abcdefghijklmnopqrstuvwxyz
ABCDEFGHIJKLMNOPQRSTUVWXYZ

Shadow:
abcdefghijklmnopqrstuvwxyz
ABCDEFGHIJKLMNOPQRSTUVWXYZ

Bold Shadow:
abcdefghijklmnopqrstuvwxyz
ABCDEFGHIJKLMNOPQRSTUVWXYZ

Name of font: Courier 14 point
Available on: LaserWriter, LaserWriter Plus

Regular:
abcdefghijklmnopqrstuvwxyz
ABCDEFGHIJKLMNOPQRSTUVWXYZ

Regular Italic:
*abcdefghijklmnopqrstuvwxyz*
*ABCDEFGHIJKLMNOPQRSTUVWXYZ*

Bold:
**abcdefghijklmnopqrstuvwxyz**
**ABCDEFGHIJKLMNOPQRSTUVWXYZ**

Bold Italic:
***abcdefghijklmnopqrstuvwxyz***
***ABCDEFGHIJKLMNOPQRSTUVWXYZ***

Outline:
abcdefghijklmnopqrstuvwxyz
ABCDEFGHIJKLMNOPQRSTUVWXYZ

Bold Outline:
abcdefghijklmnopqrstuvwxyz
ABCDEFGHIJKLMNOPQRSTUVWXYZ

Shadow:
abcdefghijklmnopqrstuvwxyz
ABCDEFGHIJKLMNOPQRSTUVWXYZ

Bold Shadow:
**abcdefghijklmnopqrstuvwxyz**
**ABCDEFGHIJKLMNOPQRSTUVWXYZ**

Name of font: Avant Garde 14 point
Available on: LaserWriter Plus

Regular:
abcdefghijklmnopqrstuvwxyz
ABCDEFGHIJKLMNOPQRSTUVWXYZ

Regular Italic:
*abcdefghijklmnopqrstuvwxyz*
*ABCDEFGHIJKLMNOPQRSTUVWXYZ*

Bold:
**abcdefghijklmnopqrstuvwxyz**
**ABCDEFGHIJKLMNOPQRSTUVWXYZ**

Bold Italic:
***abcdefghijklmnopqrstuvwxyz***
***ABCDEFGHIJKLMNOPQRSTUVWXYZ***

Outline:
abcdefghijklmnopqrstuvwxyz
ABCDEFGHIJKLMNOPQRSTUVWXYZ

Bold Outline:
abcdefghijklmnopqrstuvwxyz
ABCDEFGHIJKLMNOPQRSTUVWXYZ

Shadow:
abcdefghijklmnopqrstuvwxyz
ABCDEFGHIJKLMNOPQRSTUVWXYZ

Bold Shadow:
**abcdefghijklmnopqrstuvwxyz**
**ABCDEFGHIJKLMNOPQRSTUVWXYZ**

Name of font: Zapf Chancery 14 point
Available on: LaserWriter Plus

Regular:
abcdefghijklmnopqrstuvwxyz
ABCDEFGHIJKLMNOPQRSTUVWXYZ

Bold:
abcdefghijklmnopqrstuvwxyz
ABCDEFGHIJKLMNOPQRSTUVWXYZ

Outline:
abcdefghijklmnopqrstuvwxyz
ABCDEFGHIJKLMNOPQRSTUVWXYZ

Shadow:
abcdefghijklmnopqrstuvwxyz
ABCDEFGHIJKLMNOPQRSTUVWXYZ

Name of font: Palatino 14 point
Available on: LaserWriter Plus

Regular:
abcdefghijklmnopqrstuvwxyz
ABCDEFGHIJKLMNOPQRSTUVWXYZ

Regular Italic:
*abcdefghijklmnopqrstuvwxyz*
*ABCDEFGHIJKLMNOPQRSTUVWXYZ*

Bold:
**abcdefghijklmnopqrstuvwxyz**
**ABCDEFGHIJKLMNOPQRSTUVWXYZ**

Bold Italic:
***abcdefghijklmnopqrstuvwxyz***
***ABCDEFGHIJKLMNOPQRSTUVWXYZ***

Outline:
abcdefghijklmnopqrstuvwxyz
ABCDEFGHIJKLMNOPQRSTUVWXYZ

Bold Outline:
abcdefghijklmnopqrstuvwxyz
ABCDEFGHIJKLMNOPQRSTUVWXYZ

Shadow:
abcdefghijklmnopqrstuvwxyz
ABCDEFGHIJKLMNOPQRSTUVWXYZ

Bold Shadow:
abcdefghijklmnopqrstuvwxyz
ABCDEFGHIJKLMNOPQRSTUVWXYZ

Name of font: New Century Schoolbook 14 point
Available on: LaserWriter Plus

Regular:
abcdefghijklmnopqrstuvwxyz
ABCDEFGHIJKLMNOPQRSTUVWXYZ

Regular Italic:
*abcdefghijklmnopqrstuvwxyz*
*ABCDEFGHIJKLMNOPQRSTUVWXYZ*

Bold:
**abcdefghijklmnopqrstuvwxyz**
**ABCDEFGHIJKLMNOPQRSTUVWXYZ**

Bold Italic:
***abcdefghijklmnopqrstuvwxyz***
***ABCDEFGHIJKLMNOPQRSTUVWXYZ***

Outline:
abcdefghijklmnopqrstuvwxyz
ABCDEFGHIJKLMNOPQRSTUVWXYZ

Bold Outline:
abcdefghijklmnopqrstuvwxyz
ABCDEFGHIJKLMNOPQRSTUVWXYZ

Shadow:
abcdefghijklmnopqrstuvwxyz
ABCDEFGHIJKLMNOPQRSTUVWXYZ

Bold Shadow:
**abcdefghijklmnopqrstuvwxyz**
**ABCDEFGHIJKLMNOPQRSTUVWXYZ**

Name of font: Symbol 14 point
Available on: LaserWriter, LaserWriter Plus

Regular:

αβχδεφγηιφκλμνοπθρστυϖωξψζ
ΑΒΧΔΕΦΓΗΙϑΚΛΜΝΟΠΘΡΣΤΥςΩΞΨΖ

Italic:

αβχδεφγηιφκλμνοπθρστυϖωξψζ
ΑΒΧΔΕΦΓΗΙϑΚΛΜΝΟΠΘΡΣΤΥςΩΞΨΖ

Name of font: Zapf Dingbats 14 point
Available on: LaserWriter Plus

Regular:
❁❂❃❄❅❆❇❈❉❊●○■□❏❐❑❒▲▼◆❖❘❙❚
✡✢✣✤✥✦✧★☆✪✫✬✭✮✯✰✱✲✳✴✵✶✷✸✹

Italic:
❁❂❃❄❅❆❇❈❉❊●○■□❏❐❑❒▲▼◆❖❘❙❚
✡✢✣✤✥✦✧★☆✪✫✬✭✮✯✰✱✲✳✴✵✶✷✸✹

## Sampling of LaserJet Plus Fonts

Fonts for Hewlett-Packard JaserJet printers come either cartridge- or disk-based. There are a number of fonts available, and the folllowing is just a sample of what is available. For a complete list of Hewlett-Packard LaserJet font suppliers, see the Products listing in the Reference section of this book.

TMS RMN, 10 POINT

ABCDEFGHIJKLMNOPQRSTUVWXYZ
abcdefghijklmnopqrstuvwxyz
1234567890-=[]\;',./
!@#$%^&*()_+{}|:"<>?
ÀÂÈÊËÎÏ``¨˜ÛÜ£¯°ÇçÑñ¡¿¤£¥
§ƒ¢âêôûáéóúàèòùäëöüÅîØÆåíø
æÄìÖÜÉïßÔÁÃãÐdÍÌÓÒÕõŠšÚŸÿÞþ
—¼½ªº«■»±

TMS RMN ITALIC, 10 POINT

*ABCDEFGHIJKLMNOPQRSTUVWXYZ*
*abcdefghijklmnopqrstuvwxyz*
*1234567890-=[ ]\;',./*
*!@#$%^&*( )_+{ }|:"<>?*
*ÀÂÈÊËÎÏ``¨˜ÛÜ£¯°ÇçÑñ¡¿¤£¥*
*§ƒ¢âêôûáéóúàèòùäëöüÅîØÆåíø*
*æÄìÖÜÉïßÔÁÃãÐdÍÌÓÒÕõŠšÚŸÿÞþ*
*—¼½ªº«■»±*

**TMS RMN BOLD, 10 POINT**

**ABCDEFGHIJKLMNOPQRSTUVWXYZ**
**abcdefghijklmnopqrstuvwxyz**
**1234567890-=[]\;',./**
**!@#$%^&*()_+{}|:"<>?**
**ÀÂÈÊËÎÏ``¨˜ÛÜ£¯°ÇçÑñ¡¿¤£¥**
**§ƒ¢âêôûáéóúàèòùäëöüÅîØÆåíø**
**æÄìÖÜÉïßÔÁÃãÐdÍÌÓÒÕõŠšÚŸÿÞþ**
**—¼½ªº«■»±**

Hewlett-Packard LaserJet Cartridge Fonts.

## AVANT GARDE BOOK
abcdefghijklmnopqrstuvwxyz
ABCDEFGHIJKLMNOPQRSTUVWXYZ
0123456789[!#$%&''(:)*+,—

## CENTURY BOOK ITALIC II
*abcdefghijklmnopqrstuvwxyz*
*ABCDEFGHIJKLMNOPQRSTUVWX*
*0123456789[!#$%&''(:)*+,—*

VS HLV
abcdefghijklmnopqrstuvwxyz
ABCDEFGHIJKLMNOPQRSTUVWXYZ
{!<#>$%&''(!)*+,-.\/;?~@}=[0123456789]

## UNIVERS EXTRA BOLD
**abcdefghijklmnopqrstuvwxyz**
**ABCDEFGHIJKLMNOPQRSTUV**
**0123456789[!#$%&''(:)*+,—**

VS BHS DB
abcdefghijklmnopqrstuvwxyz
ABCDEFGHIJKLMNOPQRSTUVWXYZ
!"#$%&'()*+,-./[\]^_`
0123456789:;<=>?@{!}~™
ÀÂÈÊËÏÌ`´¨˜ÙÛ£ °ÇçÑñ¡¿ª£¥§ƒ¢
âêôûáéóúàèòùäëöüÅìØÆåíøæÄìÖÜÉïβ
ÔÁÃãÐdJÎÓÒÕõŠšÚÝÿþþ —¼½º⁰«■»±

## GARAMOND ANTIQUA
abcdefghijklmnopqrstuvwxyz
ABCDEFGHIJKLMNOPQRSTUVWXYZ
0123456789[!#$%&''(:)*+,—

Downloadable "soft fonts" from VS Software.

# Formatting Type  11

*N*ow that you have learned some of the basics of typography and have had a chance to examine the typefaces available to you on laser printers, it is time to start thinking about how your text will be formatted into type.

PC PageMaker is great since you can enter type in just about any fashion and later format it into the typestyles you will want to use. When writing, if you do not feel comfortable changing sizes and styles, you can wait until you have finished writing before worrying about formatting the page. This is also the way that you would work with text from ASCII files or from telecommunicated type that contains no formatting.

## Planning for PC PageMaker

PC PageMaker, the page assembly program you will be working with, makes full use of whatever formatting it can with your word-processing program. If you can put type in bold, that is how PC PageMaker will place it on the page if it can work with your word-processing program's formatting. When it can, PC PageMaker follows your size, font, style, tab, and alignment commands. These may be modified once you are in PC PageMaker, but remember that PC PageMaker is not a word-processing program. It is quicker to make format changes in your word-processing program.

The only area that you need not worry about with PC PageMaker is the column width. When using PC PageMaker, you will be working with a master page grid that will have defined column widths. When you place your text in PC PageMaker, it will format the type to the column width on the grid.

These are the major considerations in preparing text for use in PC PageMaker, but the real secret is deciding what type fonts you are going to use, how large they will be, and how the page will look.

## Formatting Text into Type

Before launching into PC PageMaker, let's plan what our pages will look like. Starting with a simple text file, we will take it from raw copy into a formatted state that will be ready for use in PC PageMaker and printed on a PostScript laser printer. The word-processing program will be Microsoft Word.

The first choice that must be made is what type font will be used for text, headlines, subheads, and captions. As we study the samples of type, we must keep in mind that we are going to create a simple report with a classic look. We choose Times Roman Regular 10 point for the text, Times Roman Bold 60 point for the headline, Helvetica Bold 11 point for subheads, and Helvetica Regular Italic 9 point for captions.

Fig. 11-1 shows the text file in its unformatted state. The first step is to go in and format the type into the selected type fonts. This is illustrated in Figs. 11-2 through 11-5.

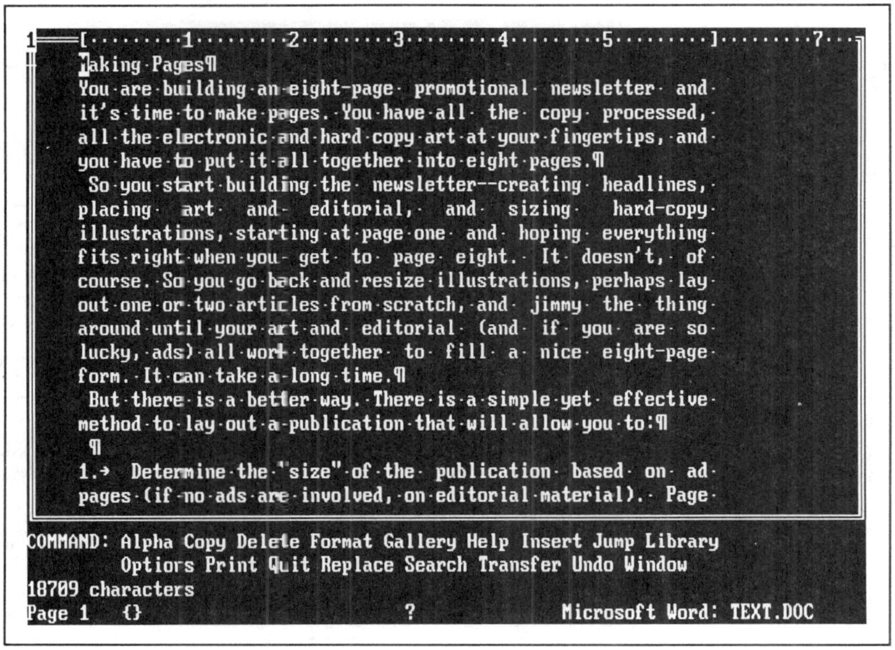

**Figure 11-1.** The text file for our report. The type shown is unformatted. The next step is to begin formatting the text file for use in PC PageMaker.

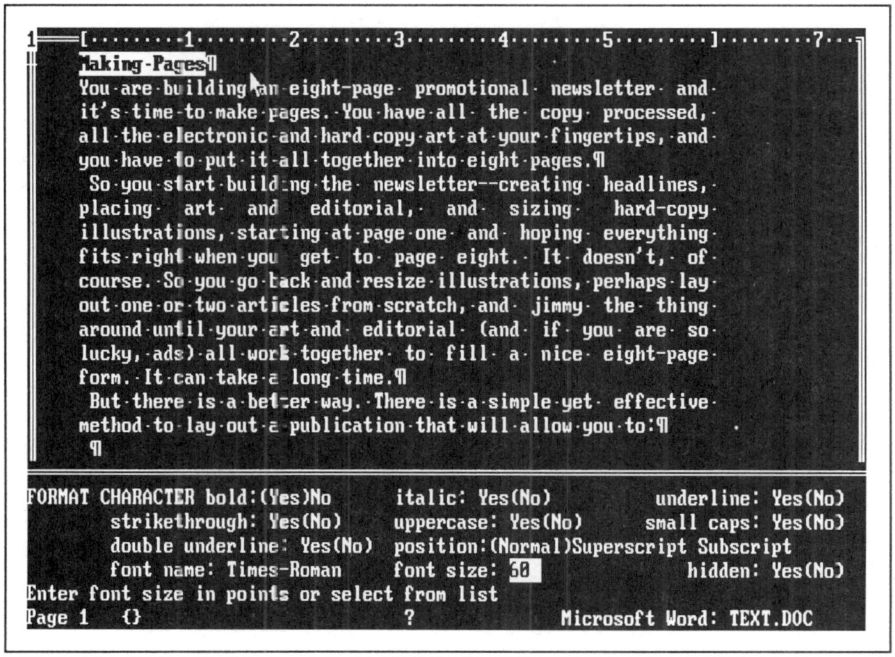

**Figure 11-2.** The headline is formatted. Note that the right-hand margin is set arbitrarily. Since we will be using the grids in PC PageMaker for our column widths, we do not have to worry about it here.

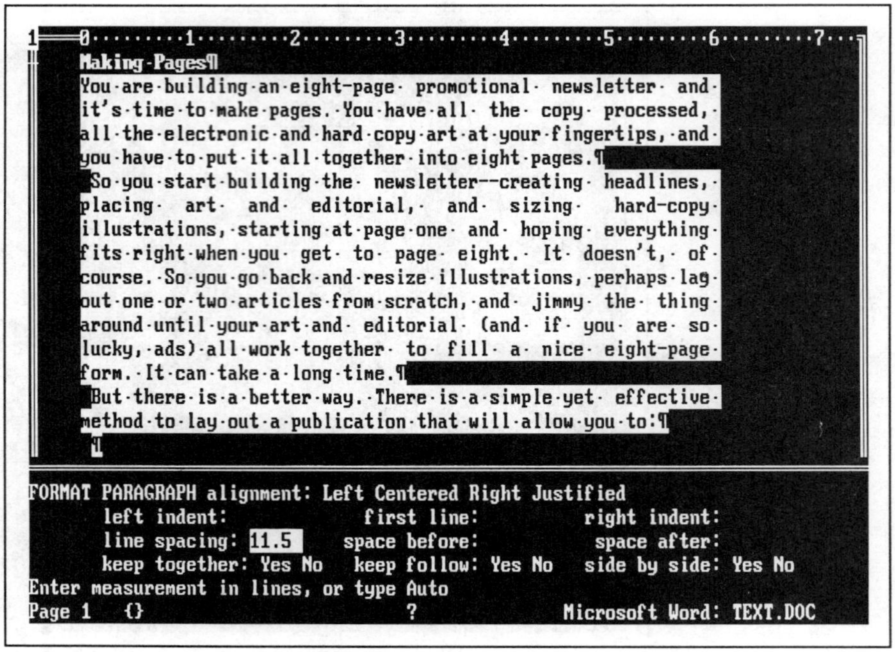

**Figure 11-3.** The body copy (text) is formatted by selecting it from format character menu and making it all 10-point Times Roman Regular. The linespacing for the entire document is made 11.5 points.

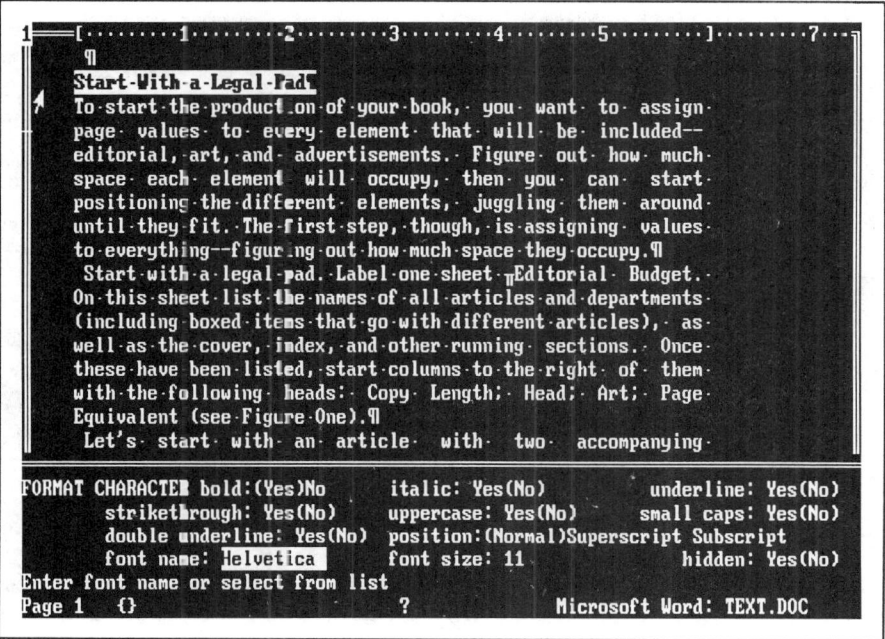

**Figure 11-4.** Scrolling down the text, subheads are selected from the format character menu and made Helvetica Bold 11 point. The F4 "repeat action" key is used to format the remaining subheads without having to return to the menu.

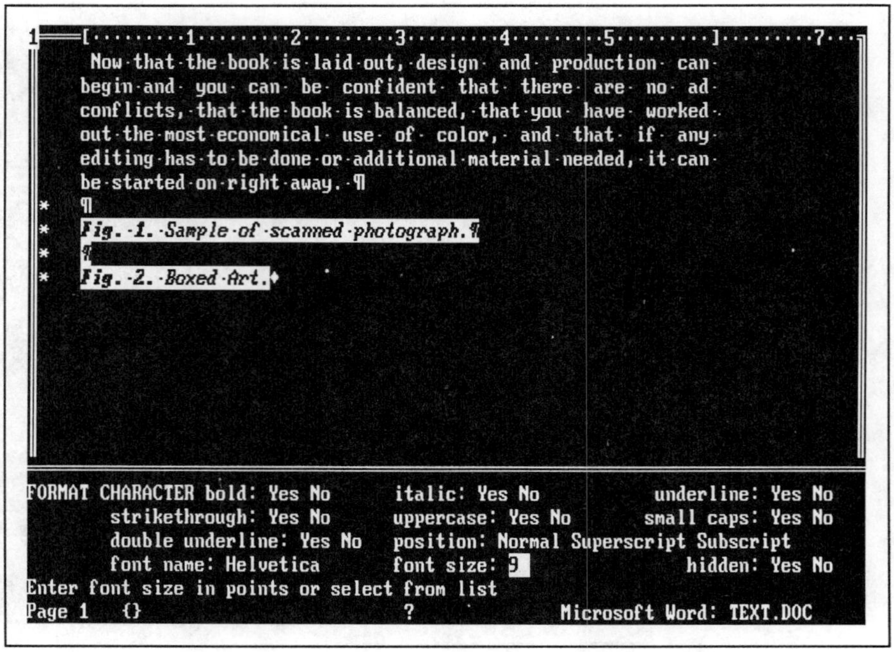

**Figure 11-5.** Finally, the report contains two illustration captions. These are made Helvetica Regular Italic by formatting them to 9-point Italic. The first words in the caption are made Bold in the same manner.

The entire text file is now saved, formatted, and ready for use in PC PageMaker.

### Helpful Hint

Consistency is the best rule for a good-looking publication. Keep all text the same size and column width. Make headlines clean and easy to read. Subheads should be strong enough to be noticed, but they should not overpower the text. Do not use more than three or four different fonts per page, preferably all from the same type family (such as Times Roman Regular, Italic, and Bold).

If you follow these simple rules, you will have a publication that is not only attractive but easy to format as well.

## Formatting from Various Word-Processing Programs

The sample in Figs. 11-2 through 11-5 shows what you can do with Microsoft Word, but you may use one of the other word-processing programs supported by PC PageMaker. The following list identifies the formatting features PC PageMaker can use in the supported group of word-processing programs.

### Microsoft Word Version 3.0
PC PageMaker supports Word's character formats, indents, justification styles, and tab stops. It uses the point-size measurement system, so type size can be between 4 and 127 points. Linespacing can start at 1 point and go up to 127 points in 1/2-point increments. Paragraph indent measures and left and right indent measures are retained, but margin widths are ignored. The file extension for Word files is .DOC.

### Windows Write Version 1.0
PC PageMaker supports Write's character formats, indents, justification styles, and tab stops, like Word. Type sizes can be from 4 to 127 points. When single or double spacing is chosen, PC PageMaker autoleads single spacing and leads 1.5 times the point size for double spacing. Since Write is a Windows program, text files can be imported from the clipboard by cutting and pasting. The file extension for Windows Write files is .WRI.

### XyWrite III
PC PageMaker supports XyWrite's character modes, indents, justification styles, and tabs. It views measurements from XyWrite as 10 units to the inch—or 10 pitch. It will support whole units (such as .5 for 1/2 inch) for measures. PC PageMaker cannot use most type information, but it does support mode commands that are embedded in the files for attributes such as normal, bold, italic, underline, superscript, and subscript. The file extension for XyWrite III files is .XWY.

## MultiMate Version 3.31

PC PageMaker supports font size, indents, tabs, linespacing, and most font styles for MultiMate. Because MultiMate measures in pitch instead of points, type size is determined by pitch. The following is a breakdown of the pitch-to-point size:

| Pitch | Point |
|-------|-------|
| 5     | 24    |
| 6     | 18    |
| 8.5   | 14    |
| 10    | 12    |
| 12    | 10    |
| 13.2  | 9     |
| 15    | 8     |
| 16.5  | 7     |
| 17.6  | 6     |

The normal, bold, subscript, superscript, and strikeout styles all can be used by PC PageMaker. Linespacing is determined by multiplying the point size of the type by quarter line (x 0.25), half line (x 0.5), single space (x 1), one and one-half space (x 1.5), double space (x 2), two and one-half space (x 2.5), and triple space (x 3). The file extension for MultiMate files is .DOC.

## Samna Word III

PC PageMaker supports Samna Word files that have been converted to DCA files. Minimal formatting is retained, left and right margin indents carry over, but hanging indents and bullets are ignored. Regular and decimal tabs are supported. Bold and underlined type are the only sizes that are recognized. Type point size is changed by pitch, which converts to point size = 120/pitch. Linespacing converts to leading = 72/lines per inch. The file extension for Samna Word III files is .DCA or .RFT.

## Volkswriter 3 Version 1.0

PC PageMaker supports Volkswriter 3 files that have been converted to the DCA format. It views the left and right margins as indents and supports up to 20 tab stops. Type style support includes subscript, superscript, and underline; it also converts overstrike to strikethru. Linespacing converts to points (leading = 72/lines per inch). The file extension for VolksWriter 3 is .DCA or .RFT.

### WordPerfect Version 4.1

PC PageMaker supports WordPerfect's tabs, indents, justification styles, most character styles, and some text alignment commands. Soft hyphens become discretionary hyphens. Hard spaces are converted to normal spaces. Character formatting for bold, underline, strikeout, subscript, and superscript are supported. Any style of underlining is converted to a single underline. PC PageMaker converts pitch to point size (point size = 120/pitch), and all text is placed single spaced and autoleaded. The file extension for WordPerfect is .WP.

### WordStar Version 3.3

PC PageMaker ignores tabs and dot commands for margins, pitch, and other formatting. As a result, text is placed with the default type font and size with autoleading and with the default alignment. Type styles are recognized from the control codes used to create bold, underscore, strikeout, subscript, and superscript. The double-strike code converts type to italic. The file extension for WordStar files is .WS.

### WordStar 2000 Version 2.0

PC PageMaker supports WordStar 2000 files that have been converted to the DCA format. The program supports left, right, and decimal tabs. Type styles that are supported are bold, underline, strikeout, superscript, and subscript. Emphasized type carries over as bold, but italic converts to normal text. Points sizes are converted as follows:

| Pitch | Point |
| --- | --- |
| Non PS 6 | 24 |
| Non PS 12 | 10 |
| Non PS 8.5 | 14 |
| Non PS 17 | 7 |
| Non PS 5 | 24 |
| Non PS 10 | 12 |

### ASCII Files

Pure ASCII text files, which can be created by most word-processing programs, are placed keeping only paragraph returns. All the default formats for size, linespacing, type style, font, and alignment are used.

# Part Four  Working with PC PageMaker

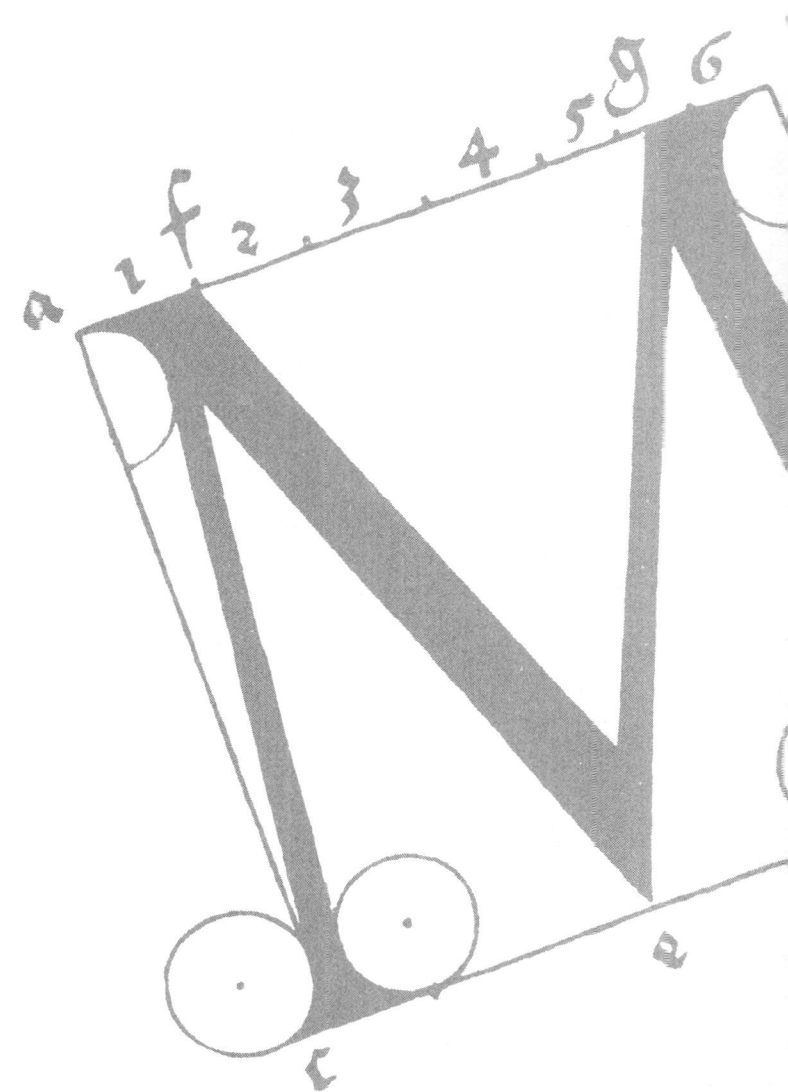

# Putting the Pieces Together 12

*I*n the past eleven chapters we have learned to assemble a variety of hardware and software into a nicely configured publishing system, gathered up the correct software to create page elements, explored the nature of a page in a multipage environment, and taken a look at the nature of type. We took raw text and formatted it into type. Now comes the point of all that work—assembling your publication.

## Page Assembly

This section will detail the use of an excellent page assembly program called PC PageMaker. In a very short time, you will see how all the concepts explored up to this point will come into play when you start using it.

PC PageMaker offers you a clean sheet of paper that you may fill with whatever you want. It offers you a tremendous number of tools to place elements in a multipage environment with ease and grace. It is a classic "power" program. To make full use of all that power, the subjects covered in the book up to now will be of great help.

Although I have gone into great detail about the equipment and basic software you will need for your publishing system, I have not yet explained the purpose of functionality of page assembly software. Along the way we have been collecting bits and pieces: text files formatted into type, headlines, captions, and subheads. We have art files, clip art, and digitized images. Now we want to take all of these elements and put them together in page form. We do not want the simple page produced by a word-processing program but rather a complex multicolumn page where elements can be intermingled and viewed as a whole, then changed quickly if you are not happy with the result.

PC PageMaker allows you to do all of this. It is simple in nature, so it is easy to learn, but it gives you all the tools and power to create sophisticated pages.

## Page Relationships

Unlike a word-processing program, PC PageMaker lets you place multiple columns on a page. If you work with large text files, your text may exceed a single page and go for several pages. When this happens, you enter the multipage environment I keep mentioning.

Let's say that you have created ten very complex pages. There are illustrations, graphic elements, headlines, and a huge text file that starts on page 1 and continues through page 10. If this had been done manually, you would have ten boards that had gone through pasteup. Done in PC PageMaker, you have built ten pages on the screen. Now, you examine the pages and find that on the first page you have repeated a paragraph when you entered the text! All that work, and you missed it, even after several sessions of proofing the pages. Let's examine how the two different systems would handle this situation.

The manual process—pasteup—would require that you go to page 1, remove the paragraph, and adjust the rest of the type on the page. The page is now a paragraph short. So you have to move a number of lines from page 2 to fill out page 1. This step is repeated on all ten pages. On page 10, you are a paragraph short, but it looks better there than on page 1! In essence, you have had to go back and manually paste up ten pages again because of one small mistake.

With PC PageMaker, you would start the same way. You would select the bad paragraph and electronically "cut" it from the page. So now what happens? Like the art board, does a hole just stare at you? No. In PC PageMaker, all the text from one file is a whole. Even from column to column and page to page, that text is one entity. If you remove a paragraph from page 1, it immediately repaginates the document. It moves all the text up without your intervention. If you go to page 10, you will see that the document is one paragraph shorter, just like on the art boards. The difference is that this took a matter of seconds, not a matter of hours.

With that type of power, you can envision that, if you can take a paragraph out, you can also add a paragraph and have all the pages adjust themselves automatically. And you would be right. But the beauty is that you can adjust for that lost paragraph anywhere. For example, you have a box on page 5 representing a photo. Instead of writing filler copy, why not make the photo bigger? So shorten the two paragraphs above the photo box and go to page 10. You will see that the type has returned to the bottom of the page. The text is now correct and ends flush. Next, go back to the photo box, click on it to get handles for stretching and pulling, and make the box larger to fill out the space. In a matter of minutes, you have electronically corrected a problem that would be catastrophic in a manual system. (See Fig. 12-1.)

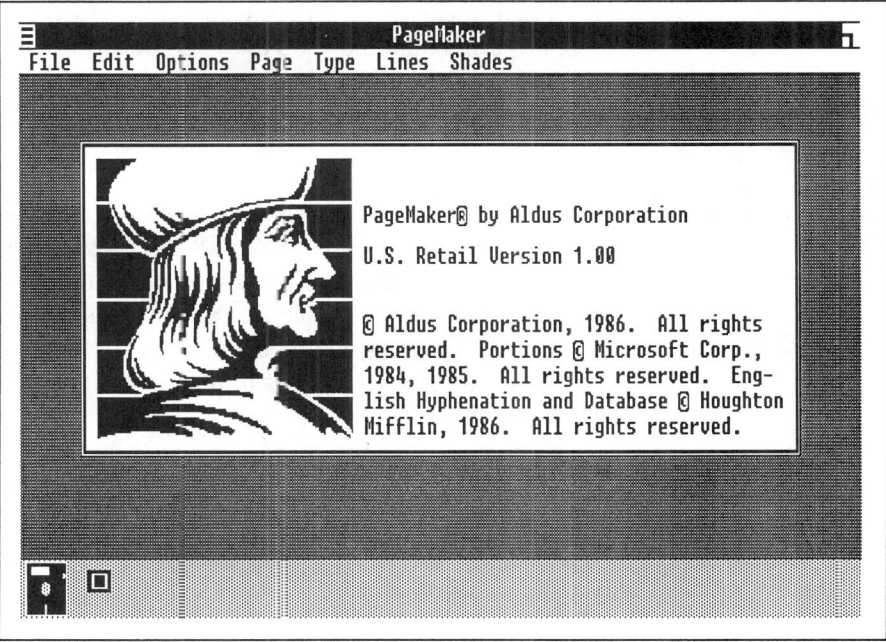

**Figure 12-1.** PC PageMaker is from Aldus Corporation. This is the opening screen that greets you when you enter the program. Aldus (pictured) stands for a man named Aldus Manutius, a Venetian printer from the 15th century who, even in those early days of print, saw the need for a more economical page assembly process. He created a small yet readable typeface called Chancery, which allowed books to be smaller and thus less expensive.

**Hot Tip**

There are a number of page assembly products on the market. Currently PC PageMaker is the most efficient example of interactive page assembly among the moderately priced programs. PC PageMaker retails for less than $700, making it one of the more expensive products for the AT. However. if you are serious about page makeup, it is well worth the money. I have used professional page assembly products designed for newspapers and books, costing over $100,000, and I find PC PageMaker to be easier to use and more logical; it also offers features that equal those on the $100,000 systems.

## PC PageMaker

PC PageMaker allows you to put all the pieces together in an organized, simple way, but it has the power to do everything you need to do. That's the easiest way to sum up why I chose PC PageMaker as the subject of this book.

The next chapters will take you from clicking open PC PageMaker for the first time to pushing it to its limits. And if you get to its limits, then you are a pretty good page maker!

# 13
## Working with PC PageMaker

*P*C PageMaker comes on floppy disks with an excellent user guide, reference guide, installation guide, and quick-reference card.

You will want to make backup copies of the disks before installing the program onto your hard disk. Installation is quite easy. You basically sit back, answer questions about your hardware, and change disks when asked. If you do not already have Microsoft Windows, a run-time version comes with PC PageMaker; you will need to install it along with the program. This version of Windows will allow you to operate PC PageMaker properly, but it does not include all the Windows functions and programs (such as Windows Paint and Windows Write). Windows costs about $100, and it is worth having the full program and its manuals.

Although PC PageMaker comes with its own QuickTour file that will show you all of the program's capabilities, I am going to start from scratch and not reference the QuickTour or sample files.

Once you have created working disks and installed PC PageMaker on your hard disk, you are ready to start. In addition to PC PageMaker, have a large text file and a few paint or draw graphic files created so you can place those elements on pages. When you have all that, you are ready to begin.

## Some Basics

PC PageMaker is an application program, and it can be started from Windows or from a file that has been created by it. The files that PC PageMaker creates are termed page files. The page files contain the text and graphics that you have formed into pages. They contain copies made from your original files, so once a page file has been created, you do not need the text or graphics files used to create the page file. It has all the information it needs.

The program can work with files from a number of programs. Text files can be had from the many word-processing programs listed in Chapter 3 or from Window's clipboard if there is any text there. Graphics files in a variety of formats (also listed in Chapter 3) can also be placed on PC PageMaker pages. (See Fig. 13-1.)

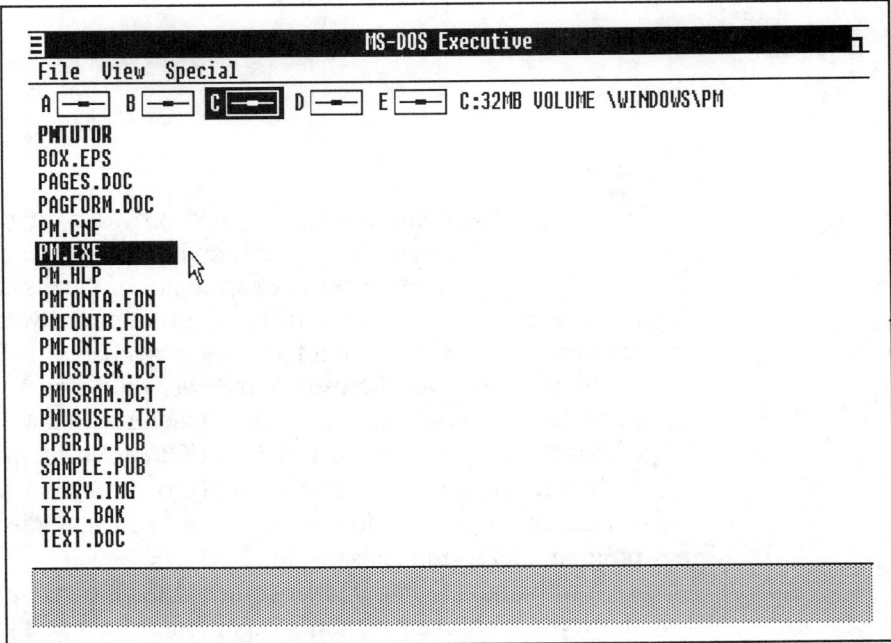

**Figure 13-1.** PC PageMaker program "PM.EXE" and page files on the Windows MS-DOS Executive screen. To start the program, double click on either the program or page files.

**Helpful Hint**

Pages will look best when printed on laser printers or typesetters. If you do plan to use a dot-matrix printer, you should consider a few factors before you begin. First, experiment with the bit-mapped fonts at their various sizes and find the ones you like best.

When using a laser printer, remember that the maximum imaging area is not 8-1/2 by 11 inches. Laser printers support various page sizes, so keep these in mind when preparing your grid:

| **Paper** | **Print Area** |
|---|---|
| Letter | 8" x 10.9" |
| Legal | 6.75" x 12.5" |
| A4 (letter) | 7.5" x 10.5" |
| Tabloid | 10.9" x 16" (tiled) |

If you are using downloadable fonts, keep the print area in mind. The fonts occupy space in the laser printer's RAM. PC PageMaker has less room to work with in the laser printer if you have loaded too many additional fonts.

You may create and print pages in either a vertical or horizontal position. The horizontal, or landscape, version allows the creation of documents such as flyers or brochures that fold one or two times and are read with a horizontal orientation instead of the standard vertical. (See Fig. 13-2.)

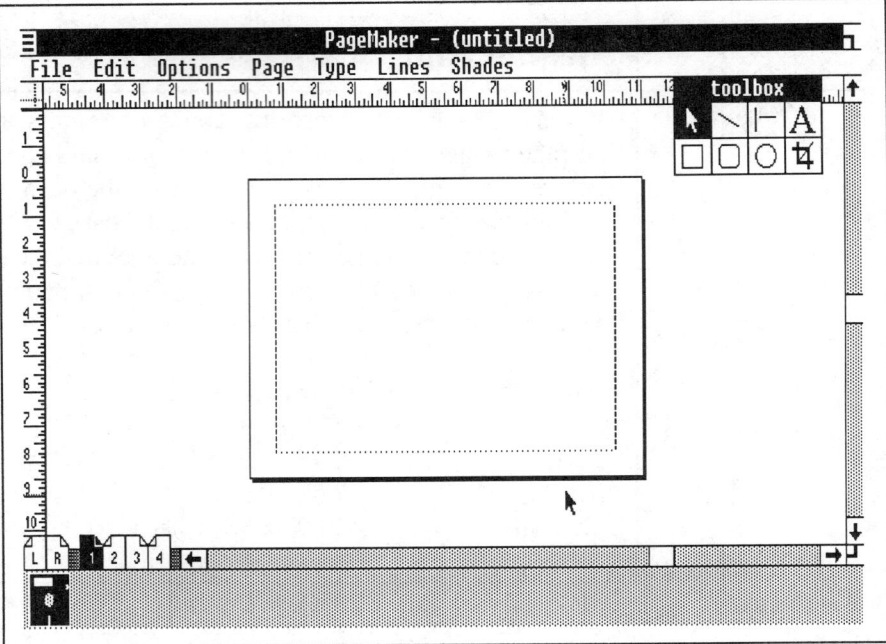

**Figure 13-2.** Landscape pages may be produced. This allows the type to be positioned vertically on a horizontal page, which is useful for brochures and 5-1/2 by 8-1/2 inch folded documents.

## PC PageMaker Tools

Working directly in PC PageMaker, you will be able to use on-screen rulers; edit type; control tabs; change type styles and sizes; draw rules, boxes, shaded boxes, and circles; and move items freely on the page or even to another page.

Most simple graphics can be created directly in PC PageMaker, so you need not prepare such elements before entering the program. Any complex graphics should be prepared in advance with a graphics program.

PC PageMaker's tools will allow you to scale or crop graphics created in paint or draw formats, so create your illustrations freely. They can be sized perfectly from within PC PageMaker.

## A Multilayered Page

A final consideration in thinking about how you place items on pages with PC PageMaker is that items can be placed on top of other items. At any time, you can move an item underneath another item to the front. Likewise, you can take an item that is on top of all others and elect to send it to the back.

This concept is very much like using paper when pasting a page together manually. If you wish, you can cover up items by pasting something over them. For example, say that you have an illustration that you would like to have a line of type run through, such as a banner. You could take the rectangle drawing tool, create a rectangle over the illustration in white with a black rule around it, then add a line of type on top of that.

You would have an illustration on the bottom layer, a white rectangle with a black border rule on the middle layer, and black type on the top layer. As you can see, you can build complex images using the layering technique.

PC PageMaker is so powerful that if you look at the finished page and think the banner and type may be covering an important part of the illustration, you can simply go to the page, click on the illustration, and from the edit menu select "Bring to the front." The illustration will now move to the top layer, covering the banner and type. If you decide that everything is all right, with the illustration still selected, you can select "Move to the back." The illustration will move to the bottom layer, with the banner and type covering it again.

This is a procedure that you will come to appreciate and will use time and time again as you create pages in PC PageMaker.

## Start Your Engines

Keeping in mind the nature of PC PageMaker as explored in this chapter, it is time to start building pages in PC PageMaker. Chapter 14 will examine building the page grid, called a master page.

# 14
# Building Master Pages

$S$tart PC PageMaker. After the PC PageMaker title screen, you will be presented with the screen in Fig. 14-1.

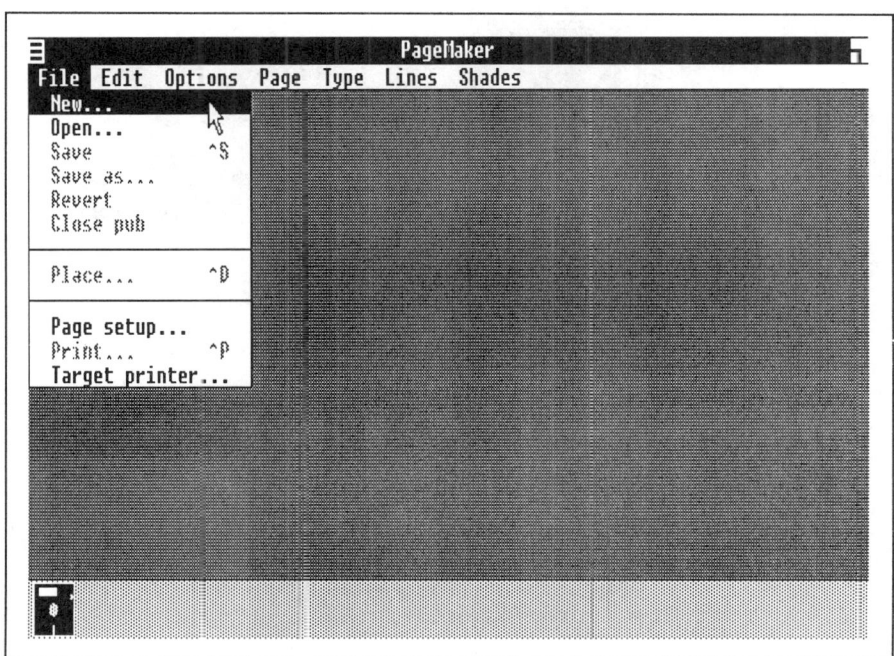

**Figure 14-1.** The screen that greets you when you start PC PageMaker directly.

**144** Chapter 14

## Choosing A Printer

The first step before creating any pages is to establish which printer you are going to use. This will allow PC PageMaker to determine which type styles are available and what sizes they may be made. It also establishes the amount of room you have for graphics on a page.

To identify the printer you intend to use, select "Target printer" from the the file menu. An on-screen menu pops up and allows you to select your printer, as shown in Fig. 14-2. This choice will affect all the options available to you, so be sure to identify your printer before attempting any other activities.

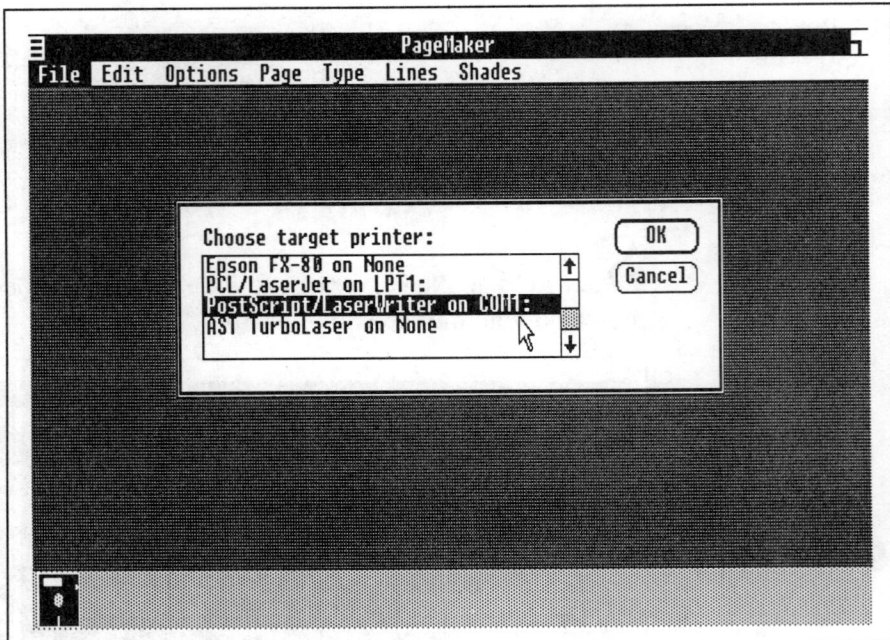

**Figure 14-2.** The menu for selecting a printer.

Next, click on the file menu. From it you can choose one of two options. The first is "New," which will create a new file for you and then allow you to create a page grid for that file. The second option is "Page setup" and is useful if you work consistently with pages that have the same size and margins. This option will allow you to enter page and margin information that will become the default every time you create a new file. For now, we will start from scratch and choose "New." PC PageMaker will automatically bring up the dialog box in Fig. 14-3.

**145** Building Master Pages

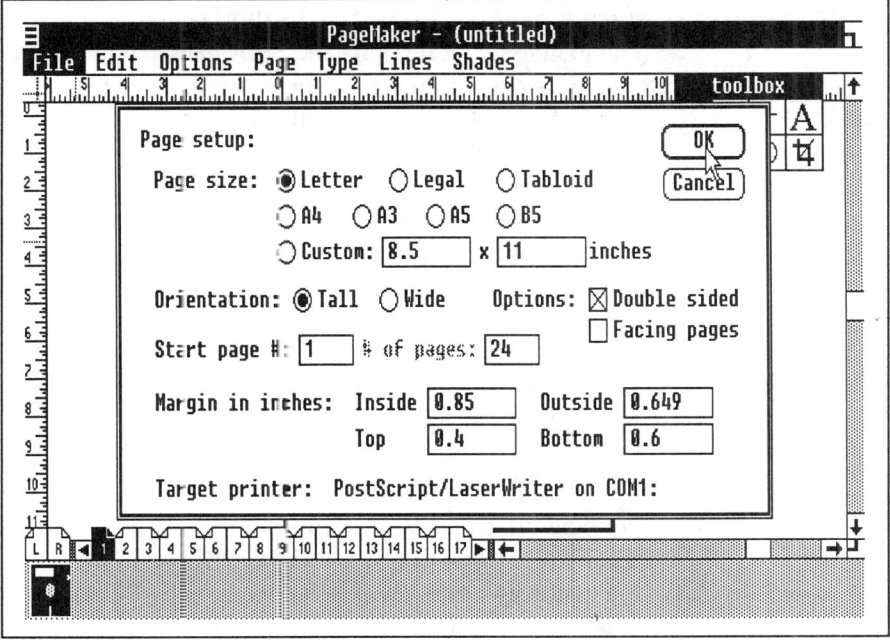

**Figure 14-3.** This dialog box is the "Page setup" for your publication. Here you choose page size, orientation, and single- or double-sided publications and set the margins.

The "Page setup" dialog box is where you will define the basic characteristics of your page. Let's examine each choice:

**Page size:** This allows you to choose the size of paper you will be printing on: Letter, Legal, A3, A4, A5, Tabloid, or Custom (where you define the page size up to 17 by 22 inches). As discussed in Chapter 13, each size of paper will give a different imaging area. For most applications, you will use Letter, which will give you a maximum imaging area of 8 by 10.9 inches (if you are not using downloadable fonts; if you are, then it reduces the imaging area to 7.7 by 10.1 inches). For now, choose "Letter."

**Orientation:** This allows you to create vertical text columns on the page positioned vertically or horizontally. "Tall" is for a vertical orientation; "Wide" is for a horizontal, or landscape, orientation. For now, select "Tall."

**Double sided:** Clicking in this box will set up the page file for right- and left-hand pages. If you do not click it in, it will set up your publication for single-sided, right-hand pages. The sample pages used throughout this book use double-sided pages. To follow along, click on this box.

**Facing pages:** If your publication is double sided, this option will allow you to display facing left- and right-hand pages, or spreads, on the screen as you are working on them. The sample pages used in this book show single pages. In most instances, you will want to work in spreads, with left- and right-hand facing pages displayed.

**Start page #:** This allow you to choose the starting page number for your file. It can be any number between 1 and 9,999. Next to that is the number of pages in the file, which can be anywhere from 1 to 128.

**Margin in inches:** This includes the margins for the inside, outside, top, and bottom. From Chapter 8, remember that you must leave room in the gutter for binding. The gutter margin is usually larger than the outside margin. PC PageMaker labels the gutter as the inside margin. The inside margin is the right side of a left-hand page and the left side of a right-hand page. For our publication, where we detailed our type formatting in Chapter 11, we will set up a 7 by 10 inch live area on our 8-1/2 by 11 inch page. This means that for the inside and outside margins we have 1-1/2 inches to work with. We will make the inside margin 7/8 inch to allow for the gutter and the outside margin 5/8 inch. The top and bottom margins leave us 1 inch to work with. Since a folio line will rest on the bottom of the page, we will make the top margin smaller than the bottom to leave room for the folio line. The top margin will be 3/8 inch and the bottom area, 5/8 inch. One note: PC PageMaker makes you enter whole numbers such as ".5" for "1/2." You must convert the values to whole numbers when you enter them. PC PageMaker also allows you to switch from measuring in inches to various other measuring standards (such as centimeters or picas) in a menu box called "Preferences." On an ongoing basis, you may find those units of measurement easier to work with. We will cover this later.

At this point you have filled in all the information needed to define your page setup. When you click OK, PC PageMaker will present you with your pasteboard, PC PageMaker's name for your page positioned on a working area.

You now see your page, as shown in Fig. 14-4.

**147** Building Master Pages

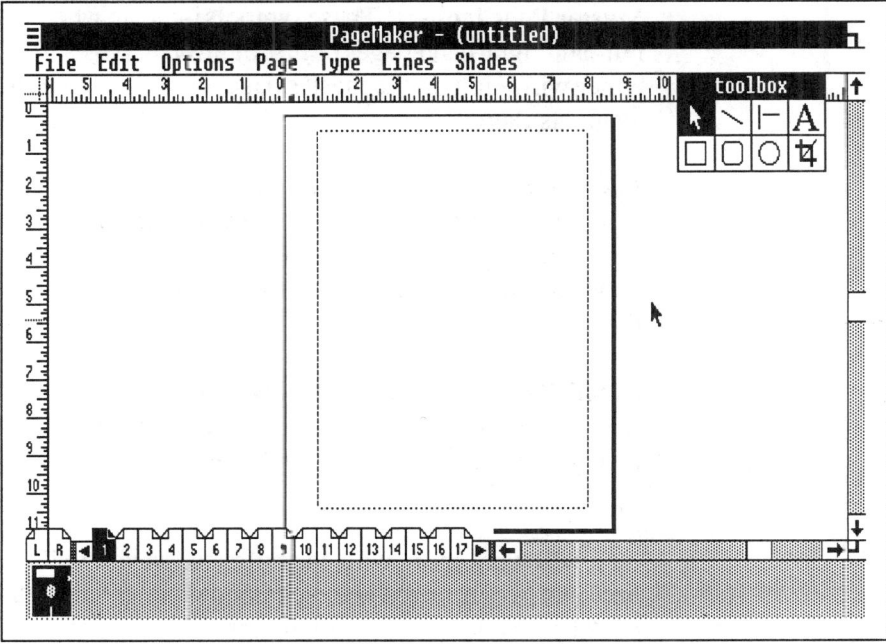

**Figure 14-4.** The page—with margins defined—on the pasteboard.

Your page is now in a fit-in-window size. You may view the page as shown or at actual size or at 50, 75, or 200 percent sizes. Most of the time, you will be working in the fit-in-window size where you may view the whole page at once.

Lets examine some of the elements on the PC PageMaker pasteboard:

**Menu Bar:** This element contains the menu listings—File, Edit, Options, Page, Type, Lines, and Shades. The options contained in each of these menus will be discussed later.

**Title Bar:** This element contains the name of the file you are working on.

**Publication:** Your publication page is represented in the center of the screen.

**Toolbox:** This element contains a number of symbols or icons that will act as drawing, pointing, and text selection tools.

**Master Page Icons:** These symbols indicate whether you are working with left- and right-hand pages or just right-hand pages. Furthermore, clicking on either will bring up the master page, either left or right, and place your grid elements there.

**Page Icon:** This symbol lets you know how many pages are in your publication and allows you to move to any page by clicking on the page number you want to go to. Only 16 pages can be displayed in the bar. Clicking on either area to the left or right of the page icons will allow you to scroll through the pages.

**Scroll Bar:** This element allows movement of the page and pasteboard. Scrolling is essential when viewing the page at actual size or at 200 percent. Moving the boxes on the scroll bar moves the page being viewed vertically or horizontally.

You will work more with each of these as you build your page. Right now, however, examine the representation of the page on the pasteboard (Fig. 14-4). The physical page is represented by the black shadowed outline. The margins we have defined are represented by the dotted lines. Note that the page icon indicates that you are on page 1, a right-hand page. Note that the left margin is greater than the right and that the top is less than the bottom. This reflects our gutter and folio adjustments.

## Creating a Master Page

The next step is to jump from page 1 to the master pages to set up the grid for the page and add some items that will appear on every page, as well as print on every page.

To jump to the left-hand master page, simply go to the L master page icon and click on it. Fig. 14-5 shows how the L master page icon is now darkened, indicating that you are on the left-hand master page.

**149** Building Master Pages

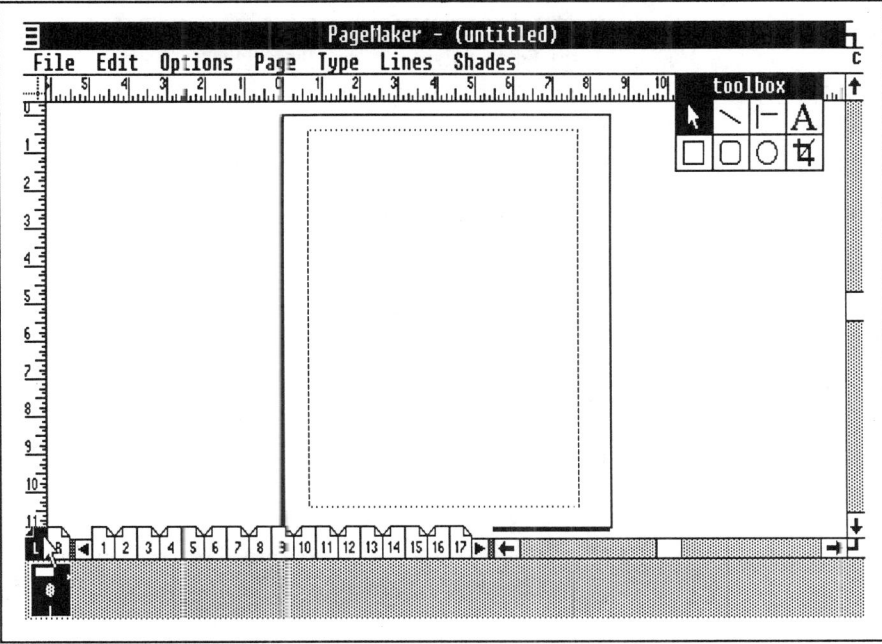

**Figure 14-5.** The left-hand master page. Here you can establish all of the characteristics and printing items that you want to appear on every left-hand page.

There are two steps that you should now take that will help you set up your master page.

The first is to call up on-screen rulers that will allow you to know the exact location of the pointer. This will let you point to any area on the page and know its exact vertical and horizontal position. This is done by going to the options menu and clicking on the "Rulers" choice. Rulers will now appear across the top and left of the pasteboard as shown in Fig. 14-6.

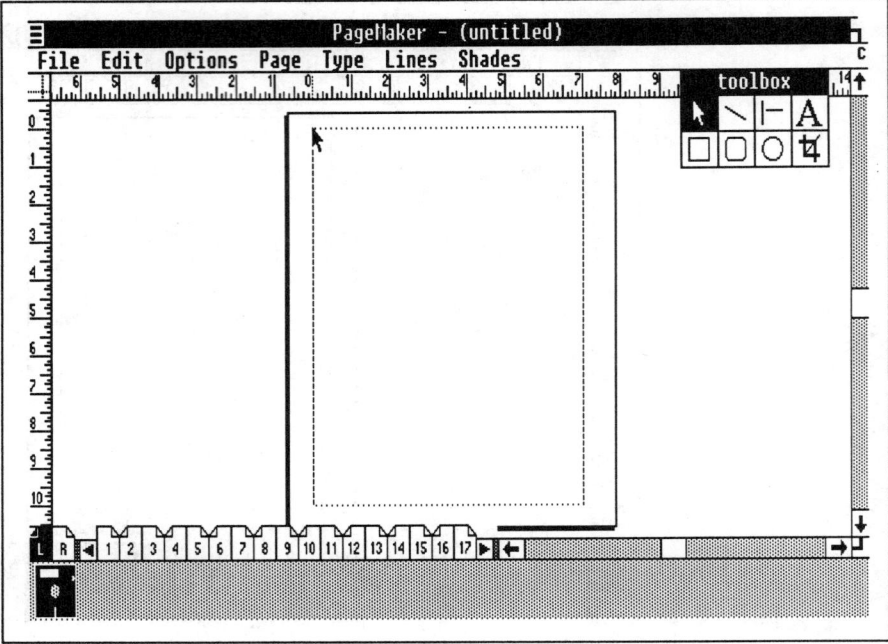

**Figure 14-6.** By choosing "Rulers" from the options menu, on-screen rulers appear, and lines in the rulers move with the movement of your on-screen pointer, telling you your exact position on the page. Note that the pointer is on the upper left-hand corner of the live area and that the dotted lines are on both zeros.

In the upper left-hand junction of the two rulers are two crossed dotted lines. From the toolbox, make sure you have the pointer tool selected. Move the pointer into the upper left-hand corner of the junction box, and place the pointer on the junction of the two dotted lines. Hold down the button of the mouse and drag the pointer to the upper left-hand corner of the live area on your publication page. When you have the pointer in the exact upper left-hand corner of the live area, release the mouse button. This action moves the zero of both rulers to the upper left-hand corner of your live area. You may, at any time, move the zero value of the ruler to any position on the page. This will help, for example, when you need to start type at an abstract point and run it three inches down.

When you first enter the master page, both rulers should have the zero set in the right spot, but this example illustrates how to move the zero in case it is not.

The next step is to establish how many columns you want your page to contain. For this example, you will want to create two columns of type with .25 inch between each column. In PC PageMaker, it is very simple to make columns. You can create one column by doing nothing. The live area would be one column, 7 inches wide. To make two to twenty columns, you go to the options menu again and select the "Column guides" option. This will bring up a dialog box as shown in Fig. 14-7.

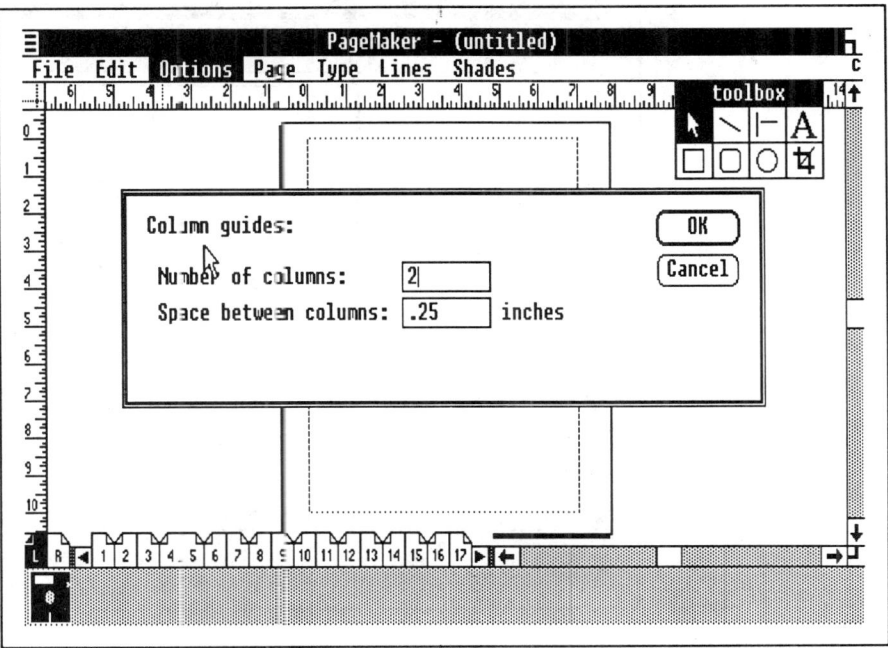

**Figure 14-7.** To create the columns on your page, type in "2" in the "Number of columns" box. For the amount of space between the columns, type in ".25," which will result in a 1/4-inch space between the columns.

Now take a look at your publication page. It shows two columns with dotted lines as in Fig. 14-8.

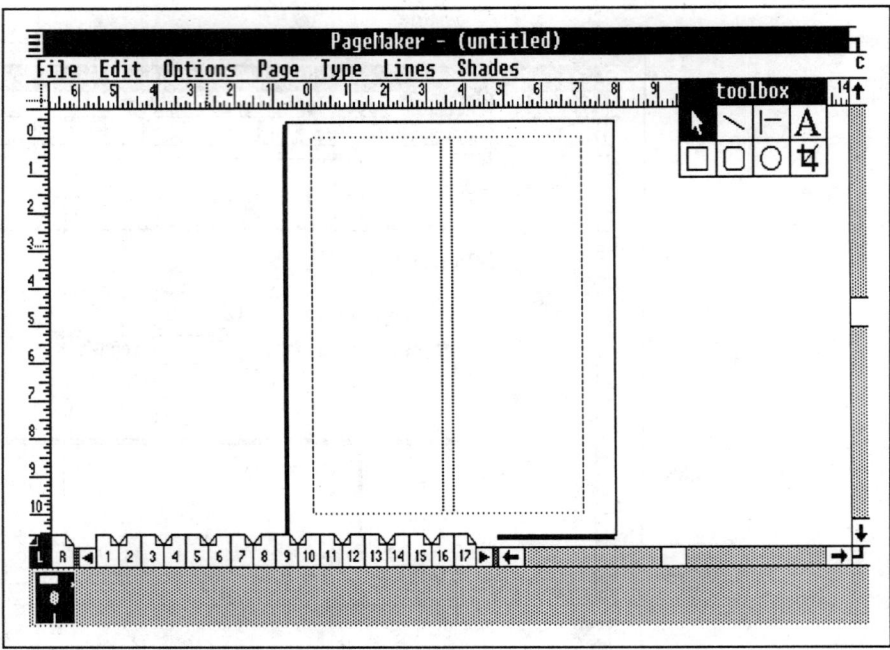

**Figure 14-8.** The columns appear as dotted lines on the publication page. The dotted lines are position elements; they will not appear when the page is printed.

The next task is to place a rule at the bottom of the page and add a folio for automatic page numbering at the bottom of the page.

You will now want to change the view of the page to actual size so you can position your rule with more precision. To do this, go to the page menu, and select "Actual size." Or with the pointer on the pasteboard, click the right mouse button, which is a shortcut toggle between "Fit in window" and "Actual size." The screen will change to the actual size. In addition, the rulers will now reflect the change, showing more increments.

Use the scroll bars to go to the bottom left-hand corner of the page, as shown in Fig. 14-9.

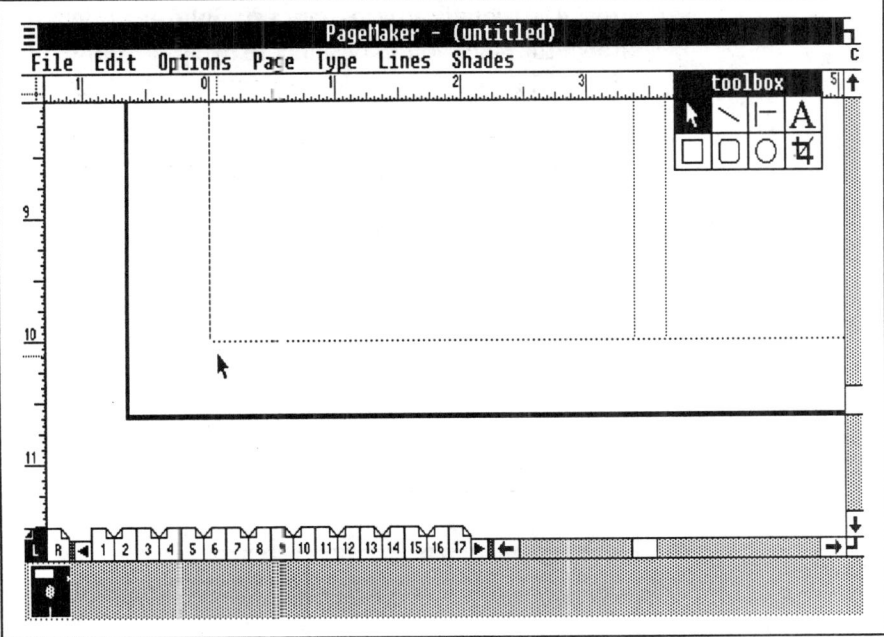

**Figure 14-9.** The publication page is now actual size, and the pointer is positioned at the bottom left-hand corner of the live area by using the scroll bars to move the page.

Fig. 14-10 details how to draw a straight-line rule on the page. After you have drawn the rule, you may select its weight from the lines menu, as shown in Fig. 14-11. A 1-point rule is selected from a variety of choices.

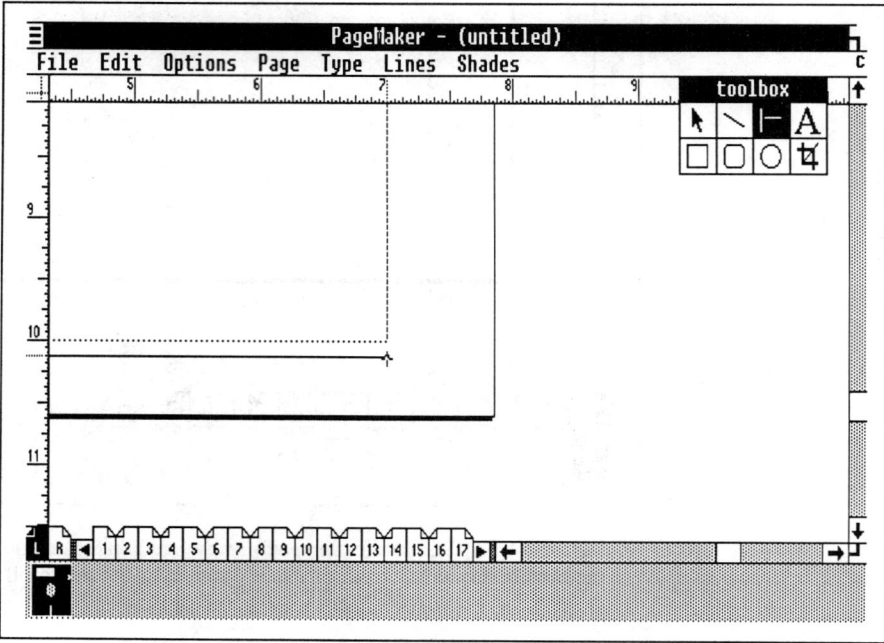

**Figure 14-10.** Move the pointer to the toolbox, and click on the straight-line icon, the third from the left in the top row. When you click on it, you will get a new pointer for drawing lines. Position this pointer at the zero point vertically and 1/8 inch below the live area. Hold the mouse button down to begin drawing your rule. Continue until you reach the 7-inch mark, or right-hand corner of the live area.

**155** Building Master Pages

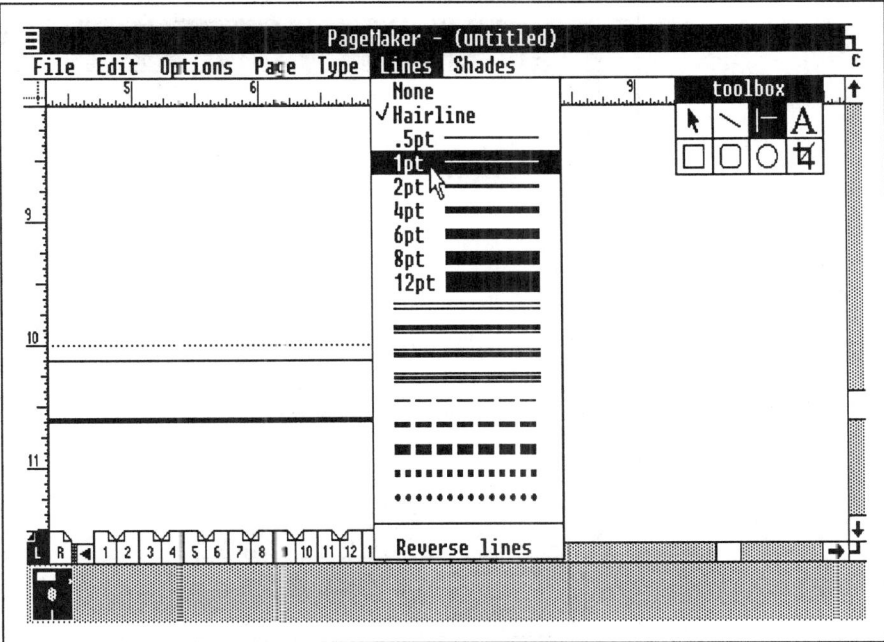

**Figure 14-11.** With the rule selected (it has handles at each end), you may go to the lines menu and change its width at any time.

To create the automatic numbering folio shown in Fig. 14-12, move to the center of the live area, between the two columns. Go to the toolbox and click on the text icon (the A). Move the text icon (an I-beam shape) to where you would like the page number to be (1/8 inch below the rule and centered between the two columns), and press "Ctrl," "Shift," and "3" at the same time. One zero will appear. The page numbering will start at this position and will use the number of the page you are working on.

 The type is in a default size and mode. For the example, you will want to change the type to Times Roman Regular 9 point. To do this, move the I-beam pointer to the left of the type. Holding down the mouse button, drag it across the zeros until they are selected (white type in a black box). With the zeros selected, move the I-beam pointer up to the type menu bar. The I-beam will change back to a pointer when you leave the pasteboard. Open the type menu and select "Type specs." A dialog box will appear as in Fig. 14-13. From here, select the size (9 points), font (Times Roman), and style (plain). The folio line will now use this type selection on every page.

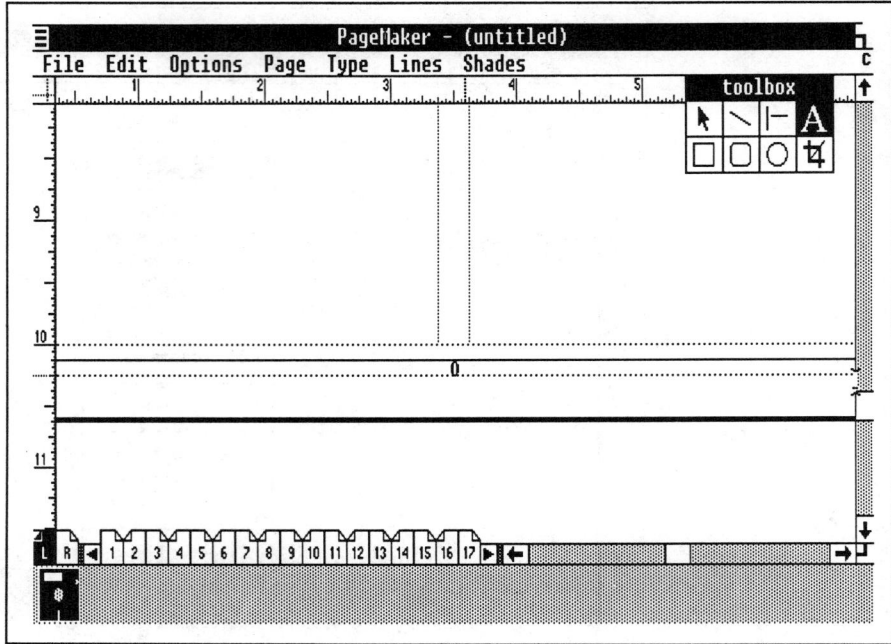

**Figure 14-12.** The final element on the page grid is an automatic numbering folio line.

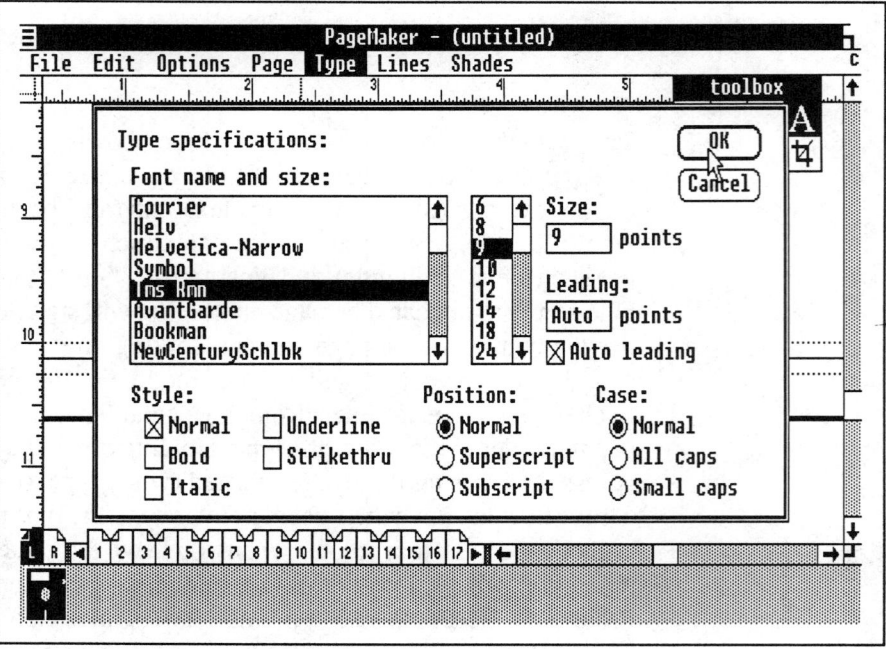

**Figure 14-13.** The type specs dialog menu allows you to choose type font, size, linespacing (leading), autoleading, and styles for the type you have selected.

The final step is to move back to the toolbox and select the pointer tool again. Go back to the folio number and move it into the exact position if it had changed at all as a result of changing type styles. You may now go to the page menu and return the page to "Fit in window." The completed master page is shown with all the desired elements in Fig. 14-14.

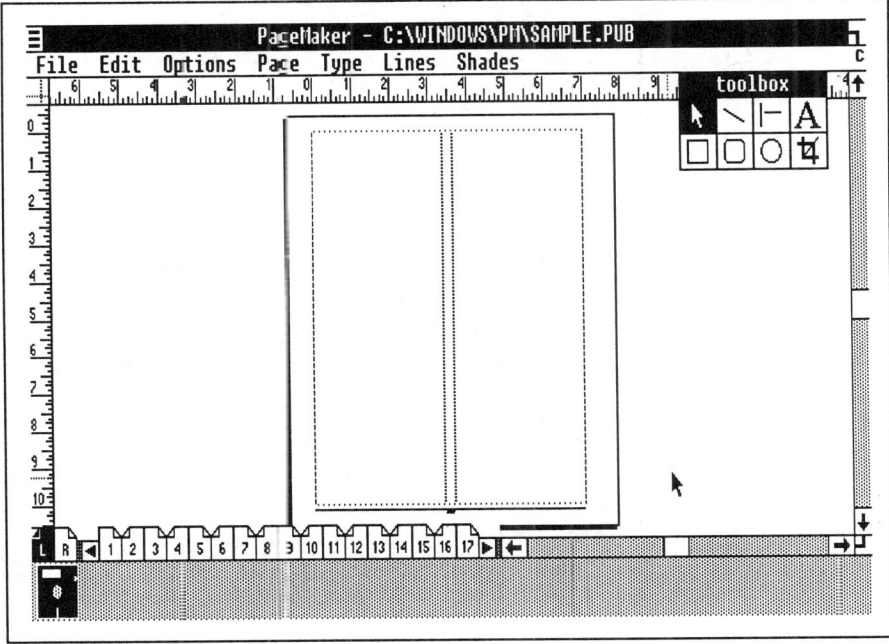

**Figure 14-14.** The completed left-hand master page. The next step is to do it again for the right-hand master page.

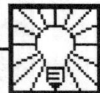

**Helpful Hint**

This takes care of the master page for the left-hand pages. Next, you would repeat this process for the right-hand page. This can be done by selecting all the items on the left-hand master page. To do this, choose "Select all" from the edit menu. All the items on the page have been made active and can be copied to the clipboard by going to the edit menu and selecting "Copy." Click on the right-hand master page, and select "Paste" from the edit menu. All the elements are placed on the page as a group and may be moved into position by moving the pointer over them and dragging them into position. Clicking outside the selected items will deselect them and allow you move each one independently. Copying the page elements does not include column guides, so you will also need to define the column guide for the right-hand master page. It is important to note that each master page is done separately even though they may be the same. More often than not, if the page is identical in margins and format, you would create the file as single sided. Most double-sided pages have folios and columns that are slightly different on each master page. An example would be a more sophisticated folio line with the date in the outside corners of the folio line. You would need to put it on the outside of each page, so each master page would be different.

## Ready to Begin

Once you have completed the same routines for the right-hand master page, you are ready to click the page 1 icon and begin placing items on your page grid. Placing elements is covered in the next chapter.

Right now is a good time to save your publication. Frequent saving is a good practice to follow, so begin now by saving your grid as SAMPLE.PUB. To save, go to the file menu, sellect "Save," and name your publication.

# 15 Placing Elements on a Page

$O$nce the master page grids have been created, the next step is the most exciting: actually placing elements on the page.

## Placing a Headline

The first element you should place is the headline. This presents the first element on the page, and it is also an element that does not fit into the two columns. It was designed to go across the entire width of the live area. If you placed it in the first column, it would break the headline to fit into the column. For such situations, there are two ways of placing such an element.

You can place the element using the "Place" command from the file menu. You will see a dialog box on your screen like the one in Fig. 15-1.

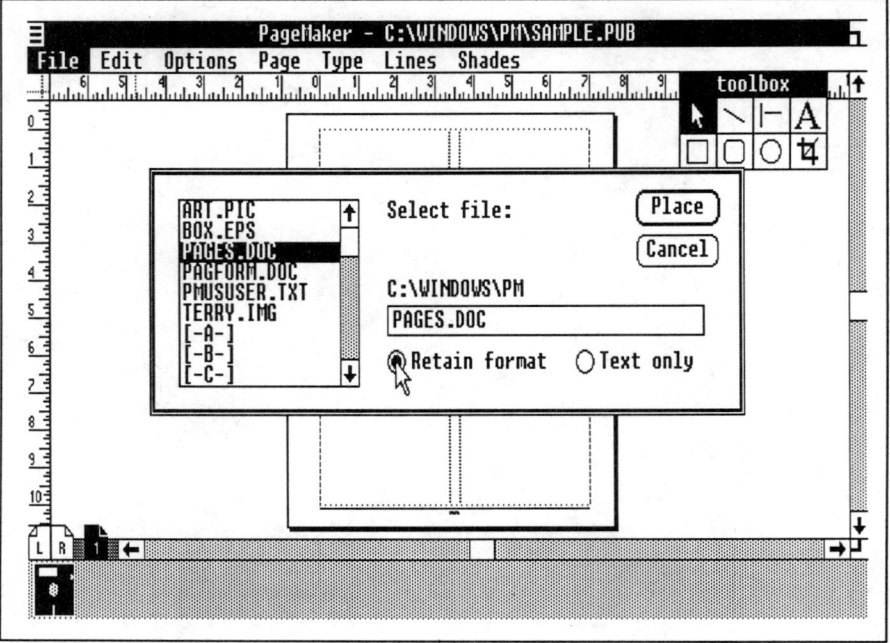

**Figure 15-1.** Choosing "Place" from the file menu presents a choice of files, both text and graphic, that can be put anywhere on the page. Here, the file "PAGES" is selected. You can choose to keep the formatting of the file by choosing "Retain format" or drop all formatting by choosing "Text only."

When you click on the name of the file, PC PageMaker presents the publication page with a new icon. Text files have icons in the shape of the upper left-hand corner of a block of text. Paint files are represented by a page corner with a paint brush in it. Draw and PIC files have the same type of icon, but with a pencil in it. Scanned images in the TIF file format are represented by an icon with an "X" in it. Finally, Encapsulated PostScript files have an icon with a large "PS" in it. If you have chosen a text file, you should get the pointer icon with the text in it.

The file chosen, "PAGES," is a Microsoft Word file, so a text icon appears on the screen, as shown in Fig. 15-2.

**161**  Placing Elements on a Page

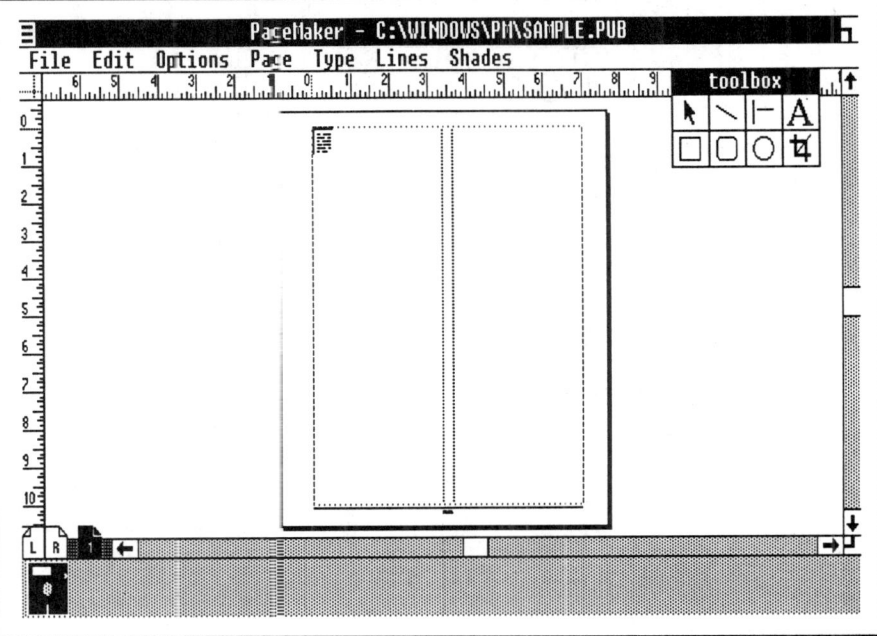

**Figure 15-2.** The text file chosen is now ready to be placed. To place the text, a text icon appears on the screen. Move the icon to wherever you wish the text to start and click the mouse button; the type will begin filling the area or column.

### Helpful Hint

To ignore the columns on the page, you can place the text in a specially sized text column that overrides the standard text columns. To do this, point to the exact place you wish the specially sized text block to start. When you click on the text icon, press the mouse button down, but DO NOT release it. Drag the mouse with the button held down. You will see a solid-line box forming in whatever direction you move. This "elastic" column can be made any size. When you have created the box you desire (such as a full-width column for the headline), release the mouse button. The text will flow into the box and not adhere to the grid columns as shown in Fig. 15-3. This is an extremely important tool for placing elements such as captions and headlines that are larger or smaller than the column size you are working in.

**162**  Chapter 15

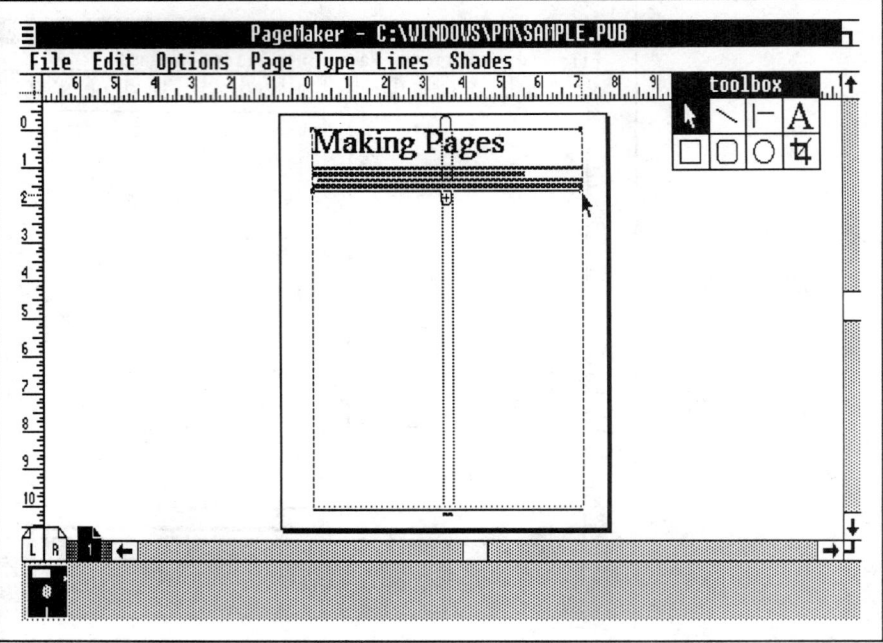

**Figure 15-3.** Placing a headline across two columns by holding down the mouse key when starting to place text, dragging the elastic box to create a custom column width, then releasing the mouse button to place the text, which ignores the standard columns.

Examine Fig. 15-3, which shows the placement of text after the headline. Note that the text, which is active or selected, has horizontal lines on the top and bottom, with very small handles on them. These handles allow you to move the excess type up and down, much like taking the bottom of a window shade and pulling it up and down. In fact, Aldus even uses the term "window shade" to describe this action.

So take the bottom handle of your textual window shade and move it up and down to see what happens. Move it up a line and stop. Move it down a line and stop. Finally, move it all the way up to the top of the first line of text, that belongs in a column and stop. Now all that should be present is the headline.

Next, make your headline larger, the goal being to fill the width of the page as best as possible. To start this process, go to the toolbox, select the text tool, and select the headline. The results should match those in Fig. 15-4.

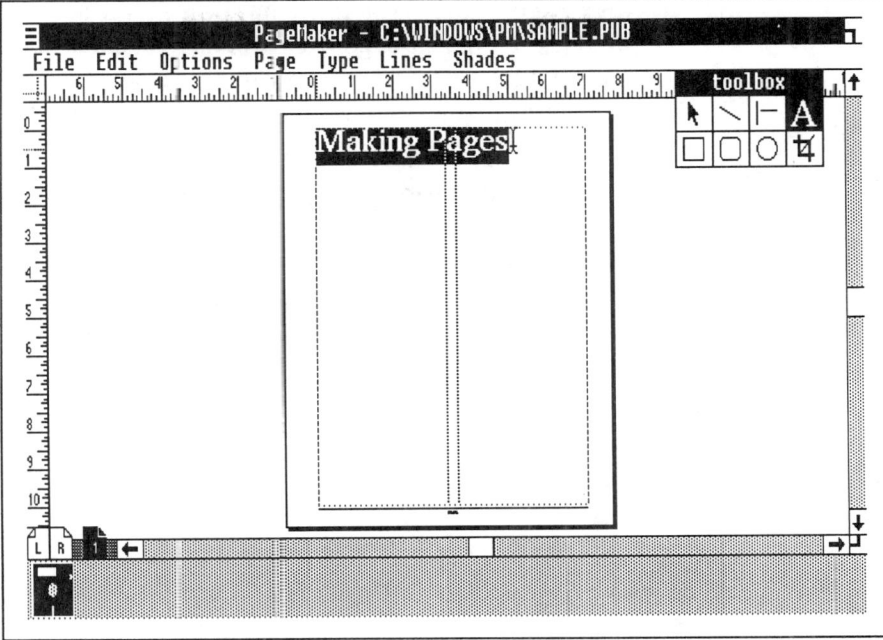

**Figure 15-4.** The text is window shaded back to the point where only the headline is on the page. The text tool is selected from the toolbox, and the headline is selected for a type size change.

## Sizing a Headline

With the headline selected, the next step is to access the "Type spec" dialog box from the type menu. The type is currently at 24 points. For the heck of it, change the size to 48 points. The dialog box goes away, and you will see the results. If the type is still not filling the line, go back and make it larger.

### Shortcut

This time, save yourself a step. Instead of moving the mouse to the type menu, press "Ctrl" and "T" at the same time. This will bring up the type box without using the mouse. PC PageMaker uses many such shortcuts, and I will point them out as we can take advantage of them.

After making the type larger, it may be too large and will word wrap, forming two lines. In that case, go back and make it smaller. It's a bit of a guessing game, but after a few tries you will get the headline to be the exact width of the live area, which will be very attractive, as shown in Fig. 15-5.

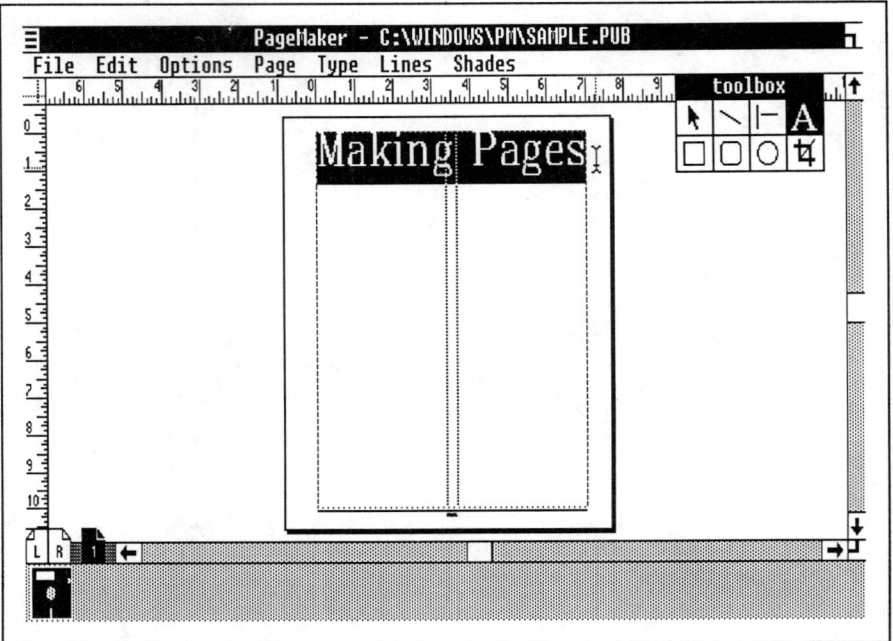

**Figure 15-5.** The headline has been sized by experimentation to be the full width of the live area. The next task is to select the headline type to get back the type handles. Go to the bottom handle. Note that the handle has a plus sign (+) in it. The plus sign means that there is more type to be placed. When all type has been placed, a number sign (#) occupies the bottom handle. Click the mouse on the bottom handle. You will then get back the text icon. This is the rest of the type that has yet to be used.

By clicking on the headline and getting back your type handles, you can click on the bottom handle and get the type icon for the rest of the text that has yet to be placed. Once you have the text icon, you can start placing columns of text.

> **Helpful Hint**
>
> Move to the first column and choose a starting point for your text. You will notice that when you move the text near a column grid line, the icon tends to move to the line by itself. That is because the snap-to-guides tool is on. You can turn this tool on and off from the options menu. The snap-to-guides tool assures you that text and graphics elements will align themselves on the nearest grid line. This tool is quite useful and, for general placement, should be left on most of the time. Turn it off for precision work; leave it on for general placement.

Even though you have your text icon back, you should note that you now wish to place two columns of type, both starting at the exact same spot horizontally. To assist you in making sure that both columns start at the same height, you can use the ruler guides.

Ruler guides are lines that are pulled from either the vertical or horizontal rulers. They act much like a column guide because they have a snap-to quality. Text placed next to a ruler guide will snap to it if the snap-to feature is on. Unlike column guides, once the text is flowing in a column, it does not stop at ruler guides. For this example, you need to place a horizontal ruler guide where the two columns will start.

Go to the toolbox, and click on the pointer. Note that you have lost the text icon. That's OK; you can get it back. With the pointer, go up to the top ruler, go anywhere in it, and press the mouse button down, but do not release it. Now drag the pointer down. Note that it is dragging a dotted line with it. The dotted line is the ruler guide. Drag it into place on your page, and release the mouse button. You now have a guide for placing your two columns. The ruler guide can be moved at any time and can be put away by dragging it back up into the ruler. (See Fig. 15-6.)

Now, go back to the headline block and click on it with the pointer to make it active. Go to the bottom handle and click on it. You once again have your text icon. Next go into the first column at the intersection of the left-hand side of the column and the ruler guide. Click the mouse button. The text will begin flowing in the column. It will fill the column completely and stop at the bottom. Change to the actual size view.

## 166  Chapter 15

**Figure 15-6.** A ruler guide is pulled down from the top ruler and aligned for the top of the type in both column.

### Shortcut

This time instead of using the menu, press the right mouse button anywhere in the pasteboard area. The screen now shows the page actual size. Note that the portion of the page shown actual size is the same area to which you were pointing when you clicked the right mouse button.

Examine how the type has flowed into the column and how it has aligned itself to the left grid line. The text is justified, since the word file was justified. Note how the column guide works as a margin on the right for the text as it flows in.

With one column of text placed, it is time to click the bottom handle on the first column of text to get the text icon for the next column of text. Fig. 15-7 shows the screen at this point.

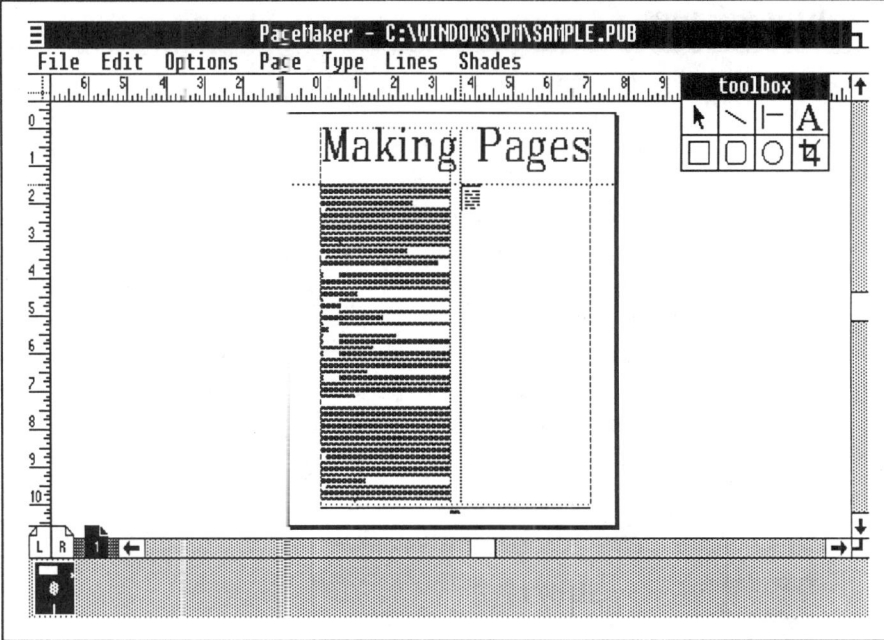

**Figure 15-7.** The first column of text is placed. It is now ready for the second column to be placed.

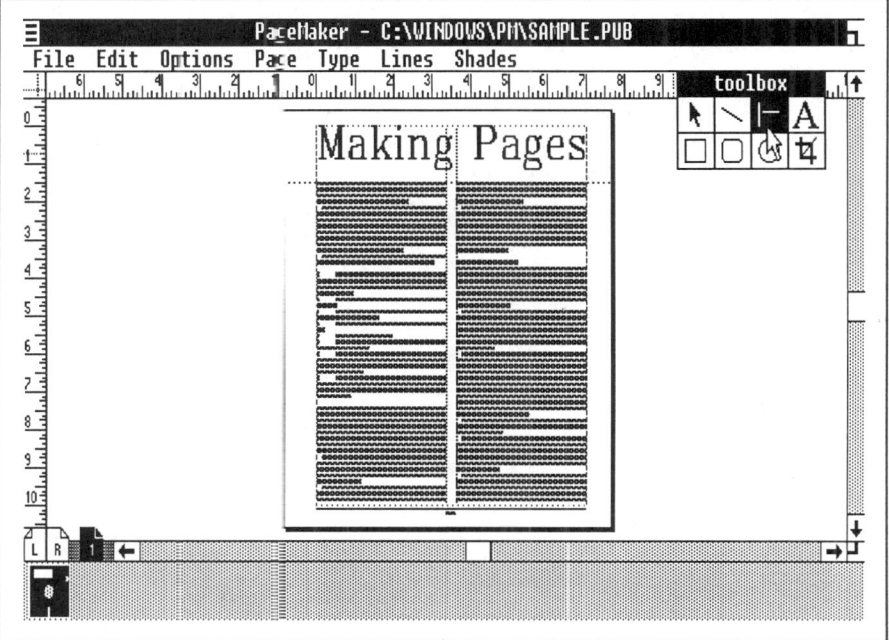

**Figure 15-8.** Both columns of text have been placed. The page has taken shape quite well. The last step is to add a rule between the two columns.

## Adding a Rule

The final step in creating the first page is to place a rule between the two columns of text. The rule will be a hairline rule centered between the two columns and will start at the top of the columns of type and stop at the bottom.

Go to the toolbox, get the straight-line icon, make your page actual size, and scroll to the center of the page, at the top of the two type columns. Position the crosshair pointer in the center of the columns, and press the mouse button down. Drag the crosshair cursor down. When it reaches the bottom of the screen, keep the button down. The screen will start scrolling and drawing the line down the page. When you reach the bottom of the columns, stop the cursor at the bottom grid. The rule is now drawn, and still selected. Go to the line menu and select "Hairline," and the rule is now drawn. (See Figs. 15-9, 15-10, and 15-11.)

### Shortcut

If the rule did not place itself in the center between the columns, press the backspace key. Any time you activate an element, you may erase it simply by hitting the backspace key.

This time, go to the options menu, turn off the snap to guide, and go back; now you will be able to position the cursor with much less difficulty. Draw the line as already described. When you are through, hit the right mouse button to view the entire page, and there is your first page!

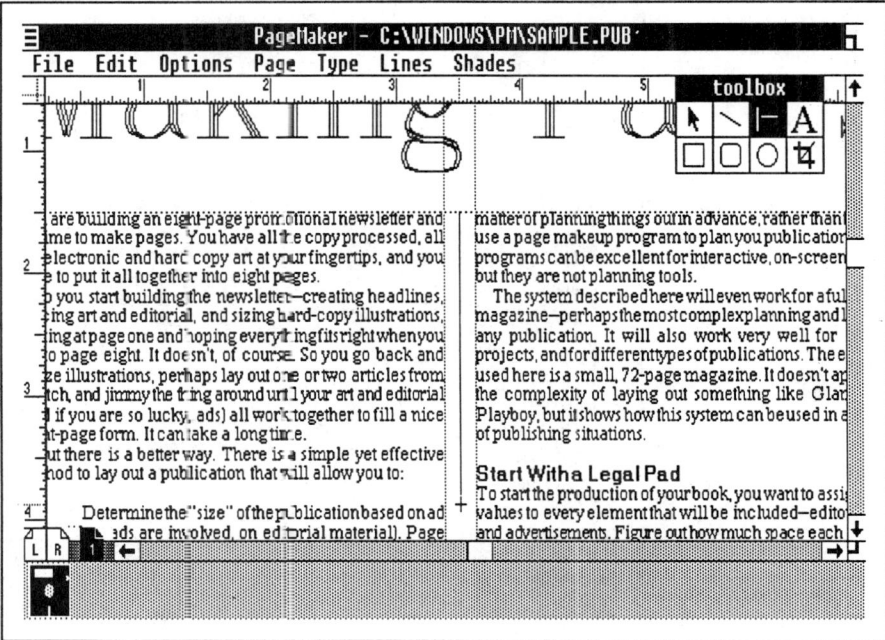

**Figure 15-9.** By selecting the straight-line icon from the toolbox, you can draw rules anywhere on the page. Here, the snap to guide has been turned off, and a hairline rule, drawn between the two columns.

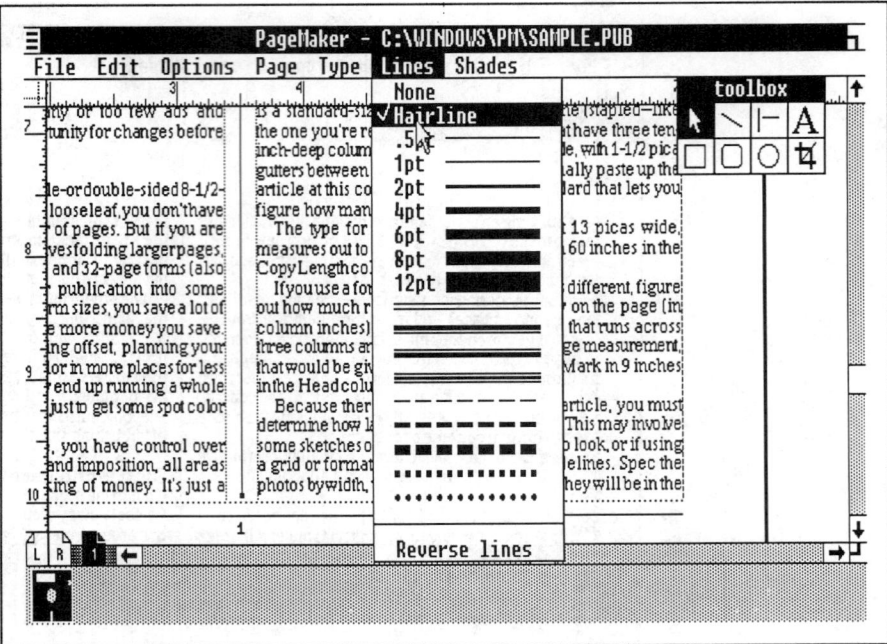

**Figure 15-10.** The rule, still selected (indicated by the handles on the top and bottom), is made a hairline width from the lines menu.

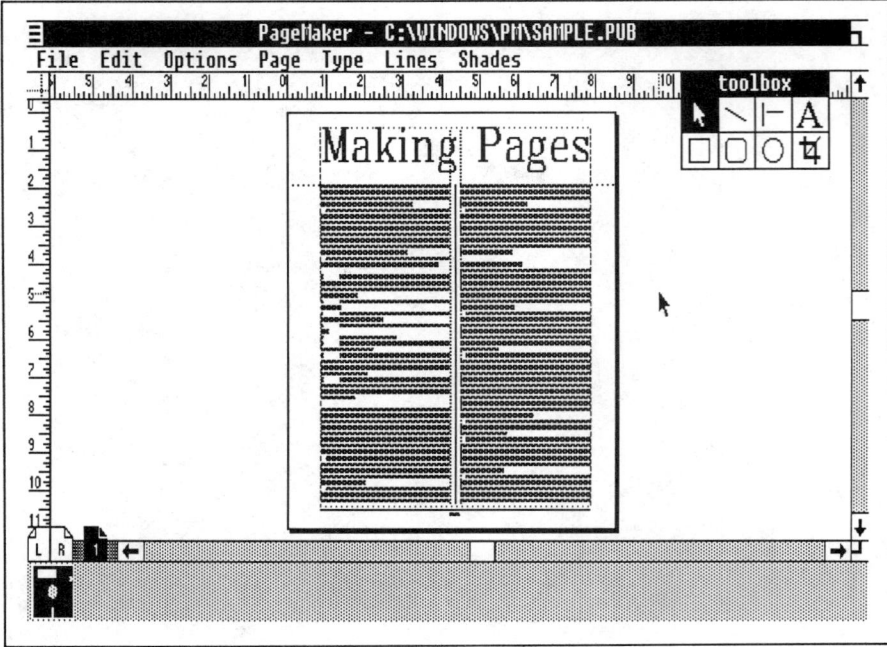

**Figure 15-11.** The finished page. Headline, body copy, and a rule have all been placed in a matter of minutes. Note that the master page items are also in place.

## On to the Next Page

With the first page complete, you can continue placing the rest of your text and graphics on the next page. To do this, go to the page menu, and select the "Insert page" choice. A dialog box will pop up and ask if you want to add a page after the current page or before the current page. Select "After current page," since you want to work on page 2. (See Fig. 15-12.)

A page-2 icon will appear at the bottom of the screen with the page icons. A new page will appear on the screen, ready for placement of text and graphics. This page will be special since you will need to place a graphic on it in addition to the remaining type.

### Helpful Hint

You can create a file by adding a page at a time. A better way is establish the number of pages for your document when opening the file and indicating the number of pages (for example, 24) that you would like your document to be. If you document is shorter than the number of pages indicated, you can remove the extra pages at any time. This will save you the task of adding a page each time.

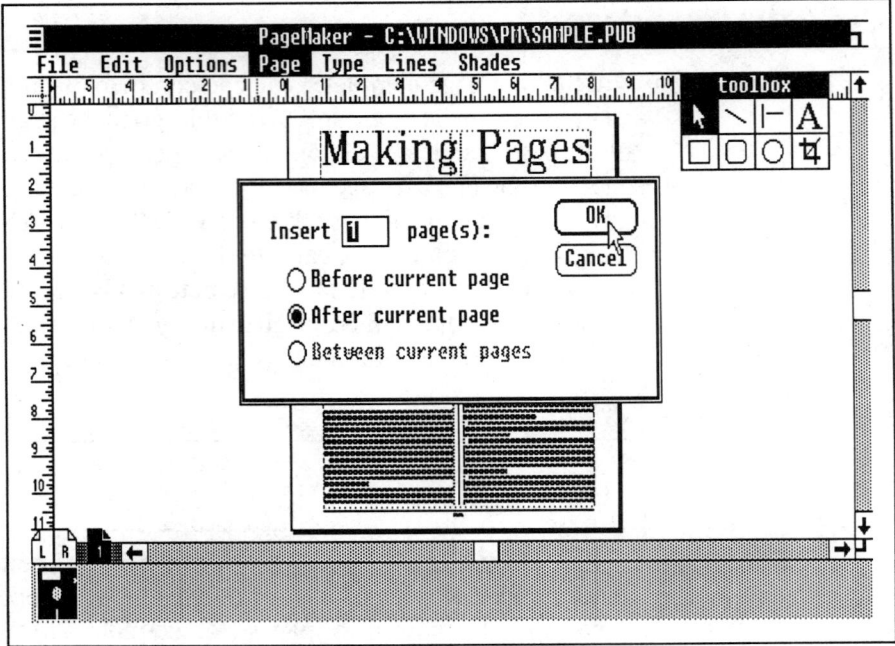

**Figure 15-12.** To insert pages, you can insert the page either before or after the page you are on.

## Placing Graphics on a Page

Placing graphics files on a PC PageMaker page is no more difficult than placing text. It is a simple matter of going to the file menu, choosing the "Place" command, and picking the name of the graphics file you wish to place. Once you click on the "Place" command, the file will appear on the screen. It will have a set of handles—one at each corner—and handles in the middle between each corner.

The handles allow a variety of edits to be performed on the graphic. You can enlarge or reduce it in any proportion, such as making it wider or taller (stretching it in only one direction as you do so) or making it wider or taller while keeping its true proportion.

Fig. 15-13 illustrates a graphics file as it is placed on page 2 of the publication.

**173** Placing Elements on a Page

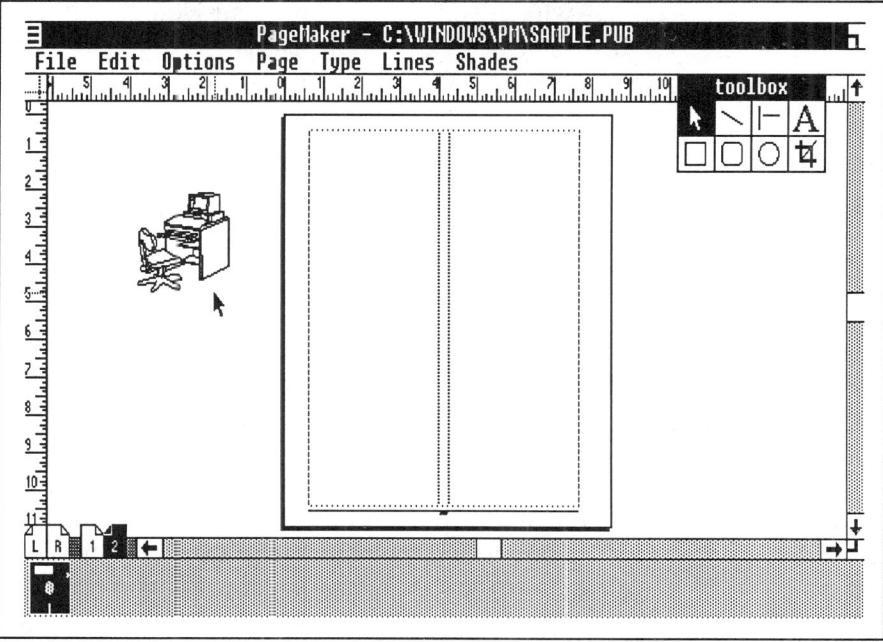

**Figure 15-13.** Graphics created with paint, draw, or scanner programs are placed just like text using the "Place" command. When they are active, they have handles on the tops, sides, and corners.

The next step is to decide where to place the graphic on the page. Since no particular placement was specified, you have a great deal of freedom and can put the graphic anywhere on the page.

The first page of the report, while attractive, was also quite plain. It contained only a headline and two columns of type. Now that you have an illustration, you may want to enhance the style of the page by using the graphic in a dynamic fashion. This could be done in a number of ways. The graphic could be enlarged, could bleed off the page (a term that means to go off the edge of the page), or, being most adventurous, could extend into the column next to it.

### Resizing Graphics

If a graphic, once placed, has areas that you would like to remove, you can crop it. Go to the toolbox, get the cropping tool, go the graphic and click on it. The handles will appear. Put any of the handles inside the cropping tool, click the mouse, and drag. You will see that the graphic is being cropped. Crop the graphic as desired.

What if you took off too much? Don't worry. The entire graphic is still there. You can see this quite easily by taking the cropping tool, going inside the graphic area, and pressing the mouse. Holding down the mouse button, move the graphic around. Note that the graphic moves freely so you can reposition it in the cropped size. It also shows that the entire graphic is still there. This means that you can take the cropping tool, go back to the handles, and resize the crop without having lost any of the graphic. This is a very handy tool. You can crop the box to the size you want, go in the graphic, press the mouse button down to grab it, and position it as desired. And you can recrop at any time.

A graphic, once placed, can be resized in a number of ways. The quickest way to understand this is to grab the bottom right handle and pull down and then to the right. Note that the graphic fills whatever size area you are creating when pulling the handle. Note also that the proportion of the graphic can change. There are times when this is desirable and times when it is not. You can control the proportion ratio and return to the original size at any time.

To reduce or enlarge any graphic in proportion to its original shape, press down the shift key as you drag a corner handle. The graphic will retain its original shape, but now at a new size. Object-oriented graphics (such as from PIC files or from draw programs) can be enlarged or reduced perfectly since they are essentially redrawn as their size is changed, so they are not distorted by a stretch in any direction. Paint, or bit-mapped graphics, do not fare as well. When stretched, they will distort due to the resolution of the original drawing versus the resolution of your printing device. You can end up with strange patterns in shaded areas, extremely ragged lines, and a pretty bad looking illustration. There are, however, certain percentage enlargements or reductions that will not cause such dramatic distortions. By holding down the control key as you resize the graphic, the paint graphic will snap to various sizes. These are sizes that, dependent upon your printer, will create the least amount of distortion.

The ability to resize a graphic, stretch it in any direction, keep proportions, and scale paint graphics to their best print resolution shows how powerful PC PageMaker's graphics handling is. If you do not like the stretched shape and want to return the graphic to its original proportions, simply get the pointer, hold down the shift key, and click on any of the handles. The graphic will return to its true proportion but not its original size if that had been changed.

When a graphic element enters a live column area, you must wrap the type around the graphic. This is a fairly complex task in conventional typesetting, but PC PageMaker has made the process quite easy. It involves several new functions, so let's create your first wrap!

# Wrapping Type

The first step is to place the graphic exactly where it is going to go on the page. This is done by simply using the pointer, moving inside the graphic, pressing the mouse button, holding it down, and moving the mouse. The graphic will now move about the page with ease. Place the graphic in the vertical middle of the page and, page 2 being a left-hand page, on the outside of the page. Place the graphic so that it both bleeds off the page and crosses over into the second column of type, as illustrated in Fig. 15-14.

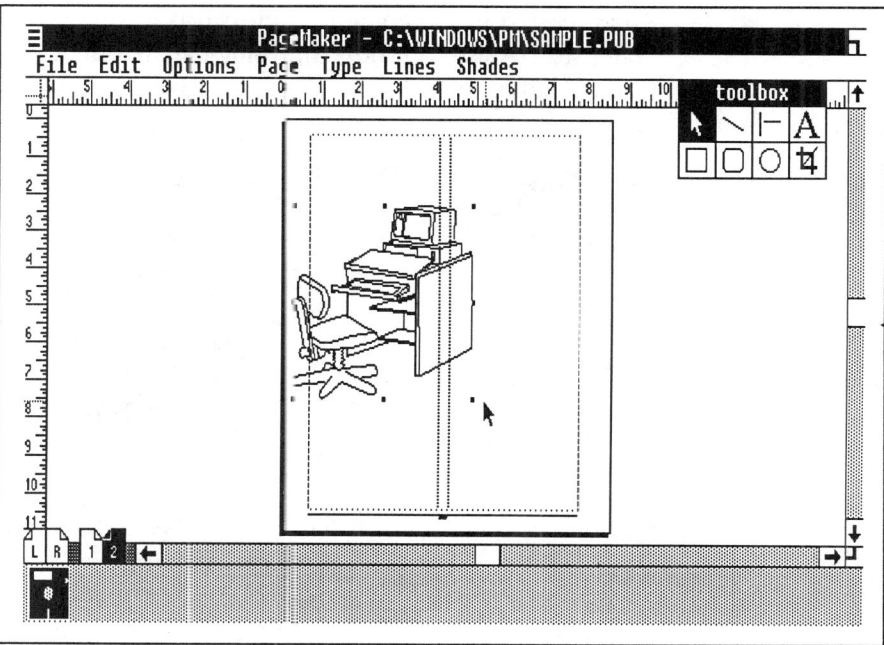

**Figure 15-14.** The graphic is placed on the page. Note that it both bleeds off the page and crosses over the column lines into the live area of column two.

When PC PageMaker fills a column with text, it will fill the column until it either reaches the end of the column or reaches a graphic element. So when you place the continued text in column one, it should stop at the graphic.

Go back to page 1 by clicking on the page 1 icon. From page 1, go to the bottom of the second column and click on the type. You will get the type handles back. Click on the bottom handle, and you will have you text icon back. Move the text icon down to the page icon area. It will change to a pointer. Don't worry; when it's off the pasteboard, it changes to a pointer. Click on page 2.

Once on page 2, go to the top of the first column, and click the mouse; the text will flow in and stop at the graphic. At the bottom handle, click again to get the text icon and go under the graphic and fill the bottom of the column. Get the text icon from the bottom handle of the column.

Go to the top of the next column, place your text icon at the top left corner, and click the mouse button. Text will begin filling the column. It will stop at the graphic. The type will now have handles on it. With the pointer, go up in the ruler and grab a ruler guide. Drag it down, placing it flush with the line of the bottom window shade. Click the bottom handle to the text icon again. Position the text icon at the upper left-hand corner of the ruler guide and the left of the column, even if it is covered by the graphic. Click the mouse. The text will flow in, filling the bottom of the column and stopping at the end of the column. (See Figs. 15-15 and 15-16.).

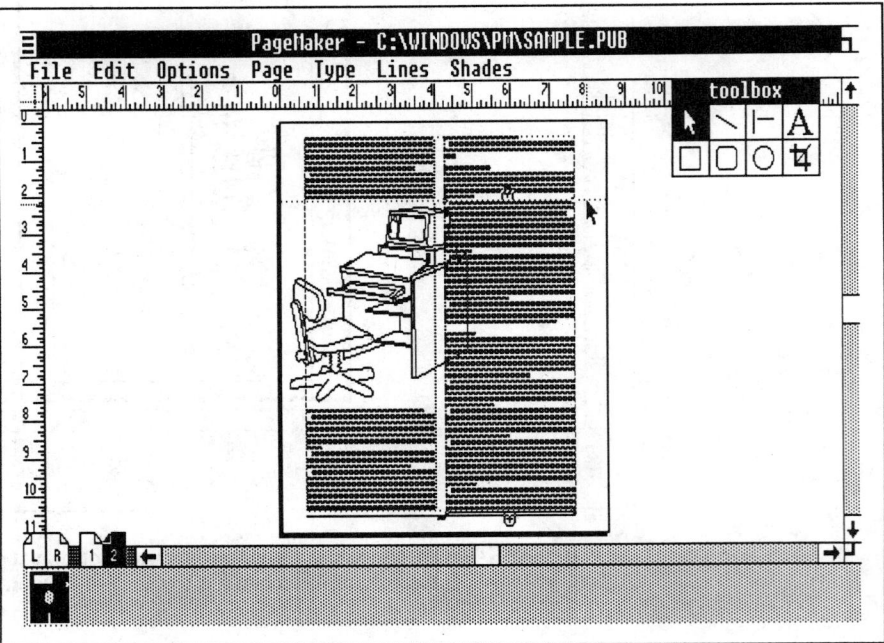

**Figure 15-15.** Page 2, with the graphic in place and text flowed in the first column and up to the intruding graphic in the second column, where a ruler guide has been placed at the bottom text handle. The text icon is gotten from the text where it stopped at the graphic and is now placed at the ruler guide and allowed to reflow over the graphic to the bottom of the column.

**177**   Placing Elements on a Page

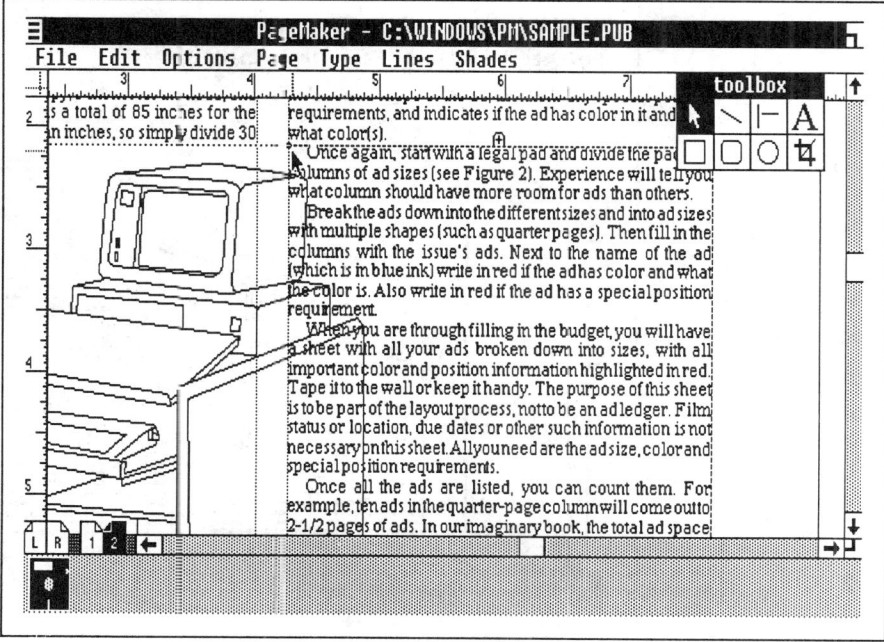

**Figure 15-16.**   At actual size, position the screen to see the area where the wrap will occur.

Now comes the fun—creating a wrap around the graphic. What happens next is quite simple. Go to either the top or bottom left handle on the type covering the graphic, and, clicking the mouse, drag it to the right. Drag until the text is to the right of the graphic. As you can see, text blocks can be resized just like graphics. Go to the bottom of the page, and window shade the text back up to a little below the graphic. Once again, drag down a ruler guide, and align it with the bottom text handle.

   Now, at the upper left-hand corner of the column guide and the ruler guide, click the text icon that you got from the text block wrapped on the right of the graphic and flow the text in under the graphic to the bottom of the column. Click on the pasteboard and study your page. You now have a perfect wrap around the graphic. By using the ruler guides to place the text blocks correctly, the linespacing in the right-hand column is correct. It should look roughly like Fig. 15-17.

**178**  Chapter 15

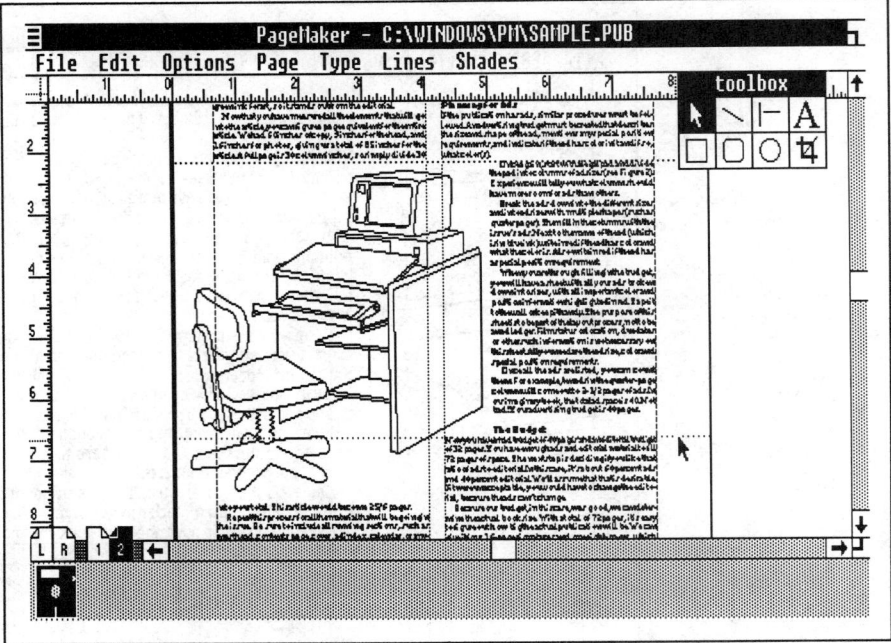

**Figure 15-17.** Text flowed into the page as a wrapped column.

Another style of handling a wrap is to change the column guides, both in wraps and in general layout and grid creation. Column guides are not locked into the gereral area they are currently in. The options menu does have a guide lock that will lock them so they cannot accidentally be changed, but you can, at any time, change the width of any column on the page (when there are two or more columns). The widths of the columns change, but the space between the columns does not. So in this example, the 1/4-inch space between the margins will remain constant.

To move a column guide to the right of the graphic, make sure that you are using the pointer. Do not get a text icon. Position the pointer in the area between the two columns above the graphic, as in Fig. 15-18, and place the pointer on either of the two column guides.

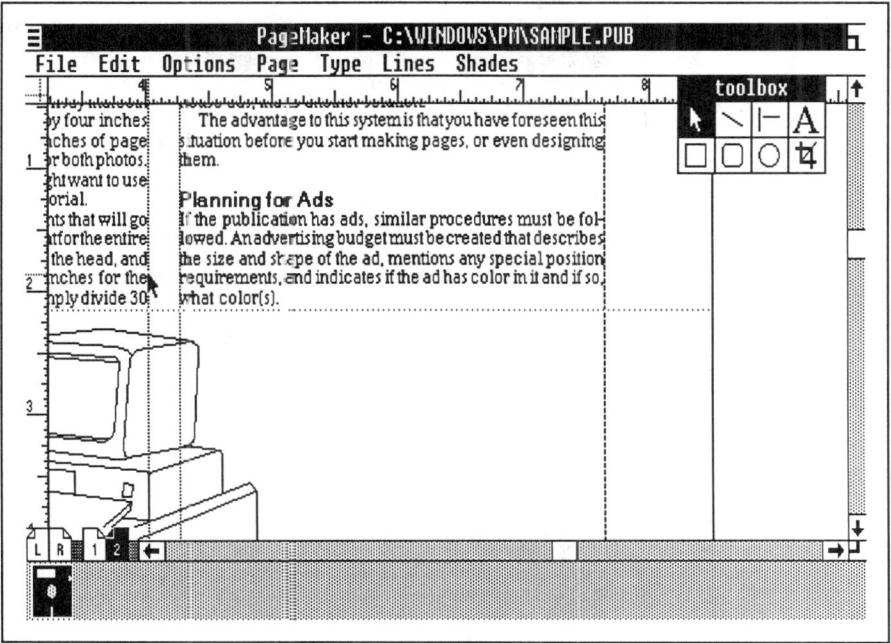

**Figure 15-18.** The pointer should rest on one of the two column guides when you are attempting to change column widths.

Now, press the mouse button. The pointer will change to a double arrow pointing left and right. This simply means that you may move that column guide in either direction. Since the goal is to create a column guide to the right of the graphic, move the column guide mover icon to the right. You will see the dotted column guide lines move with you. Using the ruler or the left column margin, determine when the right-hand column guide is 1/4 inch from the right of the graphic. When it is positioned correctly, let go of the mouse. Note that the text you have already placed does not change because you have moved the margins. The column guide should look like the one in Fig. 15-19.

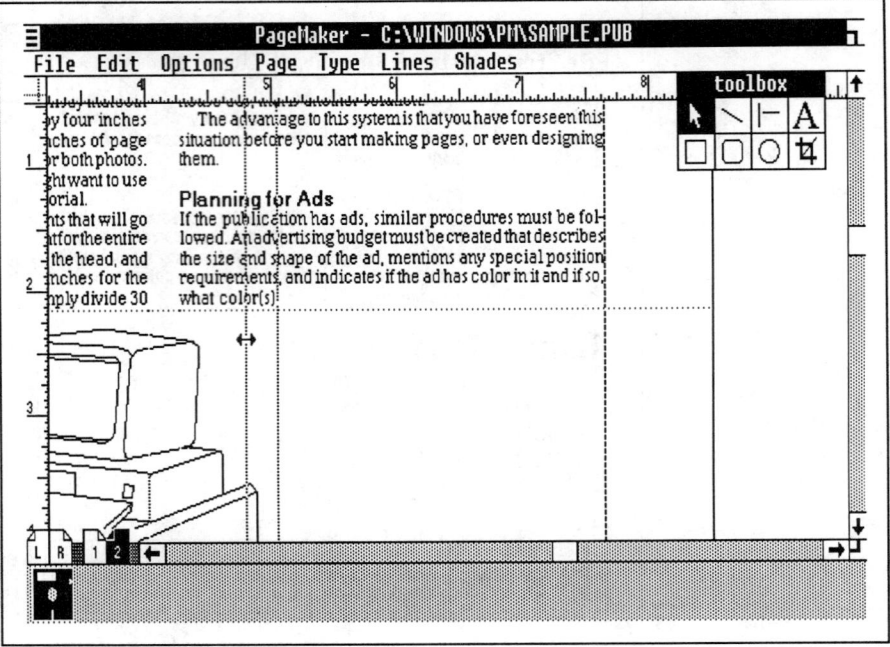

**Figure 15-19.** The column guide has been moved to the right of the graphic to form a new column to place text in, so that text will wrap around the graphic.

Here comes the amazing part. Before you begin, read the first few words in the text block below the graphic in the right-hand column.

Now, go to the text block above the graphic in the right-hand column, and click on it. You will get the handles back. Click on the bottom handle. This will give you the text icon. Position the icon at the top left corner of the new small column to the right of the graphic, as shown in Fig. 15-20.

# 181 Placing Elements on a Page

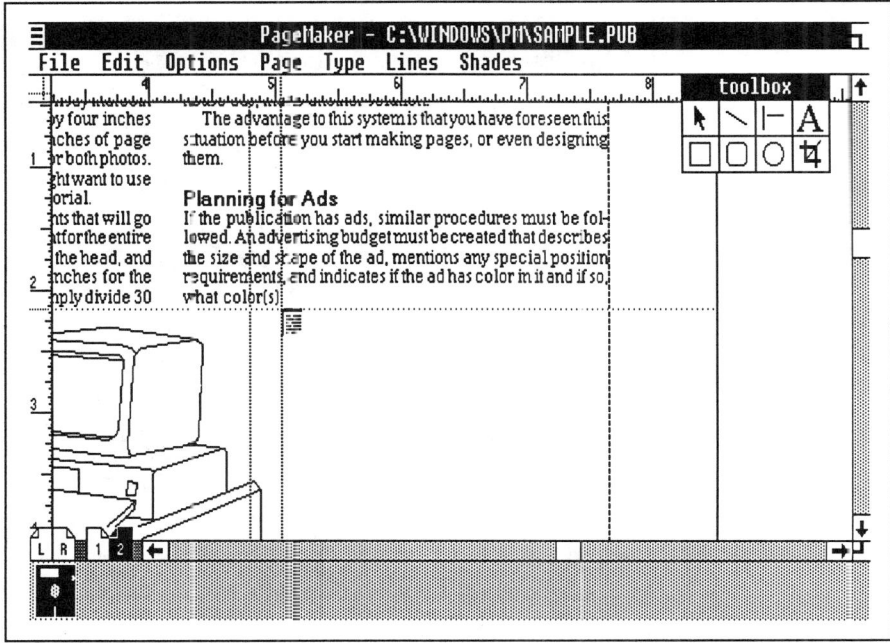

**Figure 15-20.** The text icon, taken from the bottom of the text block on the top of column two, is in place for adding text to the new small column to the right of the graphic.

Now, it's time for fun. Simply click the text icon. Text will flow into the new column and stop at the block of type underneath it. Now, take a look at the words where you started placing the text. Rather than being the word that comes after the bottom block of text (which would make sense since you placed this block after the bottom text bock), the new column has pulled the words from the bottom block up into the new block and has filled the bottom block with the text from later in the text file.

Before I explain why it can do this amazing feat, take a look at your wrap, as shown in Fig. 15-21.

**182**  Chapter 15

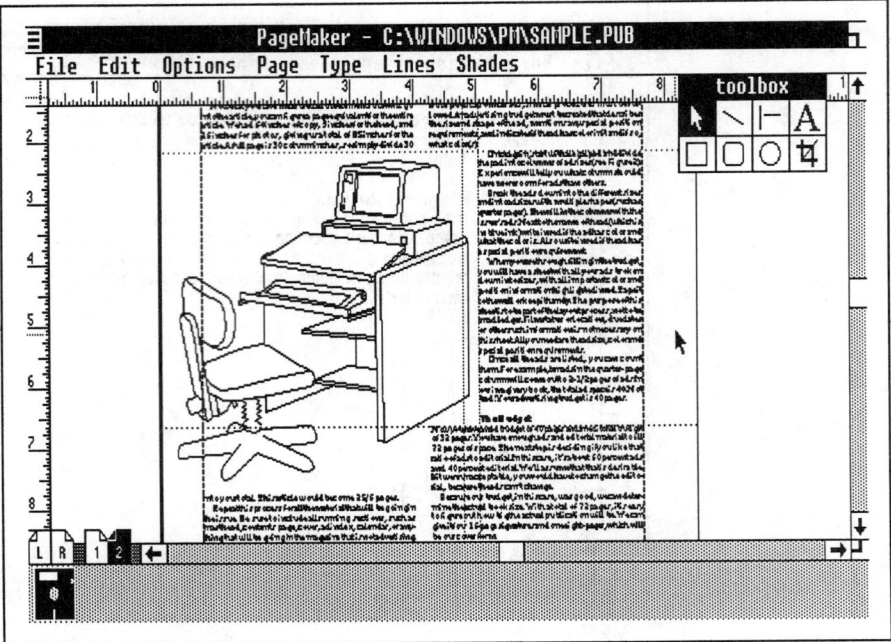

**Figure 15-21.** Text flowed into the page as a wrapped column by changing the column widths.

PC PageMaker threads the text through blocks. Since you clicked on the text block above it and then filled the column, it knew that you wanted to flow the text in a continuous stream between the text blocks. Now, here's an interesting point. What if the text block was a caption and not part of the text flow?

That is easy. Instead of going to the text block above the graphic to get the text icon, you would wait until you got to the caption (perhaps located at the end of the file), click on the caption type, and place it in the small column. It would not thread the type since the text came from a different location in the text file. It is still part of the thread of text, just located in a different area. If you were to take a paragraph out of page 1, for example, the block of text placed last with the caption (even though it is located in the middle of the text) would end up one paragraph shorter as a result. It's all part of connecting text in the threading fashion.

So, you have a pretty impressive second page. You have learned to make columns variable widths, place graphics, and do a text wrap. Not bad!

There is another form of text wrap. The one you did on page 2 was a wrap around a square shape. There will be times when you will need to wrap around abstract shapes such as circles or free-form art.

For such situations, place the text until you reach the graphic, which will block the flow of text. Get the text icon from the text block, place a ruler guide as described for the square wrap, and place the text over the graphic. Pull the text right over it so that both the text and the graphic will be visible. At this point, you must manually create your wrap by changing to the text tool. If the graphic is on the left of the column, use tabs and spaces to move the text away from the graphic, creating a free-form wrap that follows the graphic. If the graphic protrudes into the right-hand side of the column, press the return key to create the same effect by ending the line short of the graphic element. This is a bit more work, but good results can be obtained.

Finally, we will add a rule to the center of the page. This brings up the question of why, if you wanted the rule to be on every page, didn't you include it as a master page item? You could, and, in most cases, it is best to do so. This particular sample would have graphics that would cross over columns, so the rules would have shown up in the graphic.

As will be covered shortly, there are some tricks to solve this problem, but, for now, it was easier to create the rules on the page, and work around the graphic.

Draw the rules in the same fashion as on the first page. Only this time, work the rules so there are two: one above and one below the graphic. The second page is now complete, as shown in Fig. 15-22.

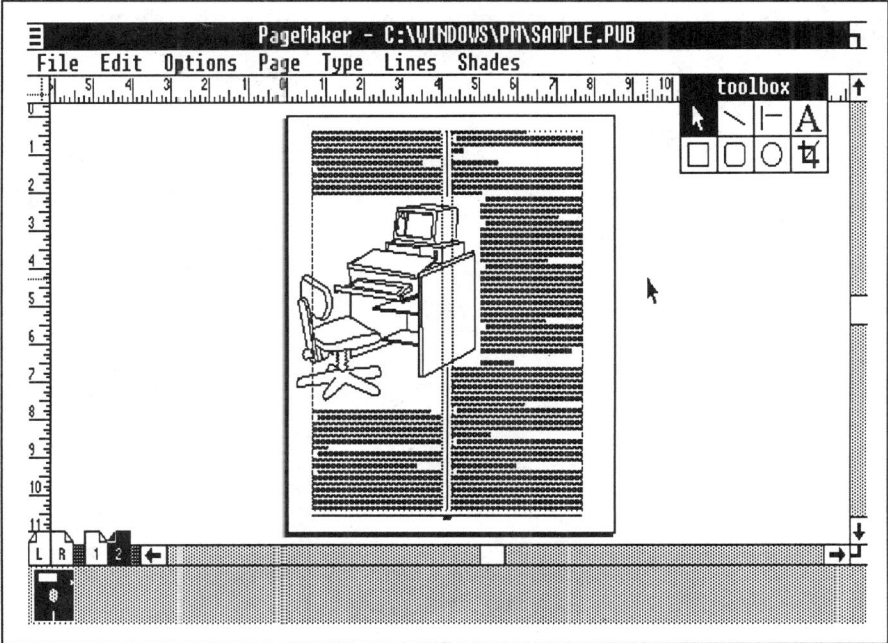

**Figure 15-22.** The second page, complete with text, graphic, text wrap, and rules.

Let's move on to page 3, the final page in our sample file, where we will complete the text and learn a basic concept of filling a page so that columns end flush.

## Making a Page End Flush

Start page 3 by clicking on the bottom of the type at the end of column two on page 2 to get the text icon. Move to the page menu and choose "Insert a page" after the current page.

Move to the top left corner of page 3, and place the text icon in the upper left-hand corner. Click the mouse button, and fill the column. Now click on the bottom handle of column one, and get the text icon. Move to the top of column two. Position the icon in the upper left-hand corner, and place the text.

The text will fill column two, but not completely. You will notice that, in the bottom of the column, the handle has a new symbol in it. Up to now, it always had a plus sign, meaning that there would be more text. It now has a number sign (#), which means that the text file has ended. So your page now has two uneven columns of type, as shown in Fig. 15-23.

### 185 Placing Elements on a Page

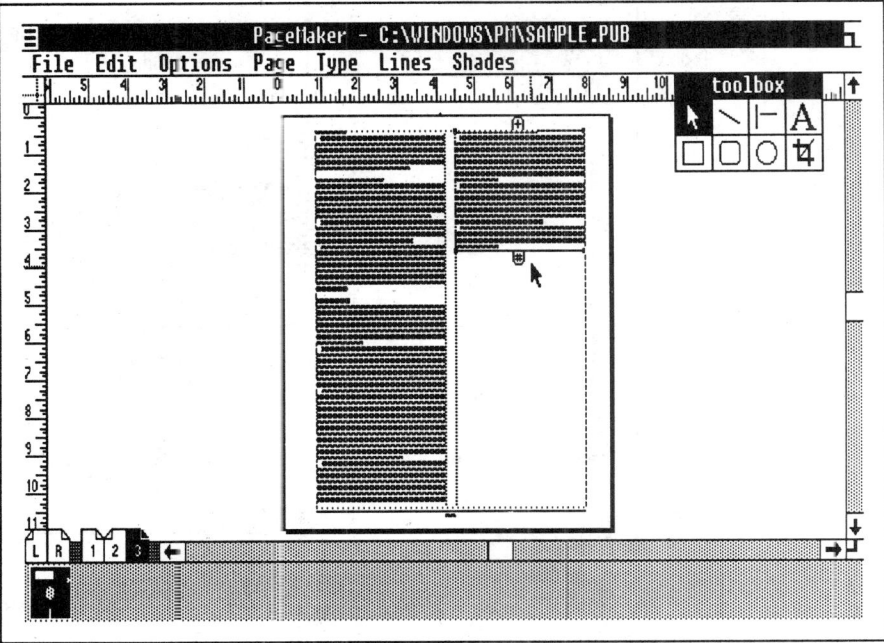

**Figure 15-23.** Page 3 with all remaining text placed in the two columns. The problem is that both columns end at a different place. The desired effect is to have both end so that they are even on the bottom.

Making the two columns end flush is quite easy. It involves clicking the columns to get their handles, shortening column one, making column two longer, and repeating the process until both are even. A first attempt at this is shown in Fig. 15-24.

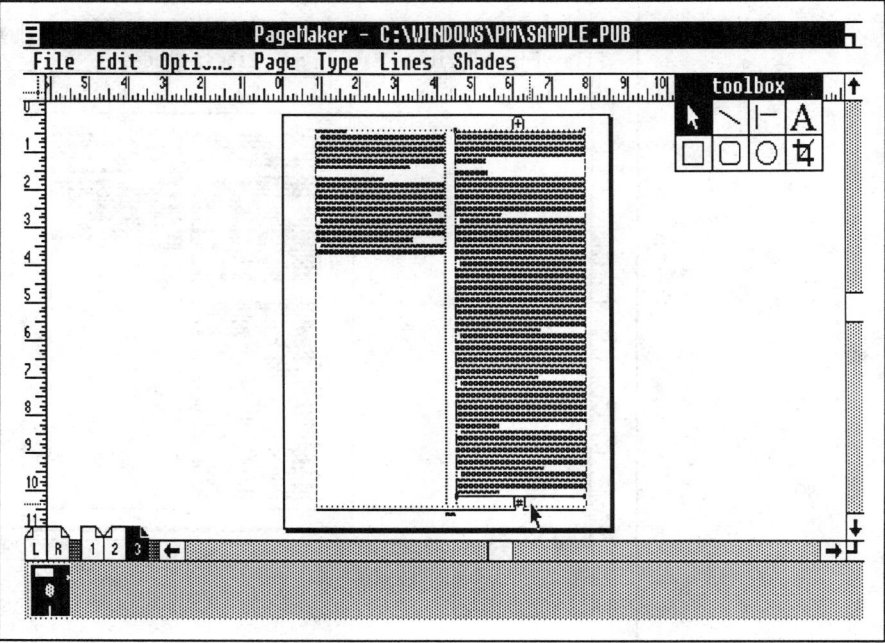

**Figure 15-24.** The first column is made shorter, and the second column made longer. The text from column one moves over to the top of column two, changing the symbol in the bottom of column two from the end-of-file sign to a plus sign. Pull the second column down, and the additional text will appear. Pull it all the way until you get the end-of-file sign.

**187**  Placing Elements on a Page

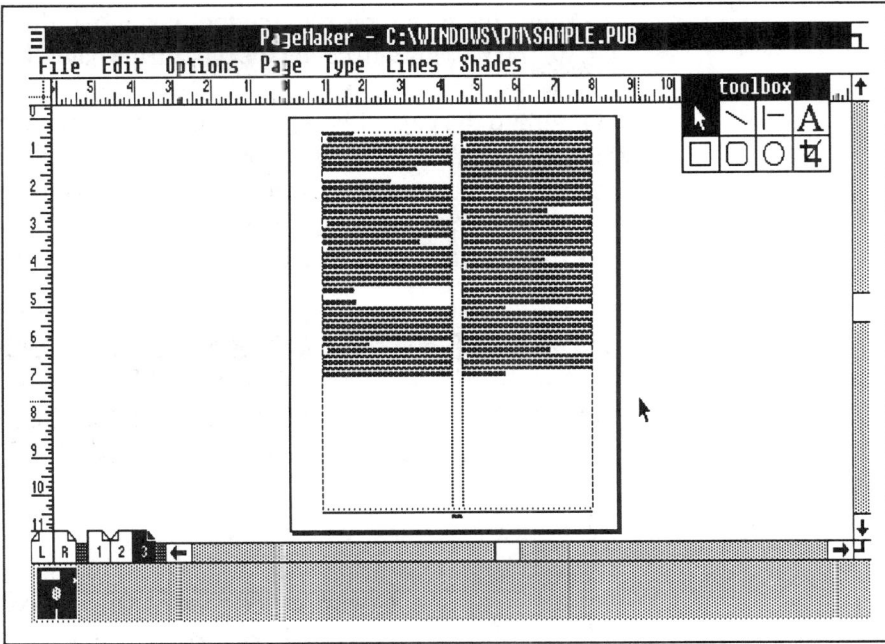

**Figure 15-25.** After a few attempts, the columns have been adjusted to where they both end flush. What is left is an empty space at the bottom of the page.

Fig. 15-25 shows the final adjustments so each column is the same depth as the other. An empty space is now available at the bottom of the page, which you will fill with a boxed message saying, "For more copies of this report, call your distributor."

## Adding Type and Boxes

The message box is not only going to contain type, it will also contain type with the type in white and the box in black.

To do this, you must first create the type. Since the message is a filler, it is not part of any text file. You will enter it from the keyboard.

The type will be centered across the page and will run across the width of the page. The first thing you need to do is go to the options menu, choose "Column guides," and select one for the number of columns. The page will contain the type, unchanged, but no column guides. Make the page actual size by pressing the right mouse button, and scroll to the bottom left-hand corner where the blank space is.

Select the type tool from the toolbox. Go to the type menu, and select "Align center." This will center the type on the page. Then go to the type specs menu; when the box appears, choose Times Roman 24-point bold. Press OK, and return to the page. Place the I-beam text cursor against the left column, click the mouse to activate text insertion, and begin typing in your message. The type will center itself in the size and style you have chosen.

When you are through, you will have type on the bottom of the page that looks like the sample in Fig. 15-26.

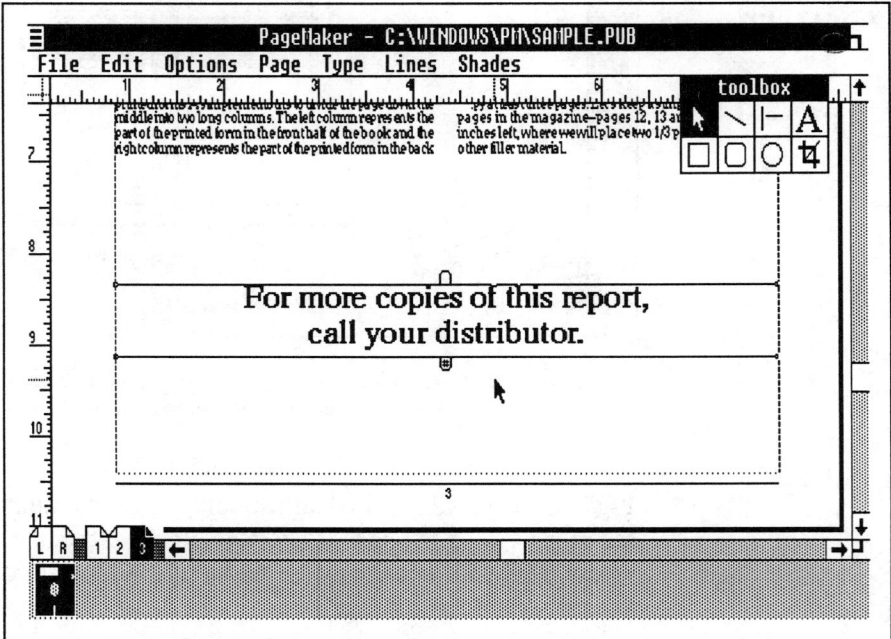

**Figure 15-26.** Type centered on page about to be boxed, with the type reversed to white. "Align center" options from the Type menu.

If the type is not perfectly aligned for height, get the pointer and move it around until the type is aligned.

The next step is to draw a box around the type. This is very easy. Go to the toolbox, and select the icon of the square. This is the box-drawing tool. Go to the left margin below the columns of type and above your new type, press the button of the mouse, and begin dragging the mouse toward the bottom right-hand corner of the live area. The screen will scroll automatically as you do this, allowing you to see when you have reached the desired spot. Now release the button. A box will be drawn around the text. It should look like the sample in Fig. 15-27.

189  Placing Elements on a Page

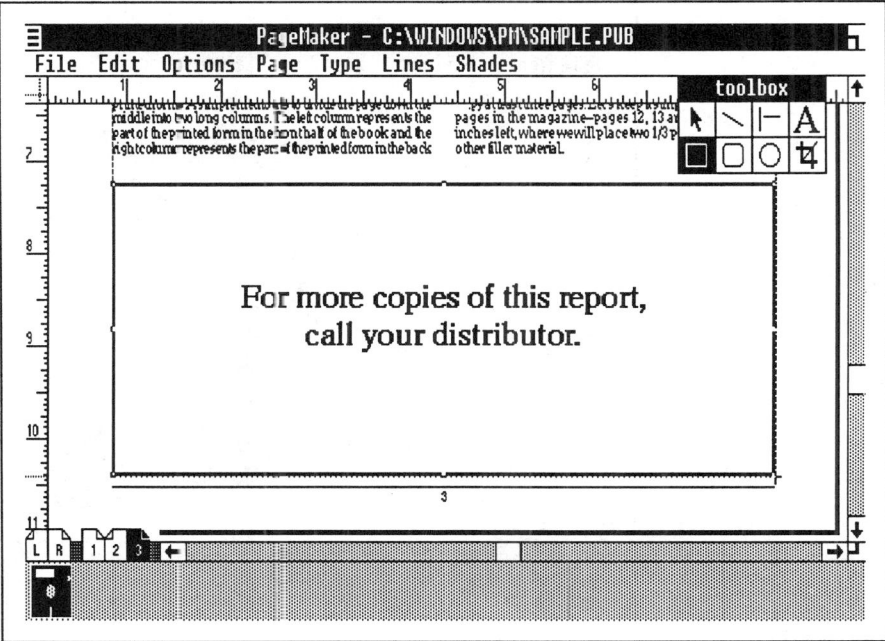

**Figure 15-27.** A box is drawn around the new type using the box-drawing tool from the toolbox.

Now comes a strange series of events. You will select the type, and, from the type menu, make it white. That's right! The type will be white, which means you will not be able to see it. To do this, get the text tool, select the type, go to the type menu, and select "Reverse Type." The type on the screen will disappear. But don't worry, it's still there, only it's white.

The second step is to get the pointer back, place it on the line of the box, and click the mouse button. The handles appear on the box, meaning that it is selected. At this point, using the lines menu or shades menu, you could change the thickness of the rule or change the shade in the box. Go to the shades menu, and select black as the shade for the box. The result will be a solid black box where the type used to be. Don't panic. The box is just sitting in front of the type. The goal is to move the box behind the type.

To do this, go to the edit menu, as shown in Fig. 15-28. On the menu are selections called "Bring to front" and "Send to back." What you want to do is send the black box to the back so that the white type is in front of the black box. Since the box is already selected, simply click on the "Send to back" command. The results should be like that of Fig. 15-28—white type against a black background.

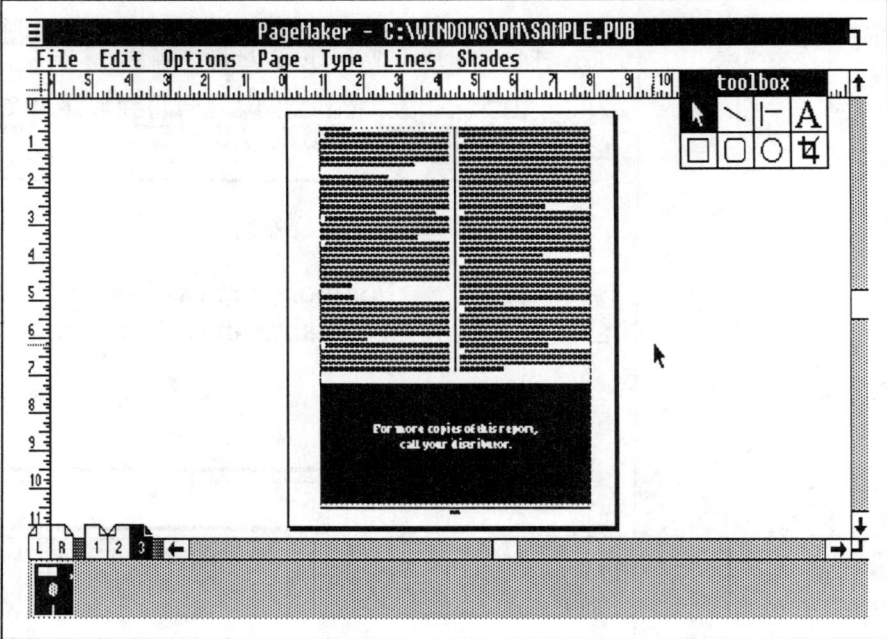

**Figure 15-28.** By sending the black box to the back, the white type is now in front of the box and shows up perfectly. For a finishing touch, the vertical rules are added between columns.

The final step is to add the rules between columns, which is also shown in Fig. 15-28.

## Publication Complete

The ability to draw boxes, circles, and other shapes; add rules; send elements to the front or back; and color type black or white all give PC PageMaker a pretty sophisticated system of handling graphics creation from within the program. The pages created used most of PC PageMaker's more basic abilities, although there are still many more subtle tricks that will be covered in the next chapters.

# Adding Graphic Elements 16

*A*fter working with placing text on pages in PC PageMaker, you will find yourself starting to explore the many graphics possibilities that the program offers.

## Using the Toolbox

With a simple set of drawing tools, termed primitives, the toolbox offers you a chance to create many different graphic elements on a page. Let's start by examining the features found in the toolbox.

The toolbox appears at the start of a PC PageMaker session in the upper right-hand corner of the pasteboard. You may move the box anywhere on the screen by clicking on the top bar and moving it to the desired location. The toolbox contains eight boxes. I will detail each one, starting from the top row and working right.

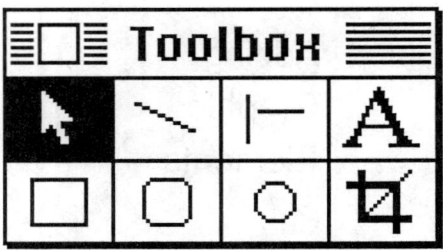

**Pointer tool:** The most commonly used tool, the pointer allows you to point to an object, such as a graphic or a column of type, and make it active, meaning that you can do things to it or with it. It allows you to move elements, window shade type columns, and remove them from the pasteboard by pointing to something, clicking the mouse, and hitting the backspace key.

**Diagonal tool:** This allows you to draw a straight line in any direction. The line drawn can be made different weights or styles by selecting them from the lines menu.

**Perpendicular tool:** I call this the straight-line tool, mainly because it allows you to draw horizontal or vertical straight lines. This is used for drawing rules between columns and across a page, for underlining heads, and for creating simple graphics. When selected, just like the diagonal tool, the lines may be made different weights from the lines menu. Additionally, you may draw rules at a 45-degree angles by pulling up or down as you are drawing the line.

**Text tool:** This tool allows you to enter text from scratch, edit existing text, or select blocks of text for modification. A simple rule is to use this tool whenever you are working in type.

**Square-corner tool:** I call this the box tool. It lets you create boxes of any size or shape by dragging with the mouse. Like the line-drawing tools, the rules can be made different weights or styles with the aid of the lines menu when the box is selected. Additionally, you can fill any box with a standard pattern, from white to light grays to dark grays to black, as well as special patterns.

**Rounded-corner tool:** This tool acts exactly the same as the square-corner tool, except that the corners are rounded. You may select various rounded styles for the corners by selecting "Rounded corners" from the options menu.

**Circle-oval tool:** This tool has all the line and shading attributes of the square-corner and rounded-corner tools but can draw ovals. By holding down the shift key as you drag the mouse, you can draw a perfect circle.

**Cropping tool:** Once a graphic is placed and selected, it has a series of handles on the sides, top, and corners. Using this tool, you can crop the photo from the sides, top, or bottom, using one of the corner handles.

The graphics you can create with these simple drawing tools are just the type of graphics you need on publication pages. You can create rules and ruled boxes and crop graphics to fit areas. Best of all, they all operate in the object-oriented programs. They are not bit-mapped graphics like those from paint programs, so they will be printed at the full resolution of the printing device used.

## Working with Graphics Files

You can, as discussed in Chapter 15, import graphics files for placement on the publication page. Such graphics can be cropped using the cropping tool as detailed here. They can also be proportioned and sized as discussed in Chapter 15.

### Helpful Hint

The most useful application of the handles is making graphics larger or smaller in proportion to their original size. For example, say that you had a scanned photograph that was on the page to show the printer where the halftone will go. If the photo is too small, by using the handles, you can make it larger to fill an area, yet keep it accurate in its proportions so that when the halftone is made, it will fit perfectly to your page version.

## Adding Shading to Areas

Shaded blocks can be created, and type can be placed over them, with the type in black or white. PC PageMaker offers you the ability to draw boxes or circles, fill them with a variety of patterns, and then place type in them.
    Many times, unless large type is used, this effect is not very good. The dot patterns are fairly large and are big enough to distort smaller type. The only exception is black, with white type, as detailed in Chapter 15. Fig. 16-1 shows both large and small type in a shaded box. You can see that this works well only with large type.

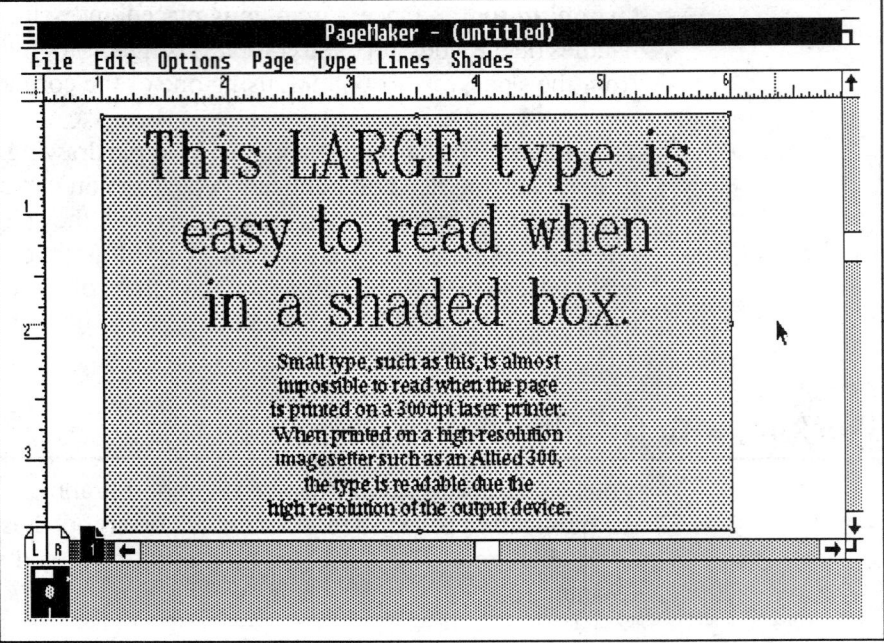

**Figure 16-1.** A shaded box filled with large and small type. Note how the large type can hold up against the coarse screen, but the smaller type becomes almost unreadable.

## Covering Master Page Elements

There will be times when there are graphic elements on a page that you want to remove or cover a small section of. A good example is a page grid with vertical rules between columns on every page. In a 24-page document, where every page is text, only the headline and one graphic on page 5 will run over the rules if you place them on the master page grids. You should place the rules on the grid and let them show up on every page. This saves you the task of drawing rules on every page.

So what about the headline and photo that will cross over the rules? Simple. Draw a box over the areas where the rules are that will conflict with the headline and photo. Draw boxes over the areas. From the shades menu, choose "White"; from the lines menu, choose "None." This acts as a form of electric white-out. Fig. 16-2 illustrates the box before changing to white with no rule; Fig. 16-3 shows the effect after changing.

# 195 Adding Graphic Elements

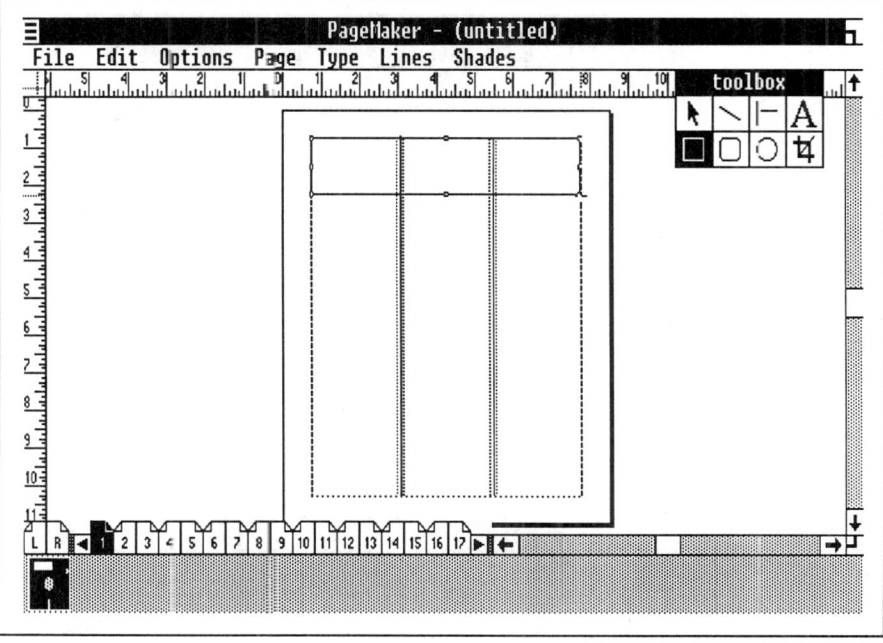

**Figure 16-2.** A box is drawn where the headline will go. Make the box large enough for the headline, with some room underneath it.

**196**  Chapter 16

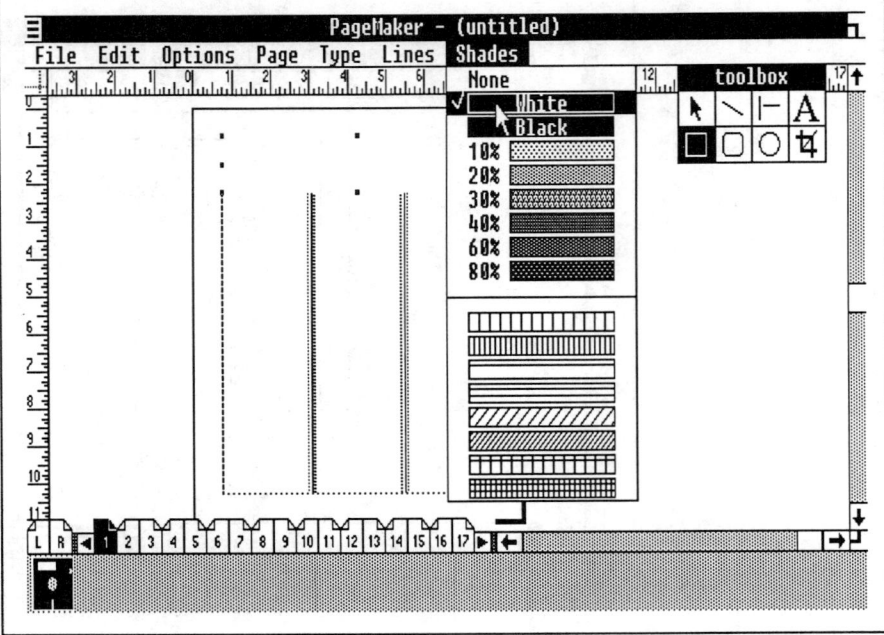

**Figure 16-3.** The box is made white by selecting "White" from the shades menu, and the rule is changed to "None" from the line menu, leaving a pure white area for the headline.

### Shortcut

You will find yourself using this white-out trick all the time. Use it to cover mistakes and even to create interesting effects such as a shadowed box. Create a black box, copy it using the edit menu, paste it down on top of itself, and fill the top box with white (with any size rule). This will create a drop-shadow box.

## TIFF and EPS Files

There are two important graphic file formats that you will encounter as you work with PostScript or begin to include digitized art or halftones in your pages.

The first format, TIFF, is a standard file format for scanned art and halftones placed on PC PageMaker pages. This file format allows you to

**197** Adding Graphic Elements

place a very high resolution scanned image on the page (such as 300dpi) yet have it represented at an accurate size regardless of the screen resolution. A paint-style image of the art or halftone will be placed on the page representing this high-resolution image, as shown in Fig. 16-4.

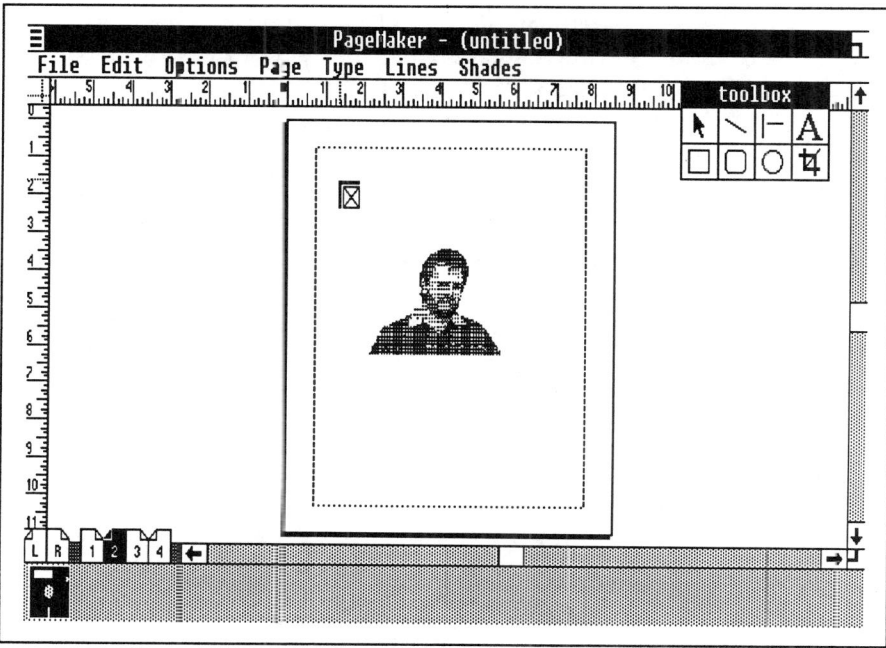

**Figure 16-4.** A TIFF file placed on a page, with its on-screen representation of the scanned graphics file.

Like all graphics, the image can be cropped, stretched, and made larger or smaller. Of course, with such an image, such changes will cause distortions since the image is bit-mapped—just a very high resolution paint file.

The TIFF file allows an image to be presented on the screen of the scanned image. Consequently, if you wish to create an irregular wrap, align it with text, or perform some other special considerations, having the screen image is invaluable.

The second file format, Encapsulated PostScript (EPS), is useful only if you will be printing to a PostScript device. Essentially, EPS is a file of the text that creates a PostScript image. When a page or graphic is printed in PostScript, there are no graphics or bitmaps, only standard ASCII text that describes the position of all elements or pixels that are in the PostScript file. As a result, a PostScript file is not a graphics file; it is simply a text file.

PC PageMaker can take PostScript files that contain art or type or just about anything and place them directly on the page as long as they have been saved in the EPS file format. This allows the addition of some of the great PostScript effects that can be created only with PostScript graphics programs or directly in PostScript.

Most often, when placed on the page, the EPS file will be placed as a gray box at the size the PostScript file states the image will be. The box will contain some simple type that tells the name of the file but most likely will not contain a screen image of the file. A screen image can be present if the file contains a metafile (a special set of codes in the file that creates a screen image), but most programs currently create just a box for size.

When the file is placed on the page, you can, as with any graphic, change the proportions. The results may be not only surprising but also unpredictable. I am simply pointing out that it can be done.

Even though the EPS file will appear as a box on the screen, when it prints to a PostScript printer, it will print to the full resolution of that printer. It is there that you will see exactly what the image looks like, as shown in Fig. 16-5.

**199** Adding Graphic Elements

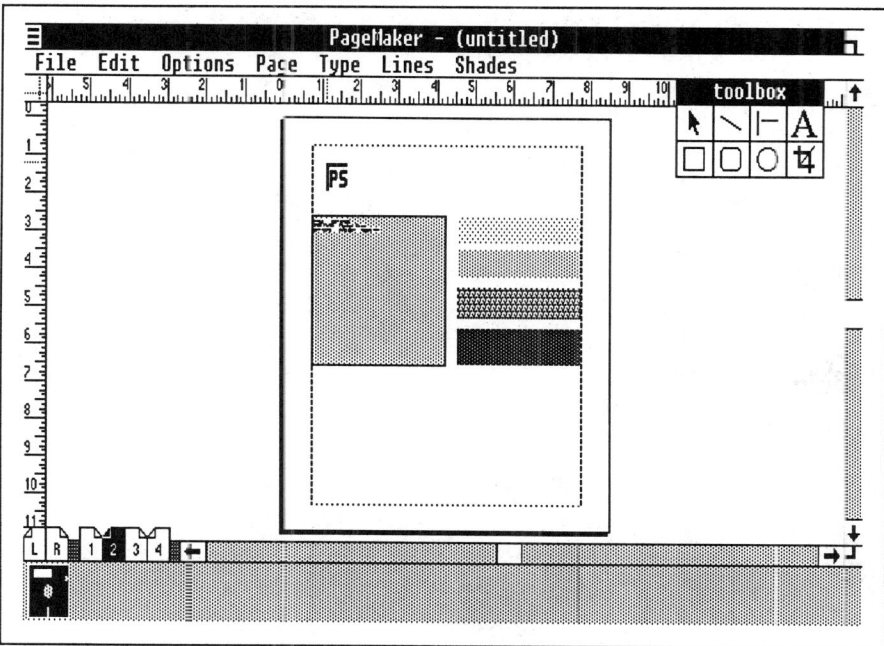

**Figure 16-5.** An EPS screen box and the resulting printed version.

## Experiment with All the Tools

There are many things that can be done with the simple drawing tools in the PC PageMaker toolbox. Each time you create a new publication you will find new uses for these tools.

# Linking PC PageMaker Files 17

*I*f PC PageMaker has one limitation in the creation of publications, it is its page file limit of 128 pages. Since many books and reports run longer than 128 pages, you will have to plan for this situation. In many cases, the file limitation size can be handled if you understand that the publications are often divided into parts or chapters.

If you have a publication with a section that runs longer than 128 pages, this chapter will help you plan your publication so as not to be restricted by the page limitation.

## The First Options

If your publication is divided in any fashion, such as parts or chapters, then make each part or chapter a single-page file. If the parts or chapters individually exceed the 128-page limitation, then you will need to split the text file (a subject to be covered shortly).

It is always best to try to structure your text files to fit in the page limit when using PC PageMaker, even if the split comes at a subhead or illustration break. Try finding logical breaks first; if your text is structured to accommodate these breaks, you will not need to read this chapter. If you have files that are always longer than 128 pages (such as catalogs, price lists, technical documentation), you will have to learn to split your text files. This will allow you to create page files that, when printed, will result in pages that look as if they all came from one file. There are some shortcomings in doing this, however.

First, let's examine how to handle a file that exceeds 128 pages.

## Splitting Text Files

For very long text files, regardless of nature (text, prices, graphics), create the first 128 pages as usual. Place all your elements. When you get to the bottom of page 128, simply stop, save your file, and print out the file if you like (at least print out the last page—page 128—so you can see where your text ended in the first page file).

Quit PC PageMaker and start up the word-processing program used to create your text file. Call up the text file you placed in the first page file, and save it under a different file name (such as FILE NUMBER 2), using the "Save as" option from your word-processing program. This will give you a second copy of the file to work with.

The next step is to enter the copy of the file (FILE NUMBER 2), define a block at the beginning of the file, and scroll down to the very spot where your text file ended in the first page file. Finish defining the text block, and delete it. This will remove the text used in the first page file and leave you with a new text file that starts where you need to begin the second page file. Select "Save" to store the file.

Now return to PC PageMaker, and create a second page file that matches the grid of the first. For this reason you may want to build a master page file, store it under the name MASTER PAGE FILE, and use it to start up each new page file, always saving the finished file under a different name so as not to erase MASTER PAGE FILE.

When you open the second page file, simply start placing text from File Number 2. Continue until you fill the next 128 pages. If you are using automatic page numbering, be sure to change the "Start page number at:" option to 129 from "Page setup" on the file menu.

If the file exceeds 256 pages, repeat this process, going back to the word-processing program and creating a third version of the text file, a fourth, and so on until all your text has been placed.

This process requires several additional steps but will allow you to use PC PageMaker for very long documents. There is one serious drawback to this solution, however.

## Shortcomings

As described in earlier chapters, PC PageMaker uses a threaded text flow in the page file. A change on page 1 will affect the rest of the text on the pages. If you remove or add text, all the rest of the pages will adjust.

Once you reach the file limitation and start a second file, that relationship is lost. A major change on page 1 will not affect page 129; it will only affect the pages of the page file it is in. For this reason, if you are working with a volatile document that may undergo radical changes throughout the file, the threading feature of PC PageMaker will not help you. In many cases, you may have to rebuild files from scratch.

Now, this is the exception more often than the rule. Although PC PageMaker has its page limitation, the same problem would occur if you were to assemble the pages manually. Remaking page files in PC PageMaker is much easier than having boards rekeylined!

### Build in "Break Points" on Long Files

Whenever possible, break up your text so that you will have some points at which to stop and start files that will not dramatically affect one another. This can be done with most publications. It is important to be aware that PC PageMaker creates 128-page blocks that are filed and cannot be linked except in layout from file to file and by sharing the master page grid file if you make one.

# 18

# PC PageMaker Unleashed

*T*he preceding chapters have discussed starting from scratch and going through to making completed page files. We have also talked about what to do if your pages won't fit in one of PC PageMaker's page files at a time.

There is more to PC PageMaker than that. It is full of shortcuts and powerful features that, once you master the above concepts, you can use all the time.

This chapter will cover each feature separately, but not in relationship to any particular page file or publication. Apply them whenever and wherever you can in your publication.

## Stretching Text

One of the best-kept secrets of both PC PageMaker and the word-processing programs is that when printing to a PostScript printing device using Post-Script laser fonts (and even bit-mapped fonts created as graphics), they can be stretched and modified the same way you would any graphic.

If you are in PC PageMaker and select type that was entered as type or as a text file, all you can do to it is make it larger or smaller and change its size and style. That is because it is treating type as type. When you import a graphic from Windows Draw (Micrografx), however, it treats it as a graphic, and you may change the size and proportions of a graphic element. So, make type a graphic element!

**206** Chapter 18

To do this, go to the MS-DOS Executive in Windows and load PC PageMaker and Windows Draw. A good example of how this feature works is the problem we had with the headline in our sample opening page in Chapter 15. The headline entered the file too small. The goal was to make the headline the width of the page.

Using the type tool, select the headline, copy it to the clipboard using the "Copy" option from the edit menu, then go to Windows Draw. Once in Windows Draw, paste the type down on the Windows Draw grid. Select the type by clicking on it; copy it to the clipboard again, and switch back to PC PageMaker. First, using the text tool, select the old headline, and hit the backspace key to remove it. You now can paste in the headline from the clipboard using the "Paste" option.

The results are that the headline is now on the PC PageMaker page as a graphic element ready to be stretched and pulled. Fig. 18-1 shows how the headline looks when it is first pasted into the page.

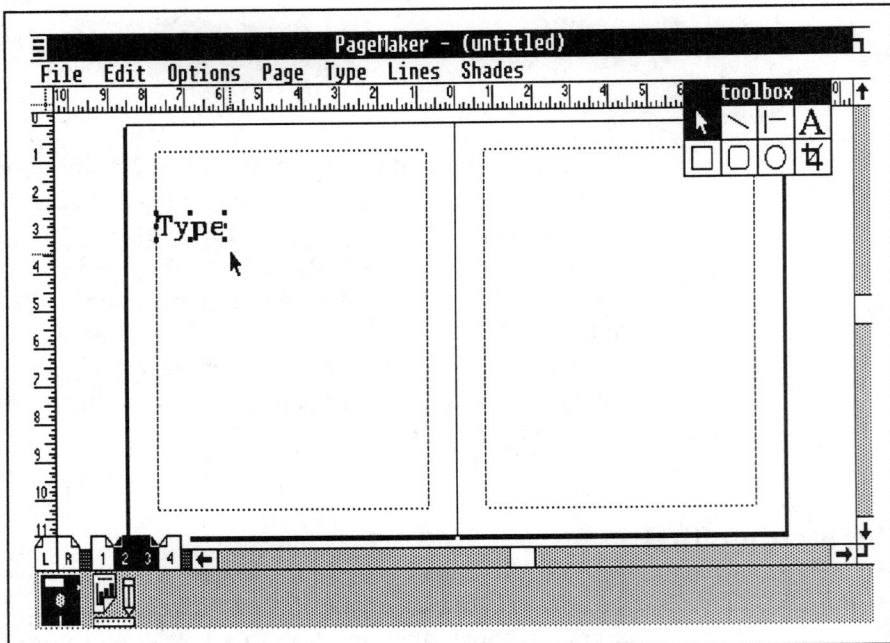

**Figure 18-1.** The headline, now a graphic from Windows Draw, comes onto the PC PageMaker page as a graphic, complete with handles for streching and changing size and proportions.

Using the pointer, move the type to the upper left-hand corner of the live area where you want the top left corner of the type to be. If you want to keep the type accurate and in proportion, hold down the shift key and drag the bottom right handle until the type is the full width of the columns as in Fig. 18-2.

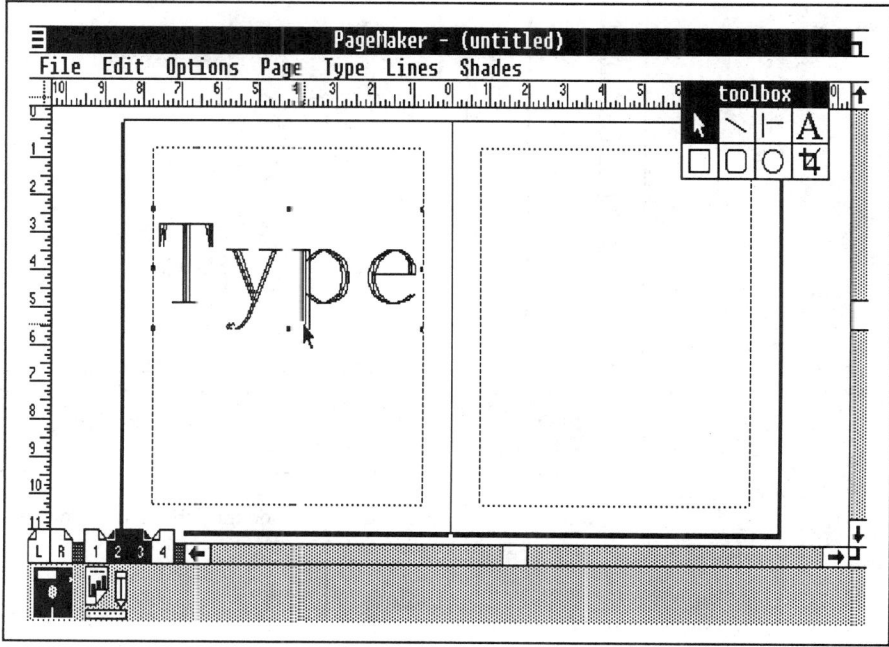

**Figure 18-2.** The type is stretched across the page by holding down the shift key and using the bottom right handle to drag the type across the page until it is full width.

This technique is fantastic for sizing headlines and for creating type of incredible shapes and proportions. By not holding the shift key and using the various handles, you could stretch the type to very creative proportions, exceeding the standard type-handling capabilities of PC PageMaker. Figs. 18-3 through 18-6 show how the same type can be stretched in a variety of fashions.

**Figure 18-3.** The type is first made the full width of the column. Using the bottom handle, it is then pulled down to create a condensed version of the type.

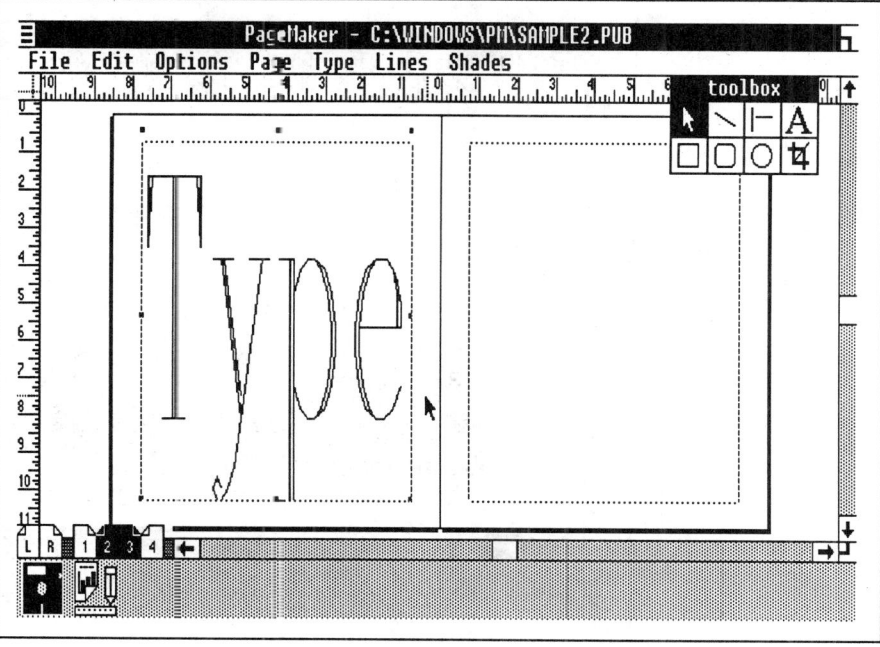

**Figure 18-4.** Stretching down even farther, the type becomes an extreme graphic element.

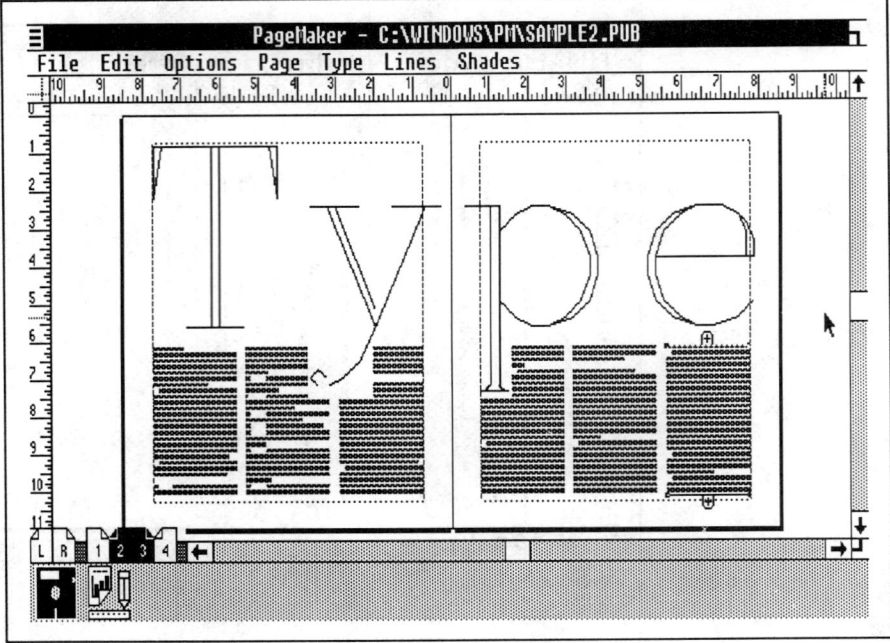

**Figure 18-5.** Using a single word and the techniques in Figs. 18-3 and 18-4, a dramatic headline is created.

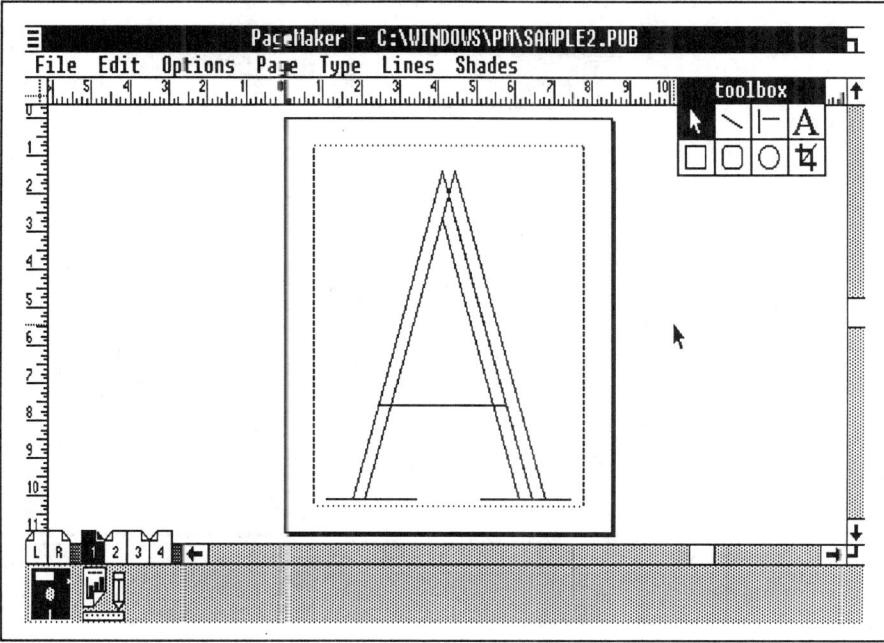

**Figure 18-6.** Using a single letter, the stretching and pulling technique allows the letter to become the size of the pages, which illustrates an unbelievable ability to manipulate type. This image prints very well on the PostScript printer or typesetter.

## Odd-Sized Columns

In the tutorial on creating a PC PageMaker page from scratch, we created only even columns, although you did learn how to create different column widths by moving the pointer between columns to one of the column guides, holding the mouse button down to get a double arrow, and then moving the columns.

Many pages use various column widths on a page. This book page, for example, has one tiny column for subheads and icons and a wide column that holds the text. You may set your master page grids to accommodate such grids. Simply use the same technique when setting up the master pages.

Fig. 18-7 shows such a page grid being created. This one uses two small columns, each one on either side of one large column.

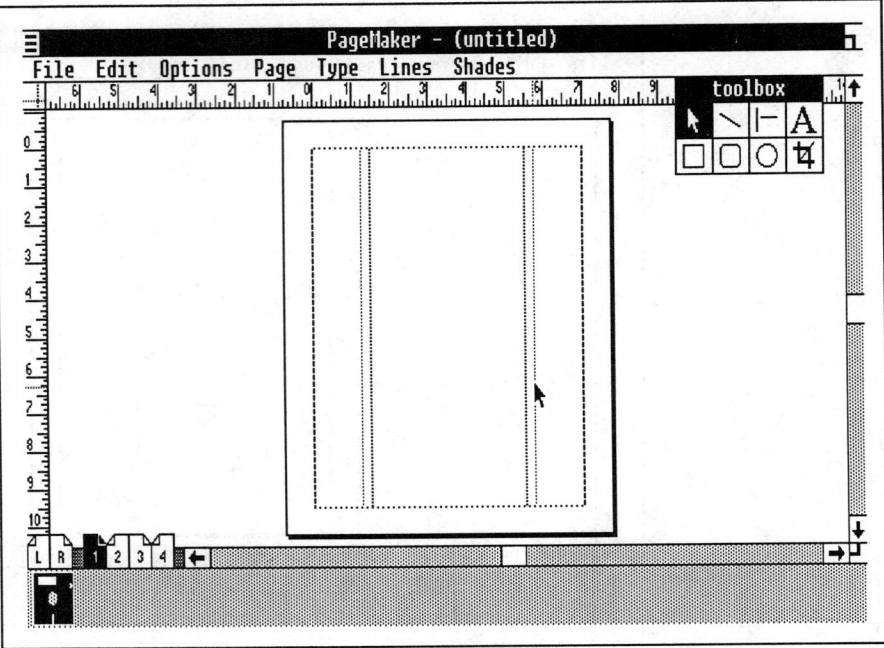

**Figure 18-7.** A master page grid with three odd-sized columns.

## Changing Column Widths with Text Placed

If you have placed a column of text and then decide later that you would like to change it, you can. Start with the first block of text on the page. The PC PageMaker manual suggests that you move the rest of the blocks off the page onto the pasteboard so they are out of the way. Using the pointer, click on one of the column handles, and resize it. This is shown in Fig. 18-8.

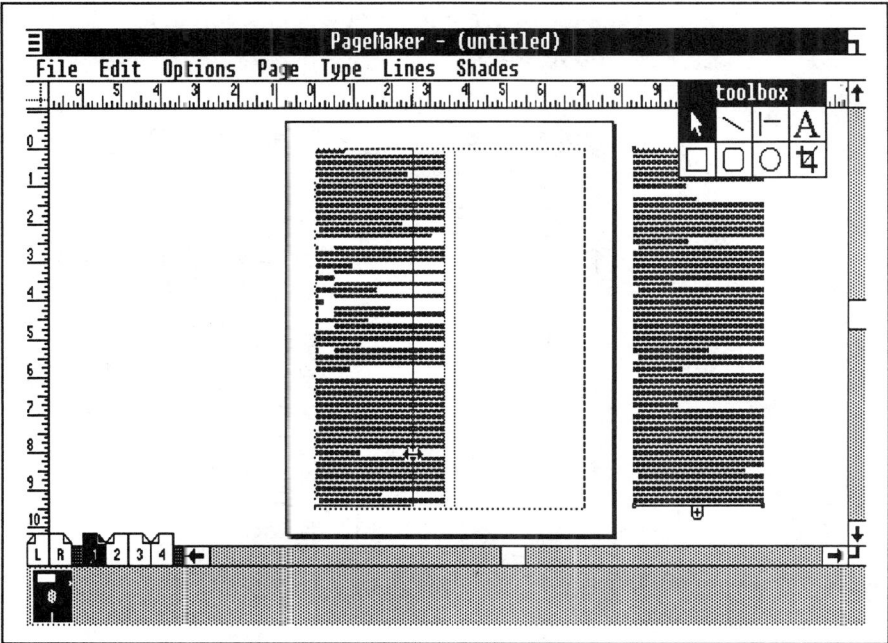

**Figure 18-8.** The first text block is selected, the other blocks have been moved off the page, and the column is being changed to a new size.

Take the next column of type, position it, grab a corner handle, and resize it as in Fig. 18-9.

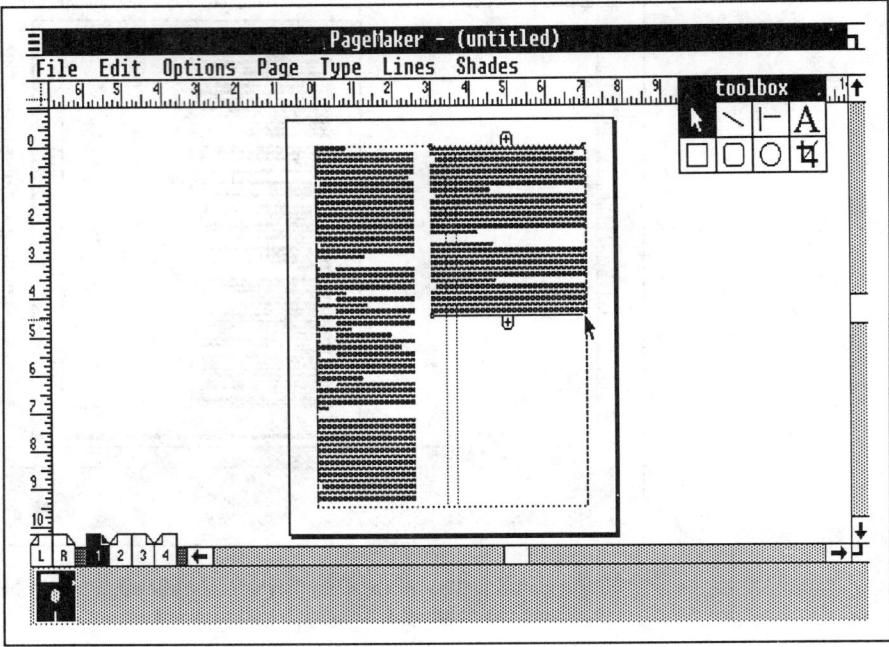

**Figure 18-9.** The next text column is resized and positioned on the page.

## Changing Size and Leading of Type

PC PageMaker offers much more flexibility in the formatting of type than any word-processing program.

When you call up the type dialog box from the "Type specs" option of the type menu, you have total control over the size and style of the type, as well as the leading (linespacing).

The type specifications box allows you to choose any type style that is available for your printer. Simply clicking on the font chooses it. The menu also features a scrollable type size menu, indicating the available sizes. This is here to let you know which screen fonts are installed and to provide a quick reference of standard sizes. Under these menus are style options for normal, bold, italic, underline, and strickthru. With discrete true fonts (such as those for the Hewlett-Packard LaserJet Plus), fonts are either bold, italic, normal, or whatever style you have. They cannot be changed by the style options as PostScript fonts can. Any combination of these may be chosen (except plain and bold at the same time, of course).

The real power comes in the next boxes on the menu. The size box will present the size of the type in its current format. Note that when you first view the box, it is reversed. For PostScript fonts, you may enter any point size in the box between 4 and 127 in one-half-point increments. That is virtual sizing of type.

The second power feature allows you to control the spacing between the lines using the leading box. This feature applies to all fonts, even the discrete-sized fonts for Hewlett-Packard LaserJets. Any point size from 1 to 127, this time in full- or half-point increments, may be selected. This gives total control over the size and spacing of type.

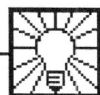

> **Helpful Hint**
>
> The "Preferences" option in the edit menu allows you to change the ruler and measurement system from inches to inches decimal (such as 5.3 inches), millimeters, picas, or ciceros. Since type is measured in points and picas (12 points) are the standard unit of measurement in typesetting, you will find the use of this measuring system helpful. You may switch measurement preferences at any time, so feel free to use whichever one works best for the task at hand.

If you choose, the default for the program is "Autoleading," which will choose an appropriate linespacing for the type size selected (such as 10-point type on 11-point linespacing). When you enter a value in the leading box, the "Autoleading" is automatically turned off. Clicking in its box will return the spacing to "Autoleading."

Finally, the menu offers position control of normal, superscript, and subscript.

PC PageMaker's type specification menu is a real power tool. Use it fully. It offers much more control of type sizing than your word-processing program. Remember, the menu only affects type that has been selected on the page by the text tool.

Fig. 18-10 shows the PC PageMaker type specification menu.

**216** Chapter 18

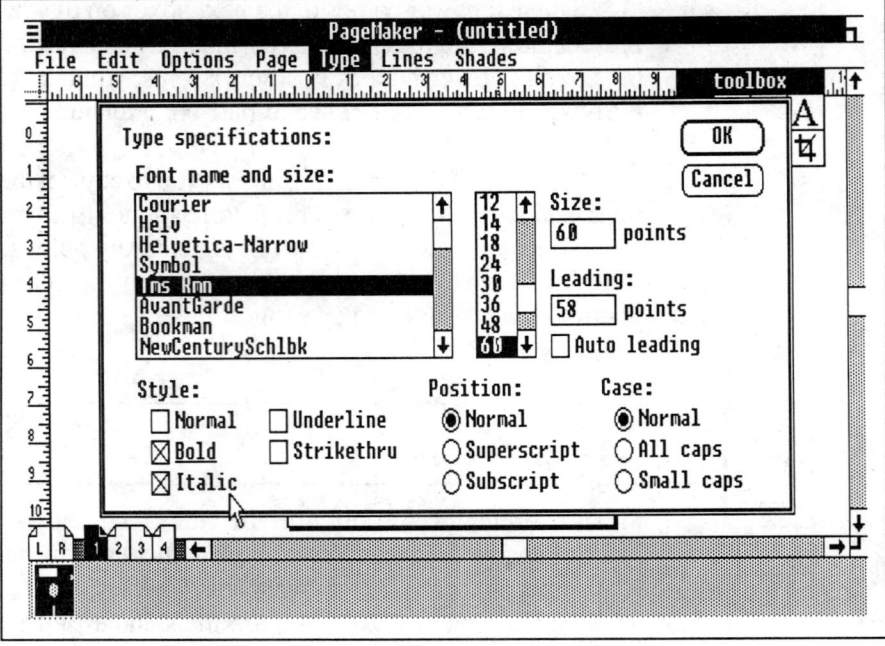

**Figure 18-10.** PC PageMaker's type specifications menu is one of the best around, offering total control over the size and spacing of type.

## Helpful Hint

Once a text block has been placed, there is no need to keep it there. You may use the pointer to click on the text and then move it in any direction or on to any page. To move a text block to another page, simply move it onto the pasteboard, click on the page you want to paste it on, and do so. Remember that if it is a part of a larger text file, it is still threaded into the file, so changes elsewhere will affect it. This is a simple but useful feature.

# Hyphenation

PC PageMaker offers fully automatic hyphenation. When a text file is placed with the hyphenation feature on, it places hyphens, actually discretionary hyphens, whenever it can to fit as many characters on a line as possible. This is especially important for justified columns of type.

A discretionary hyphen is simply a hyphen that is used only when needed to break a line. For example, the word "hyphen" could be hyphenated "hy-phen." Of course, you would only want the hyphen at the end of a justified line. To get a hyphen in the appropriate place if the word is not included in PC PageMaker's 110,000 word dictionary, such as a unique word not found in most dictionaries, press the control and hyphen (-) keys at the same time at the appropriate break point. When the word is in the middle of a line, the hyphen will not appear. If it ends up at the end of the line and the program can break the line better by using the discretionary hyphen, it will.

The program lets you embed discretionary hyphens in very long words manually so that when justifying text in a word-processing mode, it will break the long word to make a page look better.

When justifying columns in page making for publications, hyphenation should be turned on. This way, when you flow a column of text in a justified mode, it will hyphenate any words needed to create the smallest amount of space between words on each line. Because it may not have every word that can be hyphenated in its dictionary, you can opt for prompted hyphenation. This will stop text flow when a long word that is not in the dictionary and is at the end of a line is encountered. It will bring up a menu with the word, in context with the text around it. You can go and place hyphens at the correct places in the word. You then have the option of saving this word to the supplemental dictionary so you will not have to hyphenate it again. Clicking on the "Next" option will bring up the next word PC PageMaker cannot divide. So it goes until the file is placed.

This method of placement will allow you to build a large supplemental dictionary of words that you use often but that are not in the main dictionary. You can also add hyphenated words directly into the supplemental dictionary using an ASCII text processor.

The hyphenation feature is fantastic, but there are some cases where you do not want to hyphenate a word. If a word is hyphenated and you do not wish it to be, simply go to the right of the hyphen with the text tool, and hit the backspace key. The hyphen will go away. It does not remove the hyphen from the word in the dictionary, so feel free to use this option.

# Tabs

When a text file is placed in PC PageMaker, it uses the tabs set in the word-processing program. However, once on a page, the tabs do not always look right. PC PageMaker has a complete tab-handling system for its own text entry and to edit tabs from your text files.

The tab menu shows a ruler, with tabs from the current text file indicated, as well as a value for the paragraph indent if there is any.

The increments depend on the view you have selected, so use actual size as a minimum for the most accurate placement. Up to 20 tabs may be set, each one left-aligned, right-aligned, centered, or decimal, as well as leader dot tabs in periods, dashes, underline characters, or any special character that you define. It will also support hanging indents where the line exceeds the left margin. The menu also allows first line indent for paragraph indents. The complete tab menu, which is accessed from the type menu, is shown in Fig. 18-11.

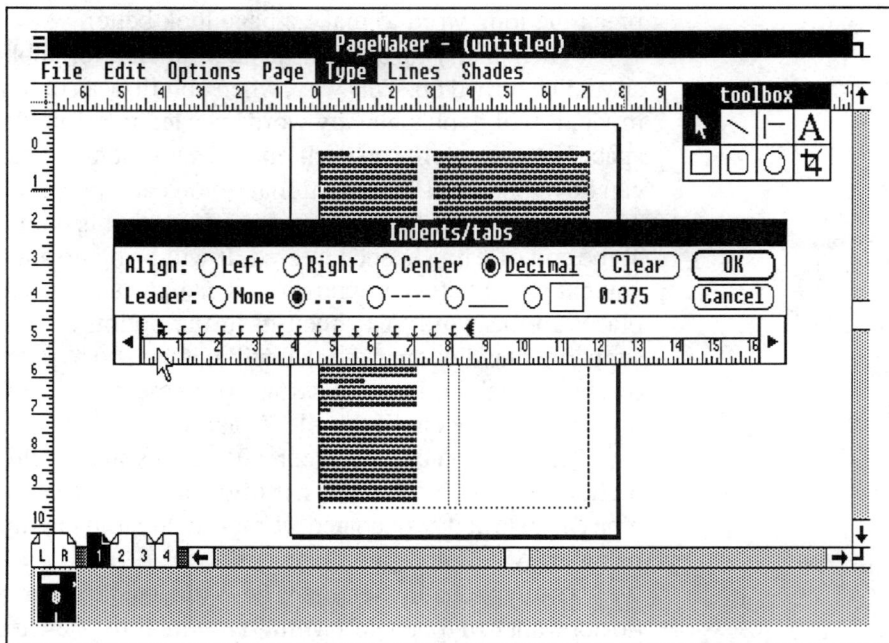

**Figure 18-11.** The tabs dialog box from the type menu.

## Kerning, Letterspacing, and Wordspacing

PC PageMaker also has automatic kerning of characters, as discussed in Chapter 9—Working with Type.

With automatic kerning on, the program will kern specific pairs of characters (such as Yo, We, To, Tr, Ta, Wo, Tu, Tw, Ys, Te, P., Ty, Wa, yo, we, T., Y., TA, PA, and WA). This set of characters will work with most printers. Some printers can kern additional sets (such as OV, OY, VA, YO, Av, Wt, and Wm). These are known as kerning pairs. Whenever they are encountered when text is placed and automatic kerning is on, they will be kerned.

Kerning can be either on or off, but you can select the minimum point size for automatic kerning. Kerning slows down the placement of type into columns. Also it is not often important with smaller type sizes, so you can select at what point size you wish characters to be kerned (such as 12 point).

When you get into larger sizes of type, especially headlines that can be as large as 96 point, you may wish to go beyond automatic kerning and kern further. This can be done manually, which will allow tighter kerning on large fonts and the ability to kern pairs aesthetically for graphic purposes.

To kern any two letters, place the I-beam text tool between the two letters, click the mouse to get an insertion point, and hold down the control key and press the backspace key for each increment (each increment is one-twenty-fourth of an em space) you wish to delete between the characters. You can also add space between two characters by holding the control and shift keys down while hitting the backspace key, resulting in adding incremental space between the characters.

Beyond kerning, menus also allow you to adjust the spacing of justified text with both wordspacing and letterspacing. Selecting "Spacing" from the type menu brings up a menu with minimum, desired, and maximum percentages of wordspacing, and minimum and maximum percentages of letterspacing. The combination of these two options allows you to have loose or tight letterspacing and more control over wordspacing, which is attempted before letterspacing.

You will need to experiment with these values for the particular type size and style you are using. the default values work well, and you can compare the changes you make with the default values.

The combination of kerning, letterspacing, and wordspacing give you ample control over the composition of the type on your page. How far you wish to push these values is up to you.

## Oversized Pages

If you want to produce pages that are larger than the standard size sheet your printer can handle, PC PageMaker can do it using its tiling feature. It divides each page into a size that is printable and prints each block or tile. When they are output, you can paste them together to form a finished page.

**Helpful Hint**

When using a large-sized page, you can print the pages out on the PostScript printer or typesetter by using the tiling feature on the print menu.

One thing to remember when printing oversized pages (such as those on the PostScript printer or typesetter) is to reset the zero point on the ruler to the farthest upper left-hand corner on the first file page of the physical publication page. Do this last, after you have finished your pages. When you go to print, choose "Tile" from the print menu, and your pages will come out in sections.

## Reverse Type and Rules

You will notice that in both the type menu and the lines menu, there are options for "Reverse type" and "Reverse lines." As the terms imply, this will allow you to place white type or rules on a black background or dark graphic. All you need to do to reverse type or lines is to select the type or line and choose the reverse feature from the menu. To be able to see the type or line, you may have to go immediately to the edit menu and select "Bring to front" if you have placed it.

## And It Keeps Coming

These are a few of the special features and powers that you will find inside PC PageMaker. As I have worked with the program, I keep seeing more and more such features, and the program is getting better all the time. Use the features here as you become more comfortable with the program.

# Printing Page Files    19

Once you have completed a page file in PC PageMaker, the file is ready for printing. There are two primary devices that you will print to on a regular basis, and printing couldn't be easier.

The first choice is a laser printer; the second, a PostScript typesetting service. Even if you do not have a PostScript laser printer, you can take advantage of the fact that PC PageMaker will let you create PostScript files that can be sent to a service for output either on a PostScript laser printer or high-resolution typesetter.

## Printing Pages and Files

From the file menu, choose "Print." A dialog box will appear. Here you will have a number of choices.

The first choice is the number of copies you want of each page.

The second is the range of pages to print. In a file you can print all, just one, or a range of pages. If the pages are oversized (such as tabloid pages), you can select "Tile" to print out the pages in single-sheet blocks. These will eventually have to be put together to form the completed page.

You can also choose to print Thumbnails. The thumbnail printout is a sheet that prints a reduced-size version of all 16 pages in the file on one sheet so that you can examine them as an entire publication.

A final option is to reduce or enlarge the page with some printers (such as PostScript printers). You can, for example, print the page at 25 percent of its actual size. Or you can print a page at 400 percent of its original size. You can turn the tiling feature on and print a giant page.

Fig. 19-1 shows the print menu.

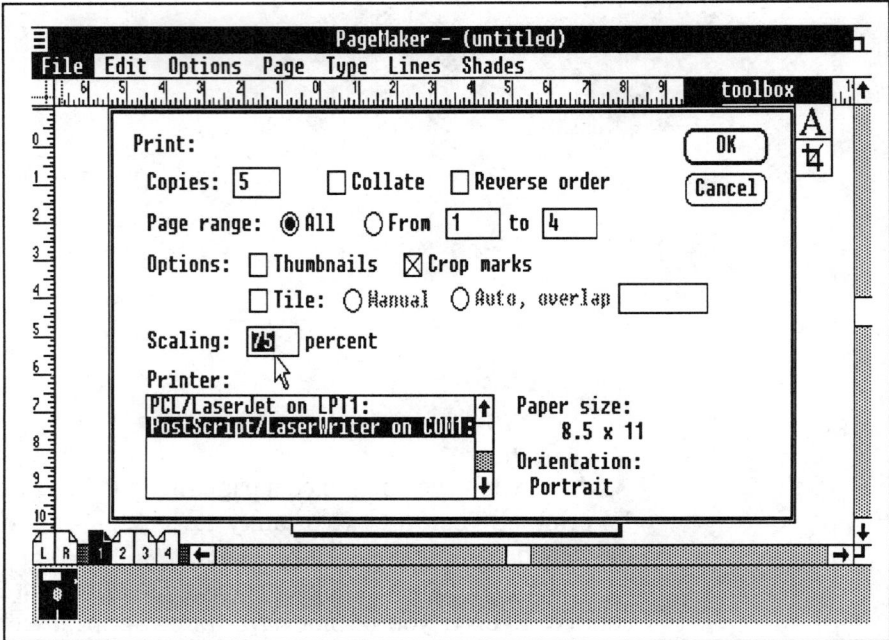

**Figure 19-1.** The PC PageMaker print menu.

The file will be sent to the printer, and in short order you will see the fruits of your labor.

When printing in Windows, the print file is sent to a printer spooler, which will print your file to disk, before returning you to PC PageMaker. Then the spooler will start printing the file to disk. Print spooling in Windows can be turned off if desired by editing the WIN.INI file per instructions in the Windows manual.

## Using High-Resolution PostScript Services

Many people are using typesetting services for their page output. These services operate in a number of fashions. Some work from your disk; others have you telecommunicate your file to them.

Most of the laser-printing services charge around $1.00 per page. If you live near one, you can go to the store and wait for your printout. Some services let you rent time on an AT and a PostScript laser printer so you can do it yourself.

If there is no such service in your area, there are services that you may send your disks to. They will output the pages for you (usually the same day) and mail the disk and the pages to you.

For a higher quality, there are now many typesetting services (some listed in the Appendix) that will typeset PostScript files created using PC PageMaker. They accept your PC PageMaker page files in two ways; first by disk, second by telecommunication. The fastest way is by telecommunication.

The typesetters will print your files on a typesetter, most likely an Allied 100 or 300. You can choose the level of resolution you want your document printed at. The LaserWriter prints at 300dpi, the Allied 100 prints the PC PageMaker file at 1,270dpi, and the Allied 300 prints at 2,540dpi.

Of course, the high-resolution printing costs more. A typical Allied 100 page averages $10-$15 per page. The more pages you have, the better the price gets.

Turn-around time is usually next day, and you should obtain an estimate of the charges before you let the typesetter create the pages for you.

## Top Quality

From the inexpensive output of PostScript laser printers to the Allied 300, which prints pages at over 2,500dpi, the PostScript files created by PC PageMaker allow you to obtain the right level of quality for your needs. If you need the highest-possible quality, it's there. If your needs are average, the LaserWriters are pure workhorses that turn out top-quality pages, even if at a medium resolution.

# High-Volume Printing 20

*F*or short-run printing, the laser printer is an excellent device. For 100 copies of a report or 200 copies of a press release, it couldn't be better. There are situations, however, where the laser printer is not the appropriate printing device for the actual printing of your pages.

## Large Print Runs

If you plan to print 5,000 copies of a page or publication created on your laser printer, you would want to have it printed in the conventional manner (such as a regular or instant printer).

Also, if you create publications such as a newsletter, you will need the 11 by 17 inch sheets that most inexpensive laser printers cannot print. I, for example, print a monthly magazine. I create my pages on the laser printer, but there is no way I could print my magazine on it. It doesn't print in color, it doesn't handle printing 32 pages on one sheet (at actual size!), and I don't think it can turn out thirty-five thousand 110-page magazines in one day like my publication printer can.

Clearly, the point is that there are jobs that you can print on the laser printer and there are jobs that you let a printer take over, working from your page master or boards.

The trick is to know when to make the jump.

## When to Print Pages with a Printer

So where does the break come for in-house printing versus going to a printer with your page masters?

First, the laser printer manual suggests that the monthly duty cycle for a typical laser printer is between 3,000 and 7,000 sheets a month. That's a good indicator. If you have an order form that you need 3,000 copies of, that would just about eat up your duty cycle for one job. Clearly that is a job best handled by an instant printer. Keep your laser printer free for what it was intended: making pages, not just cranking them out.

The second consideration concerns color. If you need multiple copies of your page printed in more than one color, you will need to take it to a printer, since the laser printer can print in only one color—black (although the next chapter will show you how to get amazing color from your laser printed pages in small quantities).

Third, if you have a publication like a newsletter or report that you need printed on larger sheets (such as 11 by 17 inches) for folding, binding, and saddle stitching or other binding methods, take your pages to a printer.

The secret is to recognize that the laser printer is a great small-run printer for print runs under 1,000. Using it for that type of printing, it will last longer, and you will free it up for general page production.

## Preparing Pages for Printing

Speaking from experience, many printers balk at printing from laser printer originals. They will look at it, and tell you the resolution is too low for them to do a quality job or that the image from the xerographic drum is not dark enough. These are the two major objections.

I have met with these, and here is how I handle it. With confidence, I tell the printer that I expect an exact duplication of the laser printer original; I do not expect an improvement upon it. If the printer can print from higher-quality originals, I am sure that this lower-resolution page will be no problem. I further say that I expect no more than that and that, if necessary, I will OK a proof of the page and take responsibility if the printed job is equal to the proof.

As for the grayness of the original, the laser-printer-produced page, especially with heavy black areas, does have a much lighter cast than type. But, I have had printers print light blue pencil marks, smudges, and many assorted things on a page that were far lighter than the laser-printed page.

Tell the printer you know that the page is lighter than real type but that it is certainly dark enough to be photographed in his reproduction process—it just takes a bit of care. Since there are no cut marks or shadows from elements being glued to the page, it has no shadows or trouble areas that will show up in the film.

Printers usually shoot a film negative slightly overexposed to remove shadow lines. The laser page does not present that problem, so they can still overexpose. This results in a fine reproduction of the original due to the fact that overexposure using film negatives will actually remove some of the ragged, very tiny pixels that give type a slightly ragged appearance. The reverse is true with instant printers who use positive-acting printing plates. They should underexpose. Remember—film negative, overexpose; film positive, underexpose.

These comments will let the printer know that you know something about the process. Use this book as an example if there is a battle. It was printed from laser-printed originals. How can there be an argument then?

Printers often grumble because you are bringing in a new set of problems. Work them out. Once the job is done and it turns out well, the printer will look forward to working with you.

# Multicolored Pages  21

When printing multicolored pages with a traditional offset or instant printer, you may find that you can save yourself money by creating pages that are color separated.

## Preparing Pages for Two-Color Printing

The pages in two-color printing have type or rules, or even graphics, in a color and black type. No matter how you format the page, you can create page originals that separate the two different colors, which will save you money. The printer will not have the table time of preparing the two film negatives needed to print the job, even though two negatives and plates still need to be made for each page.

> **Helpful Hint**
>
> First, create your pages as usual, and save the file. Second, make a backup of the page file. Then print it out, and, with a sheet of tracing paper over the printed sheet, color the areas that you will do in color. Now, go back to your page, removing all the color elements. Print the page. A page will be printed that will print all of your black elements. Now, close the file. Say NO when it asks you to save the changes! From the file menu select "Open," then choose your original file. You will see your page in its original state with both color areas in place. The black elements will return because you changed only the version in RAM, not the actual file. The backup you made is there just in case you file the changes by mistake.
>
> This time, remove all the black printing elements on the page, leaving only the elements that will print in color. Print the page. You will now have the page original for the color printing. The two sheets contain all the elements on your page. If you hold the two up to the light, one on top of the other, you will see how the page fits together.
>
> If you have more than one page, do this to all the pages that will print in color and print each color at one time.

## Creating Color Separations

Let's take the sample page we created in PC PageMaker of the report in Times Roman type with the headline on it.

Fig. 21-1 shows the full page with both colors on it.

**231** Multicolored Pages

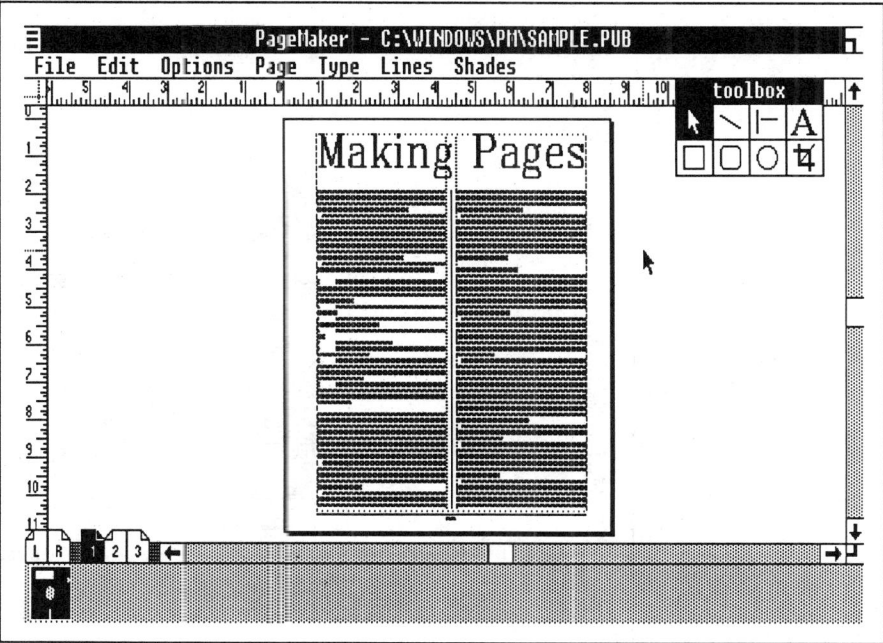

**Figure 21-1.** The sample page with both colors present.

Now, you will want to color the headline and make the rest of the page black.

To make the black page, get the pointer, click on the headline, and press the backspace key. Fig. 21-2 shows the black ink version of the page.

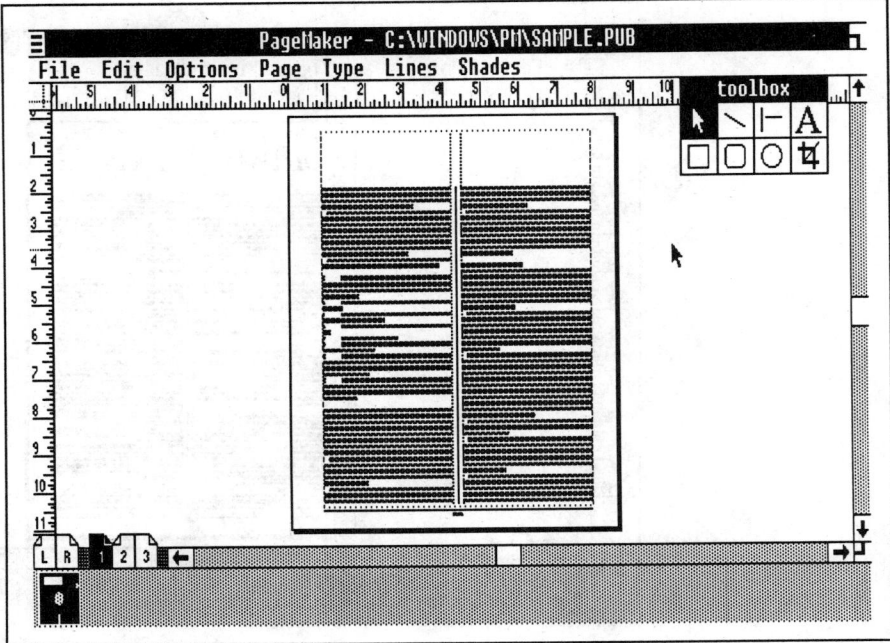

**Figure 21-2.** The black printing portion of the page.

To make the color page, close the file, say NO to keeping the changes, go back, open the file, and return to the page. This time, remove all the text and the rule you have placed on the page. A problem arises here. The master page items are still on the page. Don't worry. Go to the page menu and choose the option "Remove master items." This will completely remove the remaining black items from the page. You should now have a page as in Fig. 21-3, with only the headline on it.

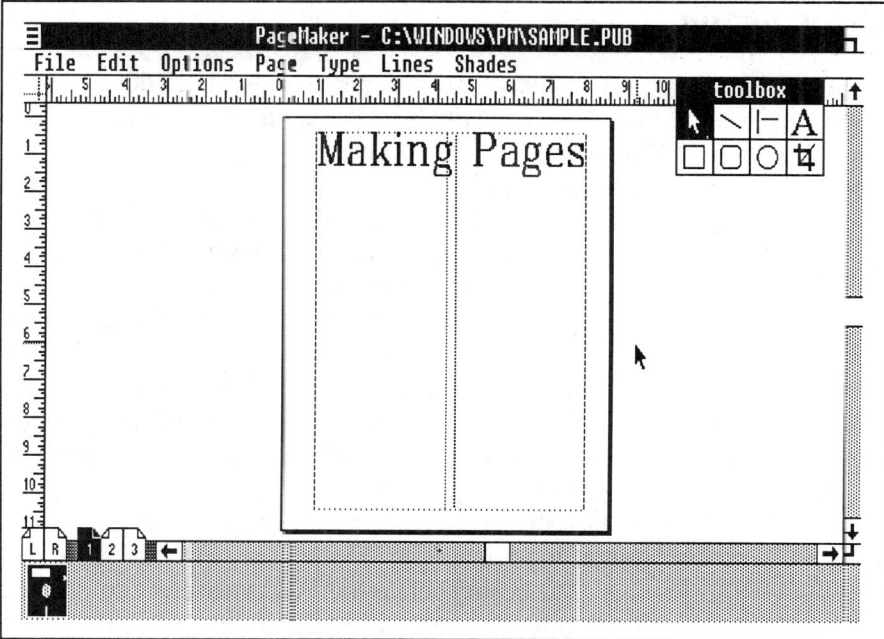

**Figure 21-3.** The color printing portion of the page.

Now you have two pages, each separated for color, that you can give to your printer. This process also works for more than one color. You can do three of four colors in the same way.

## Photocopier Printing

Doing your own color separation is also very useful for personal printing on personal photocopiers (such as the Canon PC 20) that use different color toner drums.

In the previous example, if you needed 50 copies, you could run the black page with a black toner drum and the color page with another color of toner drum by using the same sheets run through twice.

If you are using a personal copier in the method described above, creating color-separated pages is a must. This method is flawless for multicolor photocopier printing. White-out or paper masks always create shadows.

## Color Bonding

A new and very exciting system has been developed that allows you to take pages printed with black toner on your laser printer or even your photocopier and convert the black images into an incredible array of colors, even white and metallic.

How is this possible? The secret is a system that takes special color-transfer film placed on top of the laser-printed page and passes them through a hot-bonding machine. When the heat is applied, the transfer film adheres to wherever there was toner on the page. When you peel away the film, the color sticks to the toner, and the rest remains on the film sheet. The result is color type, graphics, halftones—anything that was printed with toner.

The transfer films are roughly $1.00 each and come in gloss or matte finishes, as well as white and metallic. This means you could take a black sheet of paper, print on it with toner, bond a gold transfer sheet to it, and get a black sheet with gold art and type. Note the page will be black when it comes out of the printer.

The beauty here is that you can use any color stock or paper and, getting even more elaborate, use multiple colors on one sheet. This is done by cutting the transfer film into sizes to fit elements on the page. Type could be red, a chart could be brown, art could be blue. After you have positioned pieces of transfer film to fit those areas, you simply run the sheet through the bonding unit, pull away the film, and you have a great multicolor page.

With the creative use of different colors and weights of paper and the creative application of colors, you can create truly impressive report covers, signs, ad mock-ups, or just plain art. For most of these applications, you would never have thought they could be created with a laser printer.

If you have the need for short-run color pages and really want to impress people, this is the perfect solution. The systems are available from Kroy Sign Systems and Omnicrom Systems Corporation (addresses and phone numbers are in the product reference section at the end of the book), and each bonding unit retails for less than $1000. Special papers are available, as are a wide range of transfer films that vary in price. On average, as mentioned earlier, the color comes out to about a dollar a page, so this is a system for presentation-quality pages, not hundreds of copies.

# Grids and Page Samples 22

*I* will complete this book with some examples of the type of pages you can make with your personal publishing system. As you examine them, remember that they were all created using only PC PageMaker, an AT compatible, and a LaserWriter Plus.

As much as I love the programs and equipment discussed throughout this book, I must finish my exploration of the subject with the most important consideration in using such a system: you. You are the key to a successful and good-looking publication or document. If a page comes out of your printer and looks great, it is because you have mastered the use of type and have sharpened your design skills. If it looks bad, don't blame it on the programs or equipment. Once again, you are responsible.

The secret to personal publishing is your publishing skill. The technology is just a wonderful set of tools that you use to carry out your ideas in graphic form. A personal publishing system is only useful if you use it effectively. This book was written to introduce you to the system and to prove that it can allow you to produce great publications. It is here for you to take advantage of. Let it be a reflection of yourself, and may you be proud.

## Grid

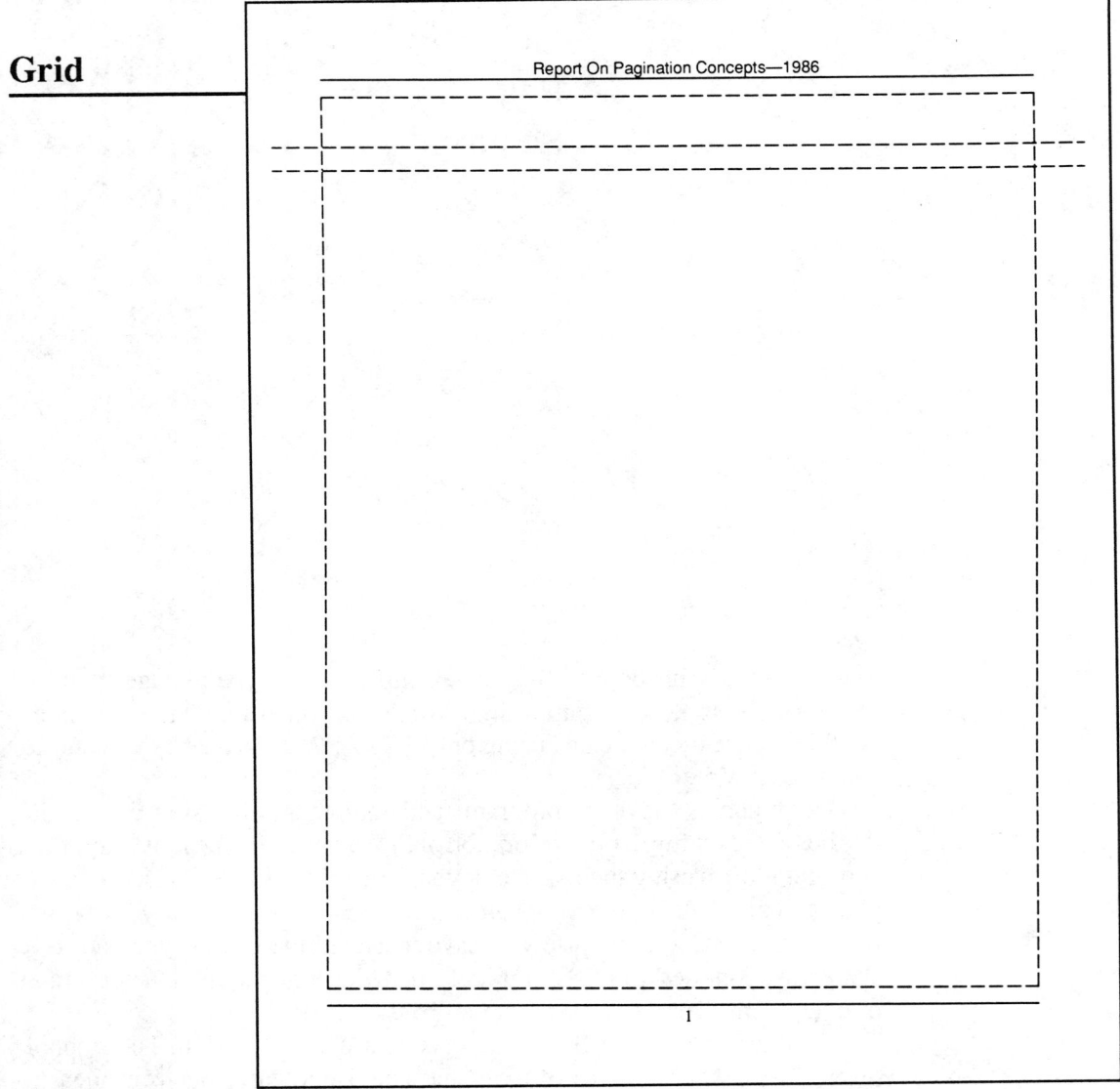

**Basic Report:** Page size: 8-1/2 by 11 inches. Live area 7 by 9 inches centered on the page. The running head rests above the live area with a 1-point rule and 12-point Helvetica type. The folio rests below the live area and has a 1-point rule with a 12-point page number centered beneath it. Two ruler guides have been placed on the master page. The top guide is the baseline for the report title; the bottom guide is the starting position for text.

**Sample**

---
Report On Pagination Concepts—1986
---

# Strategic Planning, 1986-1990

Personal publishing tools are a recent development for most personal computer users. In fact, the programs and devices that have made personal publishing a reality are only about a year old. By any standard, this is new technology, and as such has a long way to go before it is mature.

If you look back at the original VisiCalc, and take a look at the current crop of advanced spreadsheets like Excel or 1-2-3, you will see how time brings about product development. Personal publishing is so new that most of the potential has yet to be realized. Beyond that, most of the users are new to "publishing" concepts, and the programs that are available are exciting not only because they are good, but because they are new.

This article will attempt to explore the subject of "pagination," which is the art of taking text and graphics and assembling them into page blocks. When you create pages, you are actually paginating a document.

The current personal publishing programs all attempt to help you paginate documents as easily as possible. To evaluate if a program actually does help you paginate your documents in the best way it is important to understand what pagination is, what types of pagination there are, and how professional publishers have dealt with paginating the thousands of pages they process on a regular basis, using their methods as a "standard."

### Pagination Styles

There are two basic methods of pagination: Interactive and batch. The names describe precisely what they do.

Interactive pagination is the process whereby you work with the software interactively to place elements on a page. For most interactive programs, this means that every element of the page, from page numbers to lines between columns, must be placed there by your specific instruction. You control the placement of all elements. The software acts much like an electronic pasteup board on which you glue down type and pictures, and draw rules, boxes, and other graphics. When you complete one page, you move on to the next, and begin the process again. If the text you are placing continues, you "carry over" the text to the next page.

Batch processing works simply as the name implies: All elements are processed at one time, in one process. A simple example of this is the way a word processor prints pages. You create a text file, define the margins and line length for the printed pages, and tell the word processor to "print." The word processor goes into a batch pagination mode. It follows the page description you have defined, fills the first page with text, and when full, fills the second page with text, prints that, and continues until the entire file has been printed. The difference in this system is that you enter a set of instructions one time, and the program uses those rules to print the entire document without your involvement.

Batch and interactive page assembly are the foundation of automated publishing. Each is essential, yet each is quite different. The type of pagination product you use is determined by the type of document you will be processing.

### Professional Pages

Prior to developing this publication, I published a magazine for professional publishers. Even though the systems they often use can cost $100,000 and up, they still have the same basic

---
1

**Basic Report:** The design of this report is an attempt to replicate traditional typewritten reports but to enhance the page by using larger type and bold heads and subheads in varying sizes. The headline is set in Helvetica 24 point, aligned left. The subheads are set in Helvetica Bold 18 point, aligned left. The text is set in Helvetica 12 point, with autoleading, aligned left. There is one line space between items or subjects, followed by a subhead, then text with no extra space between the subhead and the text. The overall effect is a classic report, full width, no graphics, but easier to read as a result of the clean type treatment.

## Grid

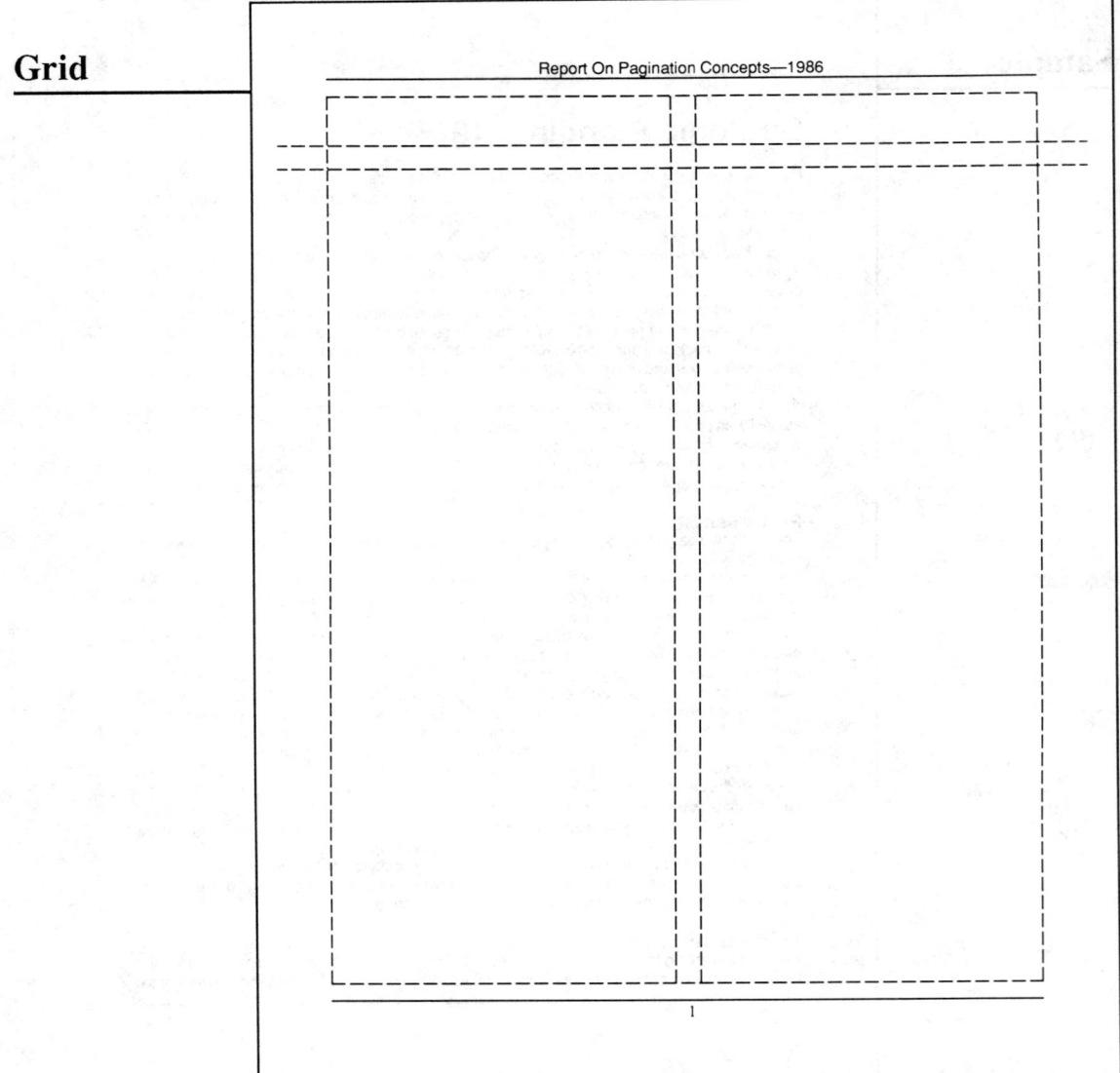

**Basic Report, Two Column:** This report is identical to the basic report grid and sample page, except that a two-column format has been introduced for the text. The page size, live area, running head, folio, and headline remain the same. From the column guides menu, "2" columns was entered with .25-inch space between columns. These are indicated by the dotted lines running vertically down the center of the page.

## Sample

Report On Pagination Concepts—1986

# Strategic Planning, 1986-1990

Personal publishing tools are a recent development for most personal computer users. In fact, the programs and devices that have made personal publishing a reality are only about a year old. By any standard, this is new technology, and as such has a long way to go before it is mature.

If you look back at the original VisiCalc, and take a look at the current crop of advanced spreadsheets like Excel or 1-2-3, you will see how time brings about product development. Personal publishing is so new that most of the potential has yet to be realized. Beyond that, most of the users are new to "publishing" concepts, and the programs that are available are exciting not only because they are good but because they are new.

This article will attempt to explore the subject of "pagination," which is the art of taking text and graphics and assembling them into page blocks. When you create pages, you are actually paginating a document.

The current personal publishing programs all attempt to help you paginate documents as easily as possible. To evaluate if a program actually does help you paginate your documents in the best way, it is important to understand what pagination is, what types of pagination there are, and how professional publishers have dealt with paginating the thousands of pages they process on a regular basis, using their methods as a "standard."

### Pagination Styles

There are two basic methods of pagination: Interactive and batch. The names describe precisely what they do.

Interactive pagination is the process whereby you work with the software interactively to place elements on a page. For most interactive programs, this means that every element of the page, from page numbers to lines between columns, must be placed there by your specific instruction. You control the placement of all elements. The software acts much like an electronic pasteup board on which you glue down type and pictures, and draw rules, boxes, and other graphics. When you complete one page, you move on to the next, and begin the process again. If the text you are placing continues, you "carry over" the text to the next page.

Batch processing works simply as the name implies: All elements are processed at one time, in one process. A simple example of this is the way a word processor prints pages. You create a text file, define the margins and line length for the printed pages, and tell the word processor to "print." The word processor goes into a batch pagination mode. It follows the page description you have defined, fills the first page with text, and when full, fills the second page with text, prints that, and continues until the entire file has been printed. The difference in this system is that you enter a set of instructions one time, and the program uses those rules to print the entire document without your involvement.

Batch and interactive page assembly are the foundation of automated publishing. Each is essential, yet each is quite different. The type of pagination product you use is determined by the type of document you will be processing.

### Professional Pages

Prior to developing this publication, I published a magazine for professional publishers. Even though the systems they often use can cost $100,000 and up, they still have the same basic problem as you do

1

**Basic Report, Two Column:** To increase the readability of the basic report and to adhere to the rule of column widths being established by the number of characters per line being best between 35 and 50, the text has been set in the same size and style, but it has been changed into a two-column format. The result is a report that retains the traditional report appearance but is simply easier to read. An added benefit is that the report has a more attractive look, moving it past the typewritten style of the full-width report.

# Grid

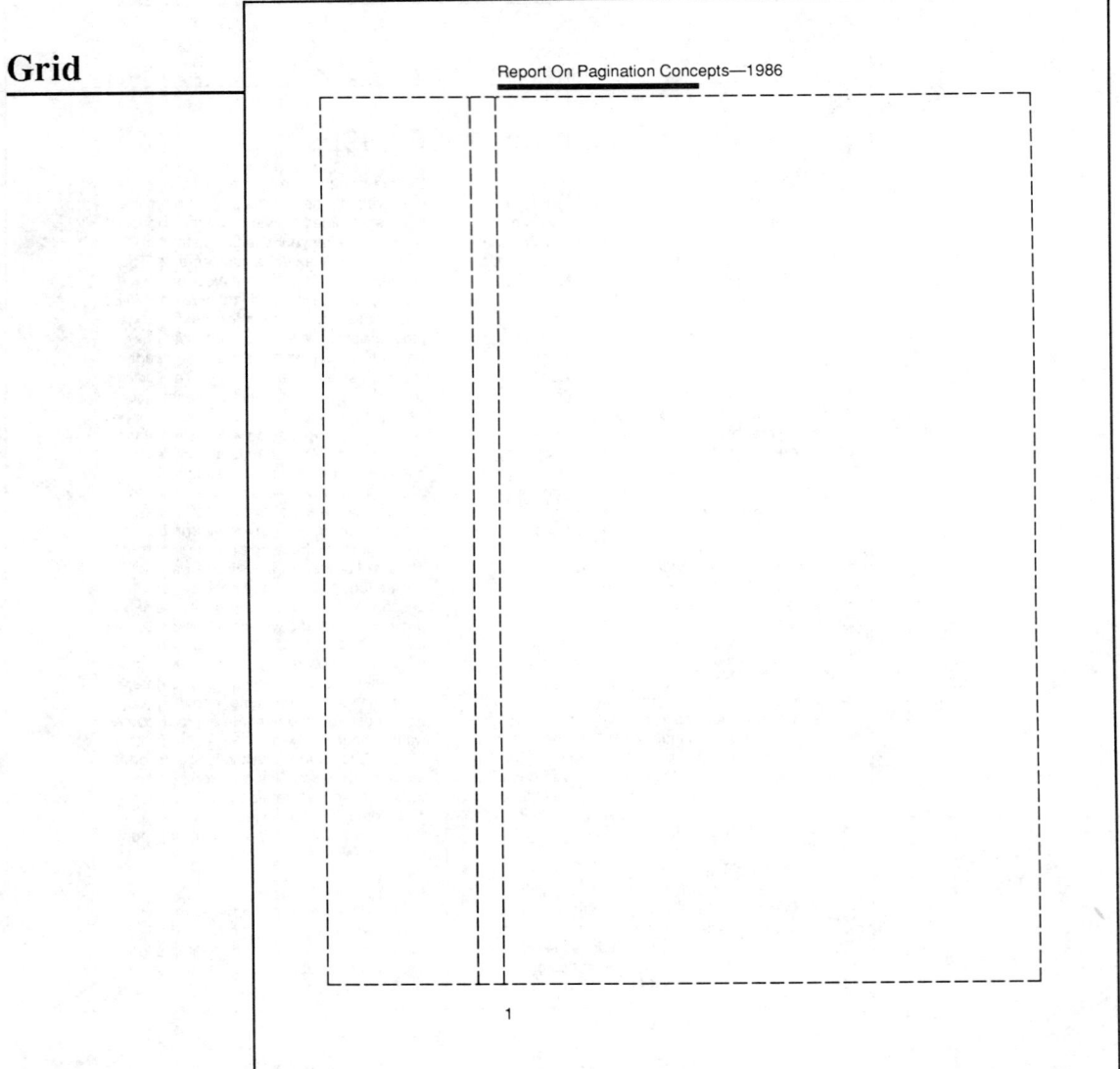

**Designed Report:** The grid for the basic report has been completely redesigned to have a more formal, designed appearance. To accomplish this, a two-column format has been established. The left column will hold hanging indent subheads. The right column, which is much wider, holds text and the headline and also establishes the ruler guide for the running head and folio. The page is 8-1/2 by 11 inches, with a 7 by 9 inch live area. The left column is 9 picas; the right column is 31 picas. The running head rests above the live area, using 12-point Helvetica resting above an abstract length bold rule. The folio is a simple page number below the live area in Helvetica 12 point.

## Sample

Report On Pagination Concepts—1986

# Strategic Planning, 1986-1990

Personal publishing tools are a recent development for most personal computer users. In fact, the programs and devices that have made personal publishing a reality are only about a year old. By any standard, this is new technology, and as such has a long way to go before it is mature.

If you look back at the original VisiCalc, and take a look at the current crop of advanced spreadsheets like Excel or 1-2-3, you will see how time brings about product development. Personal publishing is so new that most of the potential has yet to be realized. Beyond that, most of the users are new to "publishing" concepts, and the programs that are available are exciting not only because they are good, but because they are new.

This article will attempt to explore the subject of "pagination," which is the art of taking text and graphics and assembling them into page blocks. When you create pages, you are actually paginating a document.

The current personal publishing programs all attempt to help you paginate documents as easily as possible. To evaluate if a program actually does help you paginate your documents in the best way, it is important to understand what pagination is, what types of pagination there are, and how professional publishers have dealt with paginating the thousands of pages they process on a regular basis, using their methods as a "standard."

**Pagination Styles**

There are two basic methods of pagination: Interactive and batch. The names describe precisely what they do.

Interactive pagination is the process whereby you work with the software interactively to place elements on a page. For most interactive programs, this means that every element of the page, from page numbers to lines between columns, must be placed there by your specific instruction. You control the placement of all elements. The software acts much like an electronic pasteup board on which you glue down type and pictures, and draw rules, boxes, and other graphics. When you complete one page, you move on to the next, and begin the process again. If the text you are placing continues, you "carry over" the text to the next page.

Batch processing works simply as the name implies: All elements are processed at one time, in one process. A simple example of this is the way a word processor prints pages. You create a text file, define the margins and line length for the printed pages, and tell the word processer to "print." The word processer goes into a batch pagination mode. It follows the page description you have defined, fills the first page with text, and when full, fills the second page with text, prints that, and continues until the entire file has been printed. The

1

**Designed Report:** This report leaves the traditional typewritten feel behind in favor of a typeset appearance. The design allows a 9-pica-wide column of white space for every page, broken only by subheads. This use of subheads provides a very clear division of subjects within the report. The headline is also surrounded by white space, the report name has been moved to the running head, and the specific subject of the report has been enlarged into headline status. It is set in Helvetica Narrow 36 point, aligned left. The text is set in 12-point Times, providing a more formal look, also aligned left. The subheads are set in 18-point Helvetica Bold, are placed as hanging indents, and have a rule that runs the full width of the page.

**242** Chapter 22

# Grid

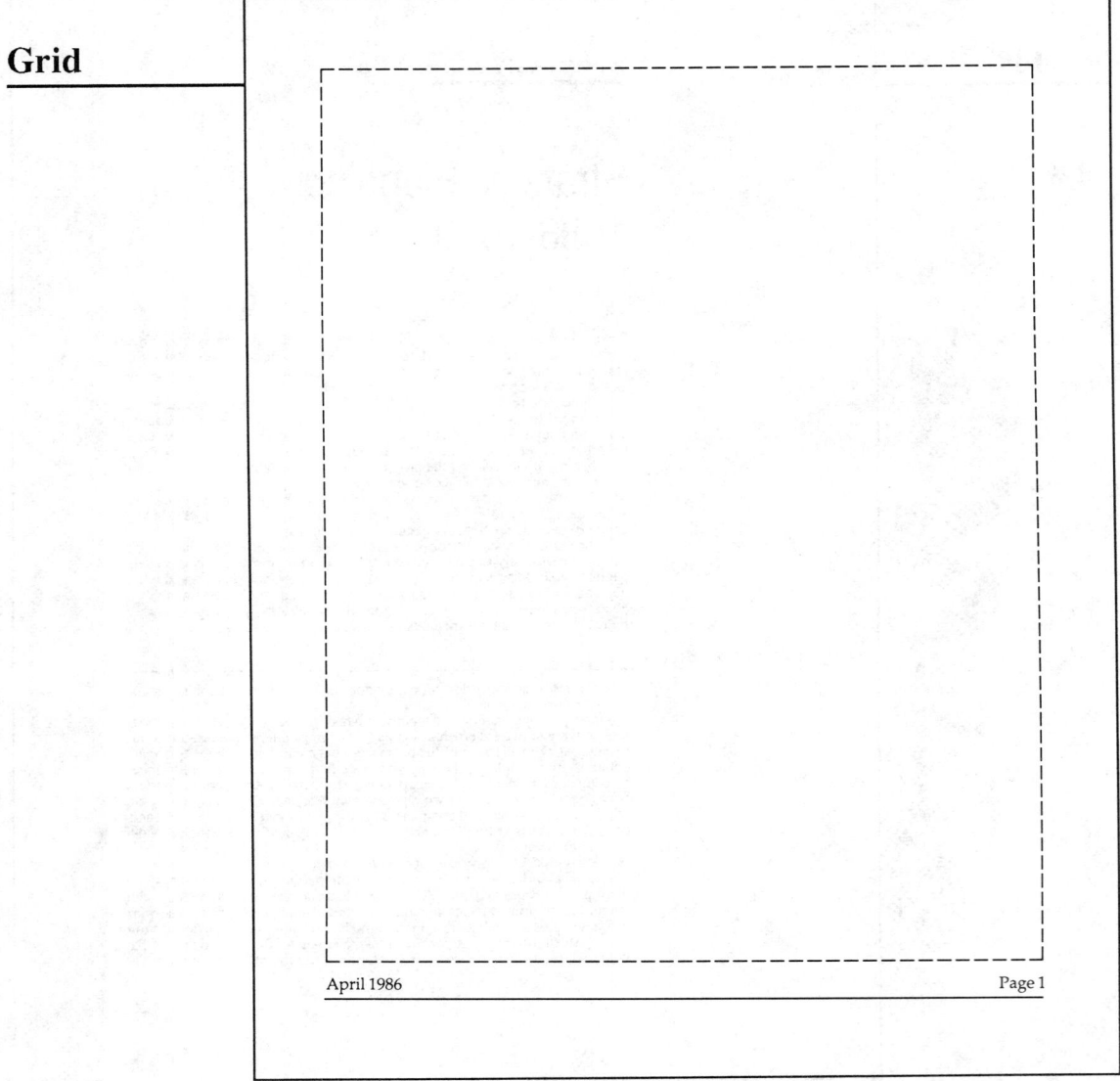

April 1986 — Page 1

**Modern Newsletter:** Although the appearance of the newsletter looks complex, the grid is very simple. Once again, it is a 7 by 9 inch live area, one column, on an 8-1/2 by 11 inch page. There is no running head, only a folio line on the bottom with the issue date on the insides of the page, the page numbers on the outside of the page, and a 1-point rule under the folio.

## Sample

**Personal publishing tools** are a recent development for most personal computer users. In fact, the programs and devices that have made personal publishing a reality are only about a year old. By any standard, this is new technology, and as such has a long way to go before it is mature.

If you look back at the original VisiCalc, and take a look at the current crop of advanced spreadsheets like Excel or 1-2-3, you will see how time brings about product development. Personal publishing is so new that most of the potential has yet to be realized. Beyond that, most of the users are new to "publishing" concepts, and the programs that are available are exciting not only because they are good, but because they are new.

This article will attempt to explore the subject of "pagination," which is the art of taking text and graphics and assembling them into page blocks. When you create pages, you are actually paginating a document.

**Current personal publishing programs** all attempt to help you paginate documents as easily as possible. To evaluate if a program actually does help you paginate your documents in the best way, it is important to understand what pagination is, what types of pagination there are, and how professional publishers have dealt with paginating the thousands of pages they process on a regular basis, using their methods as a "standard."

**Pagination Styles** There are two basic methods of pagination: Interactive and batch. The names describe precisely what they do.

Interactive pagination is the process whereby you work with the software interactively to place elements on a page. For most interactive programs, this means that every element of the page, from page numbers to lines between columns, must be placed there by your specific instruction. You control the placement of all elements. The software acts much like an electronic pasteup board on which you glue down type and pictures, and draw rules, boxes, and other graphics. When you complete one page, you move on to the next, and begin the process again. If the text you are placing continues, you "carry over" the text to the next page.

**Batch processing** works simply as the name implies: All elements are processed at one time, in one process. A simple example of this is the way a word processor prints pages. You create a text file, define the margins and line length for the printed pages, and tell the word processor to "print." The word processor goes into a batch pagination mode. It follows the page description you have defined, fills the first page with text, and when full, fills the

**Modern Newsletter:** With a simple grid, this newsletter relies on clean type treatments and a strong logo for identity. To keep an information-based feel, the type is run across the page and justified. With such a wide type measure, the type is large so that readability is kept in proportion to the 7-inch width of the type. Palatino 12 point on 14-point linespacing is used. Subheads are created by making the first few key words of each news item 14-point Palatino Bold. The logo was created with Palatino Bold 72 point for the large type, and Palatino 20 point for the the small type. The boxed area contains Helvetica 9 point. For a finishing touch, a graphic was created for the main subject matter to be placed in a black box in the upper left-hand corner. The box has rules above it, creating a feeling of motion and bringing the reader down into the page.

## Grid

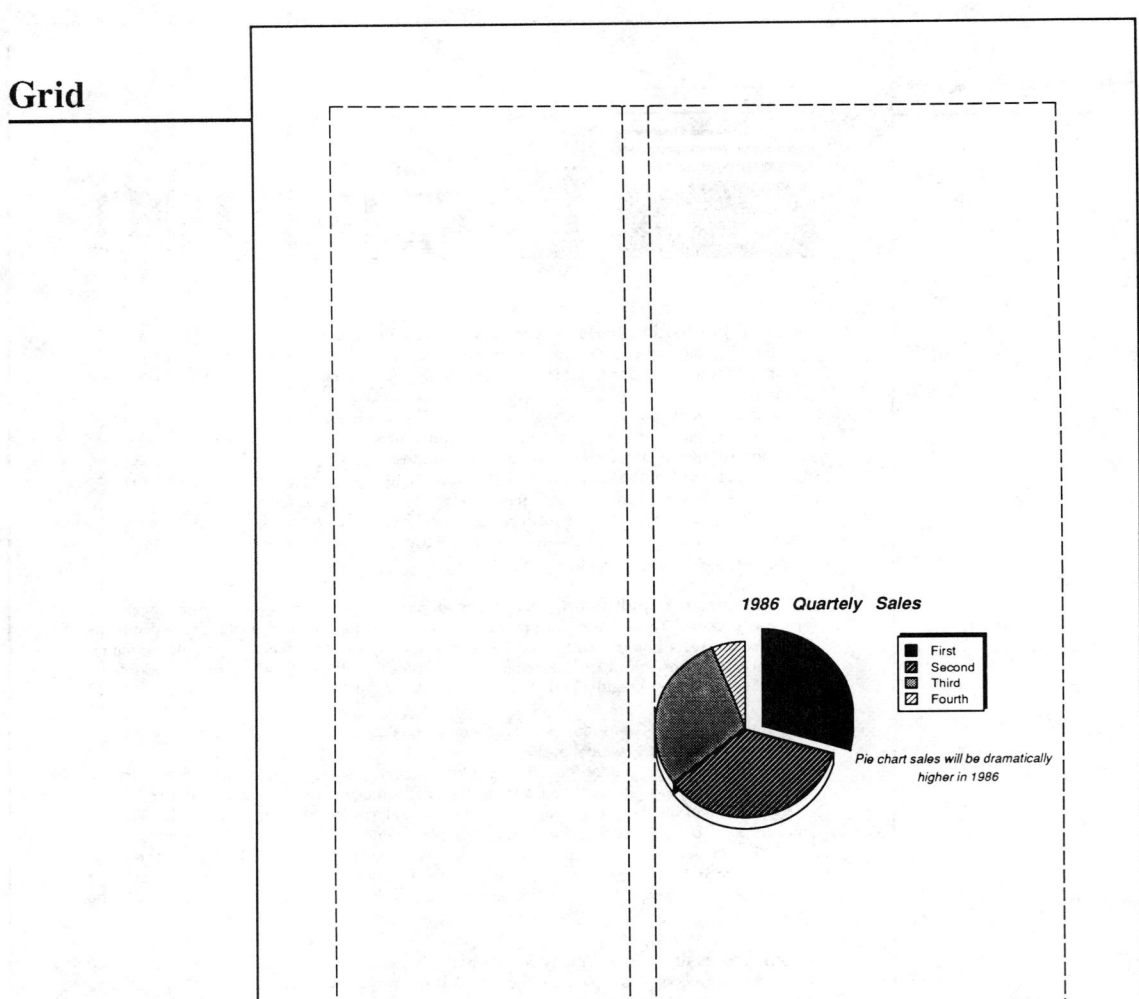

**Modern Newsletter with Graphics:** The newsletter on the previous page can include graphic elements such as a chart. This grid shows the basic grid, but column guides have been added by going to the tools menu and using the "Column guides" option, selecting two columns. The graphic is then placed on the page, and the column guides are moved to wrap the type around the graphic as shown on the next page.

## Sample

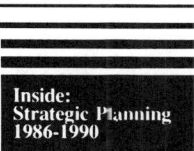

April 1986     Vol 1, No 7

**Personal publishing tools** are a recent development for most personal computer users. In fact, the programs and devices that have made personal publishing a reality are only about a year old. By any standard, this is new technology, and as such has a long way to go before it is mature.

If you look back at the original VisiCalc, and take a look at the current crop of advanced spreadsheets like Excel or 1-2-3, you will see how time brings about product development. Personal publishing is so new that most of the potential has yet to be realized. Beyond that, most of the users are new to "publishing" concepts, and the programs that are available are exciting not only because they are good, but because they are new.

This article will attempt to explore the subject of "pagination," which is the art of taking text and graphics and assembling them into page blocks. When you create pages, you are actually paginating a document.

**Current personal publishing programs** all attempt to help you paginate documents as easily as possible. To evaluate if a program actually does help you paginate your documents in the best way, it is important to understand what pagination is, what types of pagination there are, and how professional publishers have dealt with paginating the thousands of pages they process on a regular basis, using their methods as a "standard."

*1986 Quartely Sales*

First
Second
Third
Fourth

*Pie chart sales will be dramatically higher in 1986*

**Pagination Styles** There are two basic methods of pagination: Interactive and batch. The names describe precisely what they do.

Interactive pagination is the process whereby you work with the software interactively to place elements on a page. For most interactive programs, this means that every element of the page, from page numbers to lines between columns, must be placed there by your specific instruction. You control the placement of all elements. The software acts much like an electronic pasteup board on which you glue down type and pictures, and draw rules, boxes, and other graphics. When you

April 1986     Page 1

**Modern Newsletter with Graphics:** The newsletter format works well with graphic elements. Here, a simple chart, created with a spreadsheet program and saved in the PIC file format, is placed on the page. Type columns are created to run the type around the graphic. Surrounding graphics with text is very attractive. In this case, the type creates a natural box around the chart, so the chart does not need a ruled box around it.

# Grid

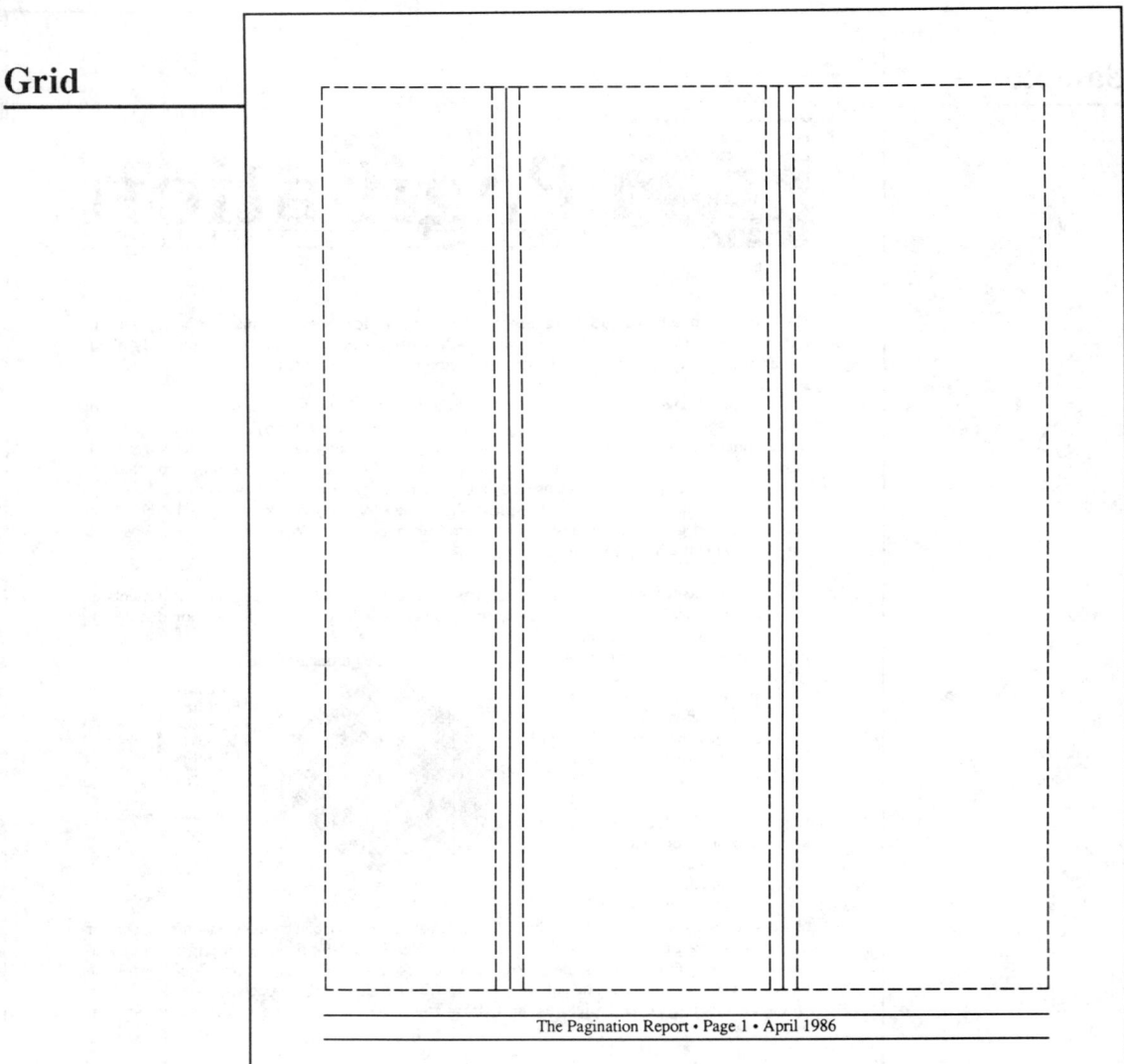

**Classic Newsletter:** This newsletter is more traditional looking but uses a more complex grid. The basic format is a 7 by 9 inch live area. Under the live area are 1-point rules above and below the folio lines; the publication name, page number, and issue date are positioned between the rules. The folio type is Times 12 point, centered on the page. There are three columns on the page, which were created by selecting "3" from the column guides menu, and then moving them to create a custom column arrangement. The two right-hand columns are 14 picas wide, and the left-hand column 10 picas wide. One-point rules are placed between the columns.

**Sample**

# The Pagination Report

*INSIDE:*

Stategic Planning: 1986-1990

Batch vs. Interactive

Adding Graphics

Creating Wraps

Designing Newlsetters

Working with a Variety of Formats

Volume 1, Number 7
April 1986

Terry Ulick
Editor

Personal publishing tools are a recent development for most personal computer users. In fact, the programs and devices that have made personal publishing a reality are only about a year old. By any standard, this is new technology, and as such has a long way to go before it is mature.

If you look back at the original VisiCalc, and take a look at the current crop of advanced spreadsheets like Excel or 1-2-3, you will see how time brings about product development. Personal publishing is so new that most of the potential has yet to be realized. Beyond that, most of the users are new to "publishing" concepts, and the programs that are available are exciting not only because they are good, but because they are new.

This article will attempt to explore the subject of "pagination," which is the art of taking text and graphics and assembling them into page blocks. When you create pages, you are actually paginating a document.

The current personal publishing

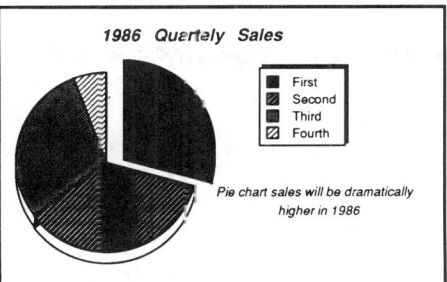

programs all attempt to help you paginate documents as easily as possible. To evaluate if a program actually does help you paginate your documents in the best way, it is important to understand what pagination is, what types of pagination there are, and how professional publishers have dealt with paginating the thousands of pages they process on a regular basis, using their methods as a "standard."

## Pagination Styles

There are two basic methods of pagination: Interactive and batch. The names describe precisely what they do.

Interactive pagination is the process whereby you work with the software interactively to place elements on a page. For most interactive programs, this means that every element of the page, from page numbers to lines between columns, must be placed there by your specific instruction. You control the placement of all elements. The software acts much like an electronic pasteup board on which you glue down type and pictures, and draw rules, boxes, and other graphics. When you complete one page, you move on to the next, and begin the process again. If the text you are placing continues, you "carry over" the text to the next page.

Batch processing works simply as the name implies: All elements are processed at one time, in one process. A simple example of this is the way a word processor prints pages. You create a text file, define the margins and line length for the printed pages, and tell the word processor to "print." The word processor goes into a batch pagination mode. It follows the page description you have defined, fills the first page with text, and when full, fills the second page with text, prints that, and continues until the entire file has been printed. The difference in this system is that you enter a set of instructions one time, and the program uses those rules to print the entire document without your involvement.

Batch and interactive page assembly are the foundation of automated publishing. Each is essential, yet each is quite different. The type of pagination product you use is determined by the type of document you will be processing.

## Professional Pages

Prior to developing this publication, I published a magazine for professional publishers. Even though the systems they

*The Pagination Report • Page 1 • April 1986*

---

**Classic Newsletter:** This format is simple, important looking, and flexible. The logo is created in Times, setting it to whatever point size will fill the full width of the page. The two right-hand columns contain the main text, which is set in Times 11 point on 13-point linespacing, aligned left. The subheads are Times Bold 14 point, with no space between the subhead and text. The left-hand column is used for special items, such as sidebars, supplemental information, and, as shown on this opening page, the sidebar that states what is in the issue. Graphics are also allowed to be extended into the area, as illustrated here. Since the graphic is not surrounded by text on all sides, a box has been added around it. The left-hand column also provides needed white space in an otherwise full page.

**248** Chapter 22

# Grid

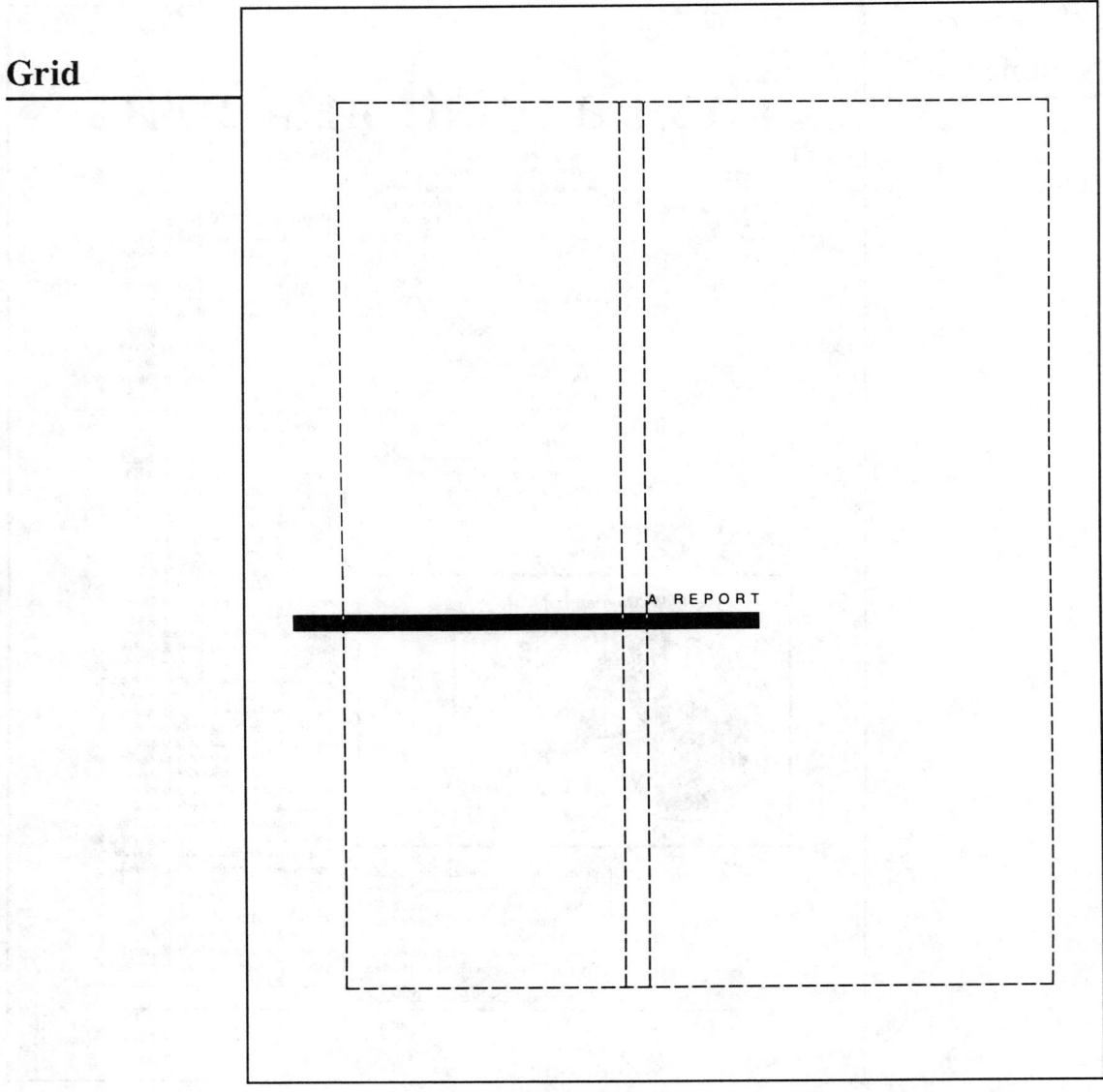

**Report Cover:** The cover of the 8-1/2 by 11 inch report can be formatted quite easily if used on an ongoing basis. This grid uses two columns, placed visually, with a bar and the type as a repeating element on all the report covers in the series. The columns will assure that the subject matter headline will always start in the same spot, as will the rule and the words "A REPORT," which is set in Helvetica 14 point, all uppercase, with two spaces between each letter.

## Sample

STRATEGIC PLANNING: 1986-1990

# Pagination Concepts

A REPORT

**Report Cover:** The grid makes the creation of this report cover quite easy. The type is placed in the right-hand column, aligned left. The first line of type is set in Helvetica 14 point, all uppercase, with two spaces between each letter. The very large type is created by setting the type in Windows Draw in Bookman, copying it to the clipboard, then pasting it on the PC PageMaker page. Once on the PC PageMaker page, it is handled as a graphic, so it may be stretched in any direction. Here, it is stretched to be very tall and condensed, giving a very modern look.

# Grid

**Directory Cover:** Since the directory cover is almost pure art, it is a simple grid. It is a single column, 7 by 9 inches centered on an 8-1/2 by 11 inch page. The only graphic element is a heavy rule across the top, which could be used on a series of report covers as an identifying element.

## Sample

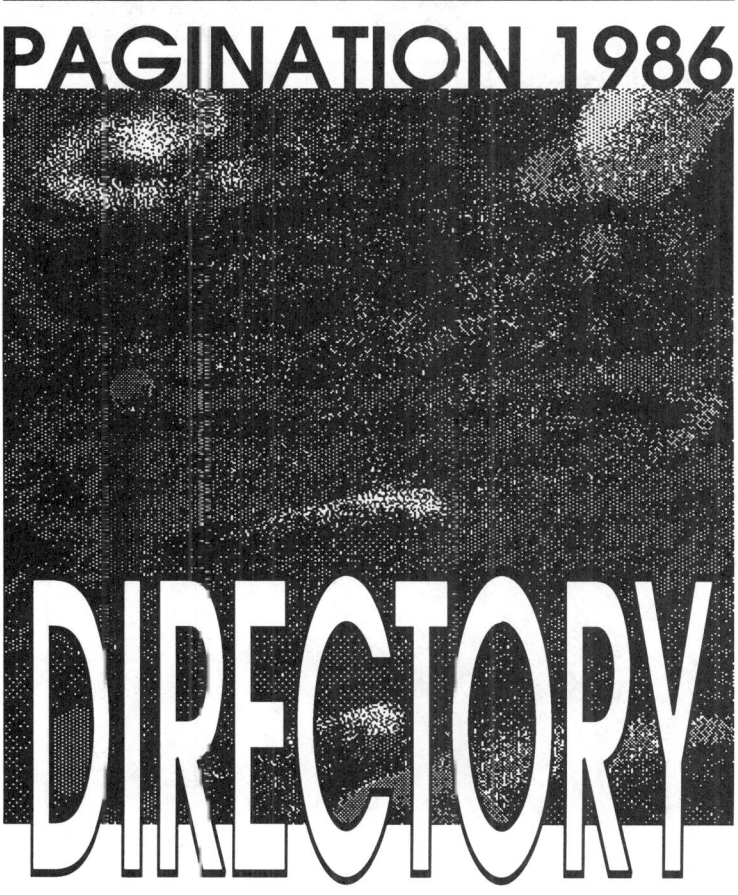

**Directory Cover:** Using type and a paint graphic, the directory cover is a highly graphic cover. First, the art was created in PC Paint. It was then placed on the page and cropped to fit the area perfectly using the cropping tool. Then, the top line was set in Avant Garde and sized to fill the width of the page. Finally, the word "DIRECTORY" was set in Avant Garde Bold Outline in Windows Draw, copied to the clipboard, and moved into PC PageMaker. It was then stretched to the desired size and effect and positioned as shown. The outline type is opaque, blocking out the art behind it.

## Grid

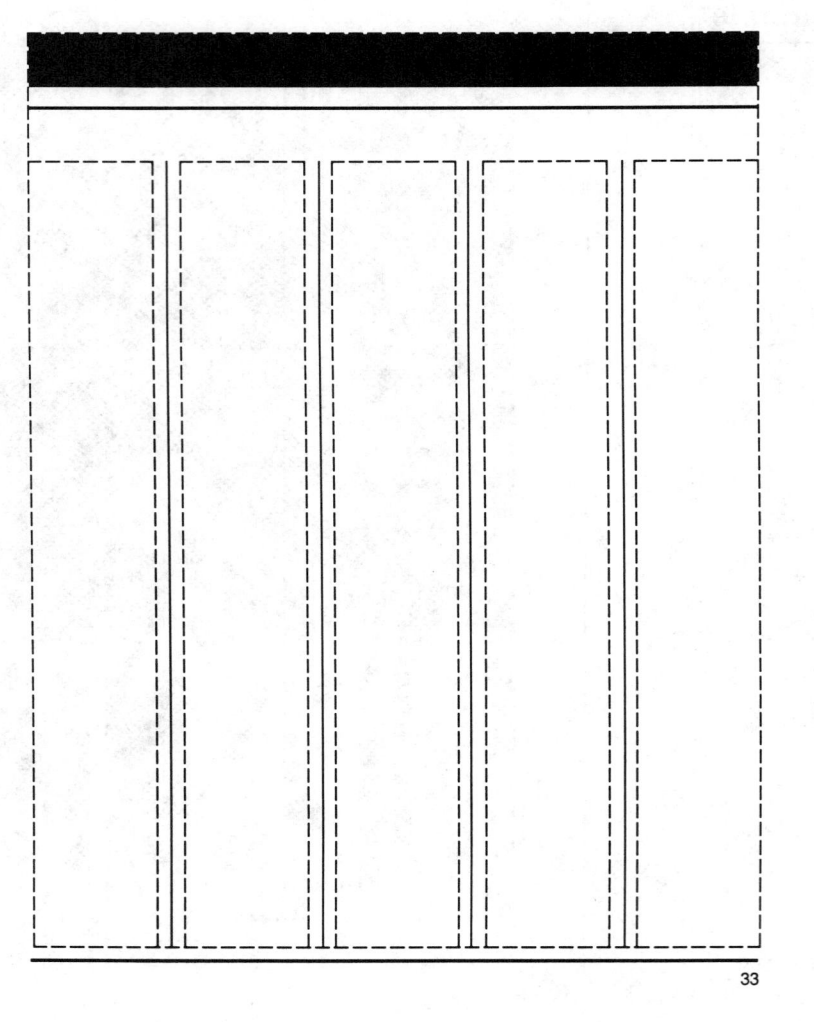

**Directory Page:** A directory can have hundreds of pages, all the same, so it is important to do as much of the work as possible on the master page. Here, just about everything except the type and division markers are placed on the grid. Five equal columns were created, then 1-point rules were placed between them. A large boxed area for reversed type is placed on the top of the page; a rule runs underneath it. A ruler guide establishes the top of the actual columns. Under the live area, a 1-point rule was placed, and a folio was created for the outside of each page.

## Sample

### Pagination Products A-C

**A**

**Product Name**
Company Name
Address Line
City, State, Zip
Description of Product
(000) 000-0000

**Product Name**
Company Name
Address Line
City, State, Zip
Description of Product
(000) 000-0000

**Product Name**
Company Name
Address Line
City, State, Zip
Description of Product
(000) 000-0000

**Product Name**
Company Name
Address Line
City, State, Zip
Description of Product
(000) 000-0000

**B**

**Product Name**
Company Name
Address Line
City, State, Zip
Description of Product
(000) 000-0000

**Product Name**
Company Name
Address Line
City, State, Zip
Description of Product
(000) 000-0000

**Product Name**
Company Name
Address Line
City, State, Zip
Description of Product
(000) 000-0000

**Product Name**
Company Name
Address Line
City, State, Zip
Description of Product
(000) 000-0000

**Product Name**
Company Name
Address Line
City, State, Zip
Description of Product
(000) 000-0000

**Product Name**
Company Name
Address Line
City, State, Zip
Description of Product
(000) 000-0000

**C**

**Product Name**
Company Name
Address Line
City, State, Zip
Description of Product
(000) 000-0000

**Product Name**
Company Name
Address Line
City, State, Zip
Description of Product
(000) 000-0000

**Product Name**
Company Name
Address Line
City, State, Zip
Description of Product
(000) 000-0000

**Product Name**
Company Name
Address Line
City, State, Zip
Description of Product
(000) 000-0000

**Product Name**
Company Name
Address Line
City, State, Zip
Description of Product
(000) 000-0000

**Product Name**
Company Name
Address Line
City, State, Zip
Description of Product
(000) 000-0000

**Product Name**
Company Name
Address Line
City, State, Zip
Description of Product
(000) 000-0000

**Directory Page:** This page was created to be as easy to read and easy to use as a directory. The large black bar on the top has highly visible type identifying the products on the page. The type is Helvetica Bold 24 point, created as White Type from the type menu and placed in the bar. The type reverses to white out of the black. The same technique is used for the division markers (A, B, C), only at a smaller size and where needed. The text is Helvetica 14 point, aligned left, with the product name in bold.

# Grid

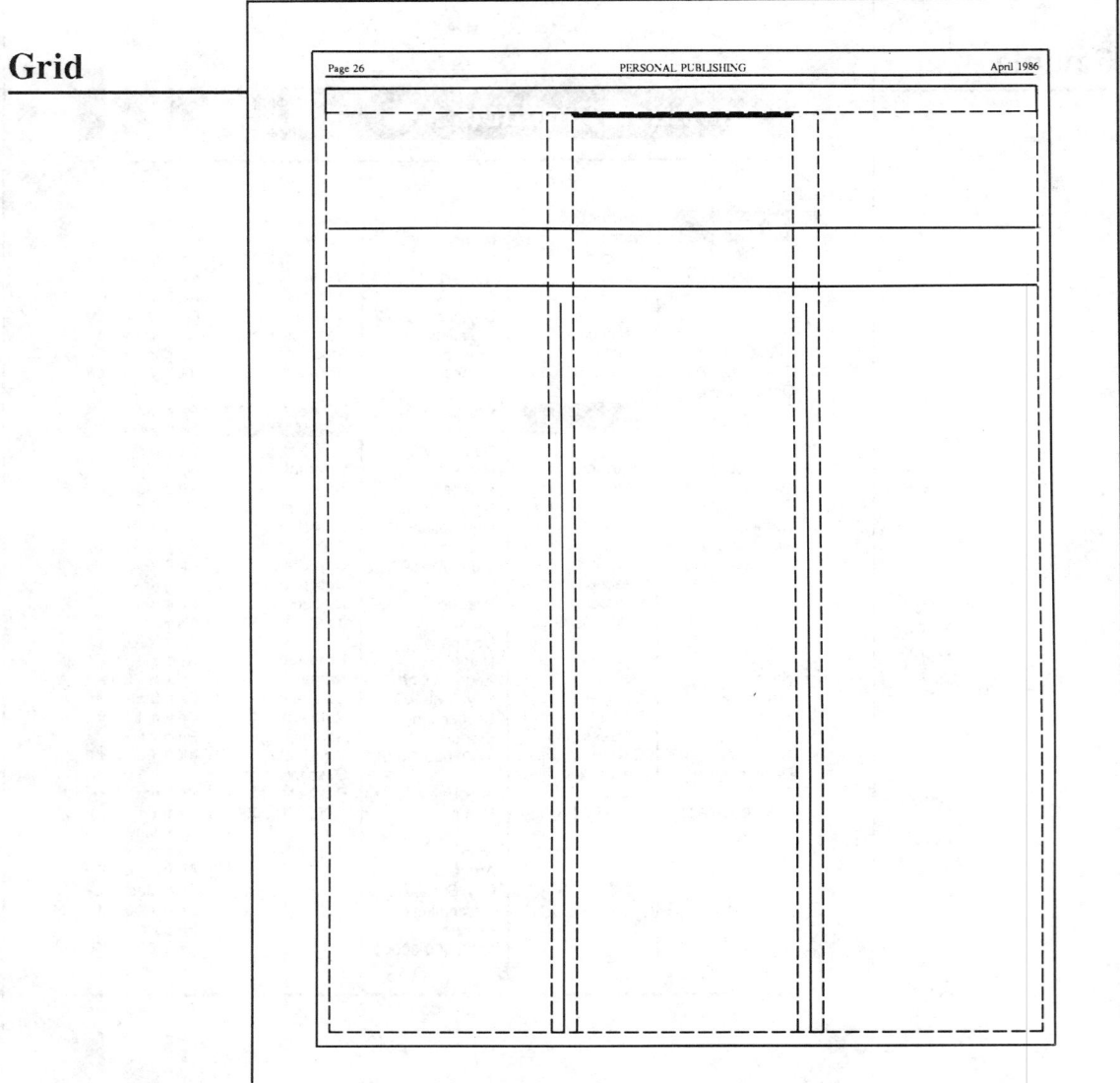

**Magazine Page:** The grid for a magazine page must be complete, yet flexible. This grid is for the opening page of a magazine article. Each page contains a 7 by 10 inch live area, surrounded by a hairline ruled box 1 pica from the live area on the bottom and sides. A hairline rule and folio line are also placed at the top of the page, with the hairline rule completing the box above it. Three 13-pica-wide columns were created, and hairlines were placed between them. A hairline-ruled box, 2 picas tall, was placed on the top of the live area, with a 3-point rule under it in the center column. Two hairline rules were drawn to surround deck copy that is located above the columns of text. That was the easy part, the hard part is putting page elements on this slightly complex grid.

## Sample

**Magazine Page:** This page uses all the tricks. It has a variety of type styles, sizes, graphic elements, a photo box, and wrapped type, and it still manages to look tasteful. The top bar contains Helvetica 14 point uppercase type with one space between each letter. The headline is Times 60 point, centered. The deck copy between the two horizontal rules is Times Italic 14 point, centered. Text is Times 10 point on 11.5-point linespacing, in 13-pica-wide columns. The caption under the black photo box is Times Italic 10 point to the width of the photo. The type is wrapped around the photo box, which was visually placed on the page for the proper balance with no specific grid rule for its location.

# Grid

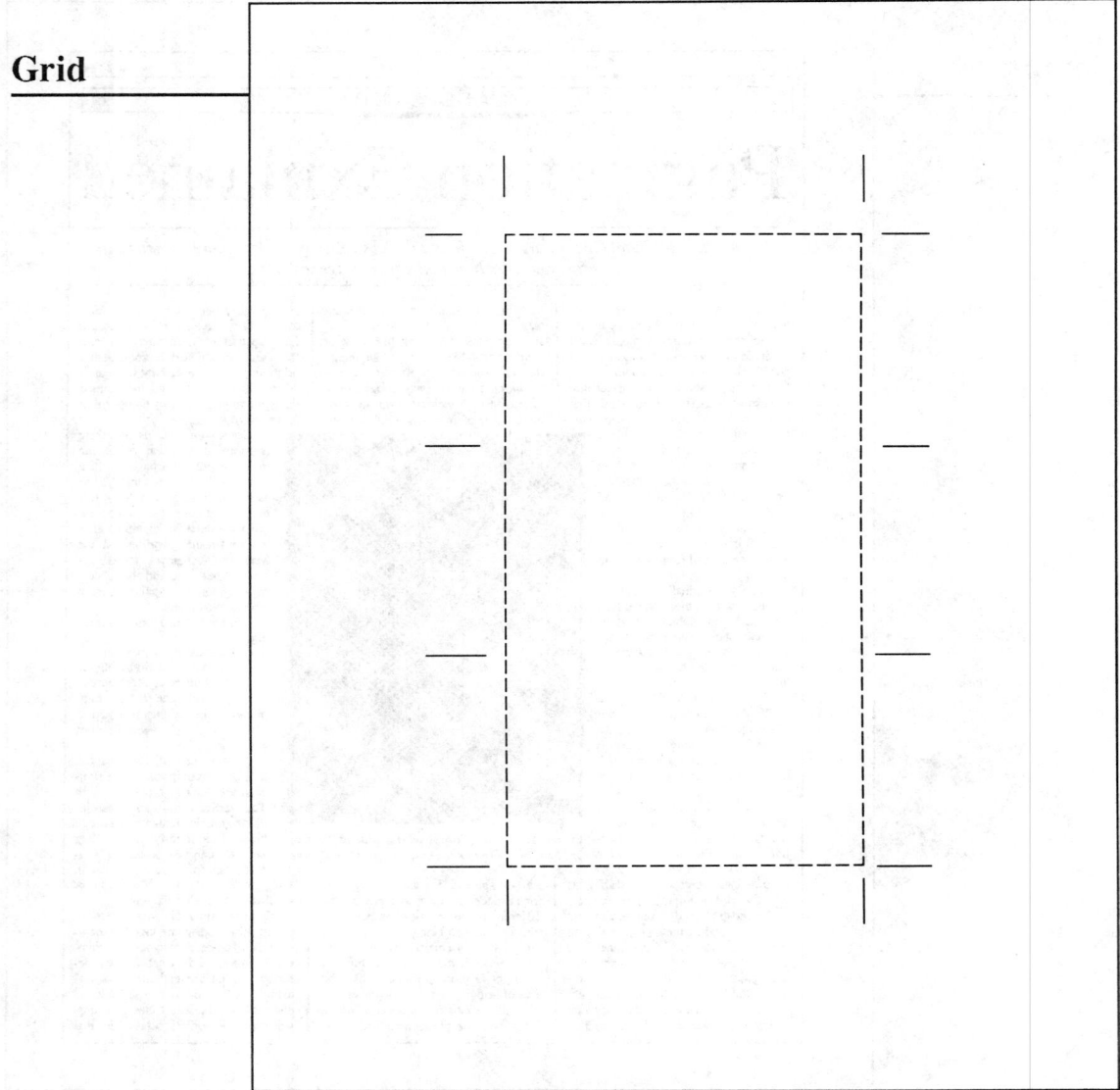

**Business Cards:** For practical applications, items prepared for traditional or laser printing may be created using PC PageMaker. This example of a business card shows how to create a grid for the live area of three business cards, and place outside of the area the crop marks that indicate where to trim the edges of the cards, and where to cut the cards apart. This was done by measuring a standard business card and adding the crop marks with the use of the on-screen rulers. All that is left is to add the type.

## Sample

**Pagination Report**
The Magazine of Pagination

Terry Ulick
*Editor/Publisher*

Published by: The Renegade Company
P.O. Box 390, Itasca, IL 60143
(312) 250-8900


**Pagination Report**
The Magazine of Pagination

Linda Ulick
*Publisher*

Published by: The Renegade Company
P.O. Box 390, Itasca, IL 60143
(312) 250-8900


**Pagination Report**
The Magazine of Pagination

Stephen F. Roth, *Associate Editor*

Published by: The Renegade Company
P.O. Box 390, Itasca, IL 60143
(312) 250-8900

**Business Cards:** The first business card is created by entering the text and then selecting and sizing the type. This card contains Times Bold 18 point for the bold name and Times 14 point for the subtitle. The rest of the type is in 12-point Times and Times Italic. All type was set aligned left. Once the first card was created, it was selected and copied, and then pasted in the next two card positions. The names were then edited using the text tool. Finally, the cards were printed at a printer and then cut apart.

# Part Five  References

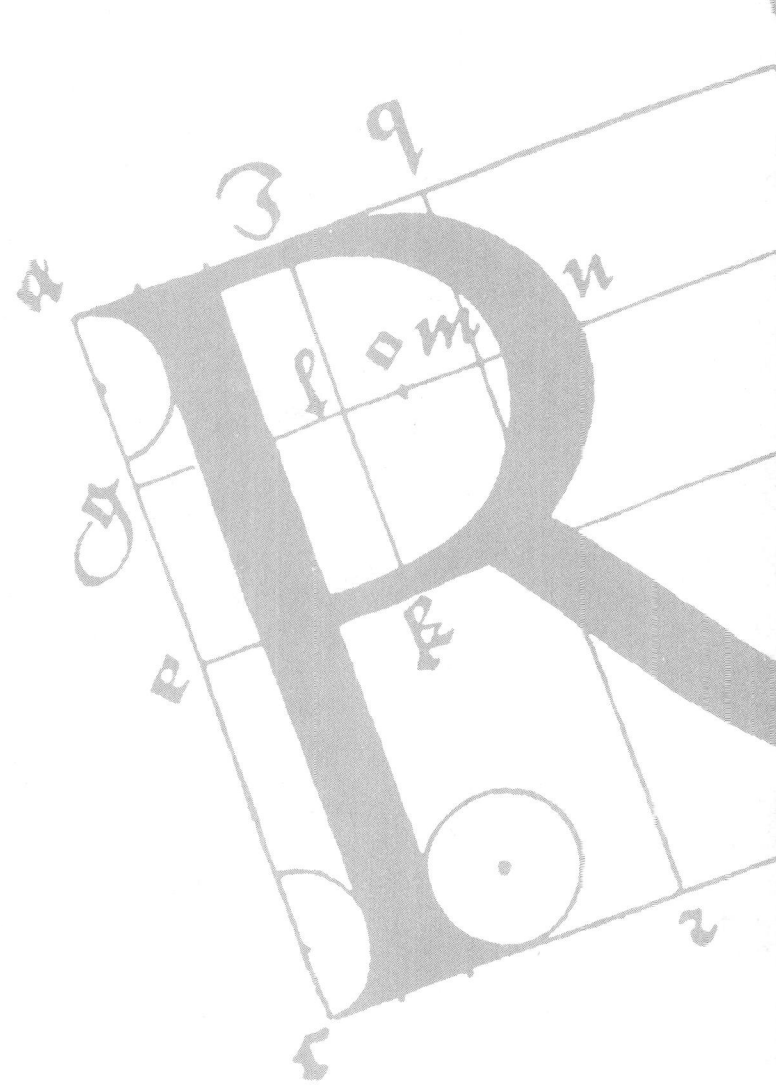

# Glossary of Graphic Arts Terms

**Alphabet Length.** The amount of space taken up by the twenty-six lowercase alphabetic characters in a particular font.

**Ascender.** That part of the character that extends above the x height of the font (as in the lowercase "b").

**Baseline.** The imaginary line that characters rest on in a line of text.

**Bleed.** An illustration, tint, or photograph that extends off the edge of the page.

**Body.** The part of a character that is between the baseline and the x height.

**Body Copy.** The main text in a document, as opposed to headlines, captions, etc.

**Caption.** Text used to describe an illustration.

**Coated Paper.** A paper with a smooth finish, varying from eggshell to glossy.

**Color Separation.** The process of separating a color photograph or illustration into its component colors. Full-color illustrations are broken down into four colors: magenta, yellow, cyan, and black.

**Condensed.** Referring to type, a face that is narrower in relation to its height than the regular variation of that face.

**Continuous Tone.** An illustration that includes grays as well as black and white.

**Copyfitting.** The process of determining how much copy will fit in a given space or adjusting copy through editing or formatting to fit a given space.

**Crop.** To cut the edges of an illustration to fit in a given space.

**Crop Marks.** The cross hairs placed in the corners of a page to show the printer where to cut.

**Descender.** A part of a character that descends below the baseline (as in the letter "g").

**Display Face.**  Any typeface, particularly when used in a larger size, that is appropriate for headlines and other special uses.

**Dummy.**  A rough layout of a page, document, or publication.

**em.**  A relative unit of measurement that is as wide as the point size of the current face.

**em Dash.**  A dash that is one em wide. Used like a comma or colon.

**em Space.**  A space that is as wide as the point size of the current font. Used primarily for first-line indents on paragraphs.

**en.**  A unit of measurement that is half the width of an em.

**en Dash.**  A dash that is longer than a hyphen, but shorter than an em dash. Used in things like the Boston—New York Express and 9 AM—5 PM.

**Expanded.**  Referring to type, a face that is wider in relation to its height than the regular variation of that face.

**Flush Left and Flush Right.**  Type that lines up with the left or right margin, also called ragged right and ragged left, respectively.

**Folio.**  Page number.

**Hairline.**  Technically, the thinnest rule that you can get from your equipment. On a 300dpi laser printer, it is one three- hundredth of an inch.

**Hyphenation.**  Adding hyphens to columns of text so excessive amounts of white space aren't left between words in justified type and ragged type is not too ragged.

**Galley.**  Type that is set in long narrow strips the width of a column, before the columns are made up into pages.

**Gutter.**  The space near the spine (the right side on left-hand pages, the left side on right-hand pages) allowed for binding in a double-sided publication.

**Gray Scale.**  A strip of standard gray tones, ranging from white to black.

**Halftone.**  A continuous tone image that has been photographically converted to a pattern of very small dots.

**Imposition.**  The layout of pages as they will be printed, taking into account how the paper will be folded and cut.

**Italic.**  A typeface variation in which letters slope forward. True italic typefaces are designed, as opposed to oblique faces, which are just slanted versions of the regular face.

**Justification.**  Setting type with both left and right margins even.

**Kerning.**  The process of moving together letters that would normally look too far apart. Used especially in large type sizes and with certain letter pairs (such as the capital "A" and the capital "T").

**Leader.**  A row of dots or dashes used to separate items in tables (as in a phone directory).

**Leading.**  Traditionally, the the thin strips of lead that were placed between lines of type with hot type. This term is often used synonymously with linespacing, though incorrectly so.

**Linespacing.** The distance from the baseline of one line to the baseline of the line below it. Technically, it is the amount of leading plus the point size of the type.

**Mechanical.** Camera-ready boards, with all text and graphics in place, that are sent to the printer.

**Moire.** An undesirable pattern resulting from incorrect halftone screen angles.

**Oblique.** A term used to described typefaces that are slanted a number of degrees to the right. Similar to, but not the same as, italic faces.

**Opacity.** A property of paper, referring to how hard it is to see through it.

**Orphan.** A single line of type from the bottom of a paragraph left alone at the top of a column or page.

**Pagination.** The process of creating pages from text, graphics, photographs, and illustration.

**Pica.** A unit of measurement equal to one-sixth of an inch, or 12 points.

**Point.** A unit of measurement equal to one-seventy-second of an inch.

**Process Colors.** The four colors used in four-color separations: Yellow, Magenta, Cyan, and Black.

**Ragged Right and Ragged Left.** Type that does not align on one side. Also referred to as flush left and flush right, respectively.

**Rule.** A line of any width, varying from a hairline to a wide, dark bar.

**Running Head.** Text that repeats at the top of successive pages.

**Scaling.** Reducing or enlarging an image or piece of type.

**Scanner.** A device used to read images into digital form so they can be manipulated electronically.

**Screen.** A fine mesh used to create halftones.

**Serifs.** The fine strokes at the ends of letters in many typefaces.

**Small Caps.** A set of capital letters that is the size of lowercase letters.

**Widow.** A single line of type from the top of a paragraph left alone at the bottom of a column or page.

**Wrap.** A section of text that runs around a graphic or illustration. Also called a run-around.

Glossary of
Special Terms
Used in
PC PageMaker

**Actual Size.**  On-screen presentation of page at the same size at which it will print (100% size).

**Alignment.**  The positioning of text within columns. There are four ways to align text: flush left (ragged on the right), flush right (ragged on the left), centered (ragged on both the left and right), and justified (flush on both the left and right). Text may be selected at any time and aligned in any of the four styles from the type menu.

**Bitmap File.**  A file usually created with a paint program that creates an image using pixels that are either black or white and, in some cases, color. Such files will usually print to the resolution of the printer selected for use. A bitmap image created at a screen resolution of 60dpi will be printed one-fifth its original size on a 300dpi laser printer.

**Cicero.**  European unit of measure for type size equaling 4.55 milimeters.

**Clipboard.**  An area of memory where text and graphics may be copied to and from. Elements may be cut, copied, and pasted from the clipboard within PC PageMaker or to and from other Windows programs. The clipboard information is only retained when the computer is on.

**Column Guides.**  A menu option where you may choose anywhere from one to twenty columns on a page or master page. The space between columns may also be selected from the same menu. The column guides appear as dotted lines on the screen.

**Crossbar.**  An icon that represents the cursor for drawing lines and boxes.

**Custom Column.**  A column width that has been changed to differ from that on the column guides on the master grid.

**Diagonal-Line Tool.**  A drawing tool from the PC PageMaker toolbox that allows lines to be drawn at any angle.

**Discretionary Hyphen.** A hyphen placed in a word using PC PageMaker that will be used only at the end of a line. This is useful when the "Justify column" command is used. If the word containing a discretionary hyphen appears in the middle of the line, the hyphen will not be visible nor will it print.

**Double-Sided Page.** Choosing the "Double sided" option in the page setup menu creates left- and right-hand master pages and alternates the gutter (inside) margin.

**Draw Files.** Graphic and text files created in a draw program that plots coordinates for graphics, allowing you to take full advantage of the resolution of the printing device used.

**Enlarge and Reduce.** Use of the handles defining the boundaries of the graphic to enlarge or reduce any graphic element. You can make the graphic larger or smaller by moving the pointer with the mouse button held down. Holding the shift key when clicking on any of the four corner handles will reduce or enlarge the graphic proportionally to the original. Holding down the control key while resizing a point-type graphic will optimize the graphic for reproduction on your chosen printer.

**Facing Pages.** In a publication or on the pasteboard of the PC PageMaker screen, two pages that face each other when printed and bound.

**Flow.** Movement of text into a column. Using the "Place" command to place a text file presents you with a text icon. Placing the text icon in a column and clicking on the mouse will flow the text into the column.

**Font Substitution.** Substitution of an existing font for a type font that is not on your system, if this print option is selected.

**Guides.** A nonprinting guideline that appears on the screen as dotted lines. There are three types: margin guides, ruler guides, and column guides. When the snap-to-guide feature is on, text and graphic elements will align themselves to guides.

**Handles.** A device to shorten or lengthen text and to reduce or enlarge graphics. Handles for text blocks appear at the top and bottom of a column of text. Graphic handles are small square boxes on the corners and the centers of each side of the graphic.

**Insertion Point.** The creation of an insertion point to add or edit text, using the text icon to place the blinking vertical cursor text.

**Inside Margin.** The gutter margin. On left-hand pages, it is on the right side of the page; on right-hand pages, it is on the left side of the page.

**Kerning.** Taking a pair of letters that would appear too far apart if left with normal letterspacing and moving the right character closer to the left character to appear more natural looking.

**Leading.** The amount of space, measured in points, between the baselines of type. Also called linespacing.

**Letterspacing.** The amount of space between letters in a typeset column. The amount of space is usually controlled by minimum and maximum values.

## Glossary of Special Terms Used in PC PageMaker

**Master Page.** Grids for pages are created as Master Pages. On the screen, they are represented by page icons with a L or R. A single-sided publication will have only one page icon, a double-sided publication will have two. Clicking on the icon will bring you to the master page, where columns, ruler guides, and printing elements may be placed that will appear on all pages in the file.

**Measurement.** From the preferences menu from the edit menu, you may switch the ruler measurement default between inches, inches decimal, picas, millimeters, and ciceros.

**Page Icon.** The small representation of the pages in a file that appear on the bottom of the screen. Clicking on a page icon will bring you to that page.

**Pasteboard.** The general work area surrounding the page on the PC PageMaker screen. Items may be placed on the pasteboard and, when changing to another page, will remain on the pasteboard for use on other pages.

**Place.** The command that allows you to call files from a menu and place them on your page. Both text and graphics files may be placed. With text files, there is the option to place the text with or without formatting.

**PostScript.** The page description language that is used by PC PageMaker to send all the information needed by a PostScript device to print a page.

**Publication.** The production of a page file. Also referred to as a "pub."

**Ruler Guides.** A nonprinting guide that can be used to align items. With the "Rulers" command on, moving the pointer into the vertical or horizontal ruler, clicking, and dragging onto the page will bring a ruler guide onto the page.

**Selection Box.** Creation of a box around a number of items that may be moved at one time by using the pointer, clicking in one spot, dragging to another, and releasing the mouse button.

**Snap-to Guides.** When turned on, text or graphics placed next to a margin, ruler, or column guide will jump to align with the guide.

**Spooler.** A Windows program that prints a page file to disk, returns the user to PC PageMaker, and then prints the file in a background mode.

**Story.** The entire set of text blocks threaded together in a publication. There may be as many stories as you wish in a publication.

**Text Block.** Text, when placed, with handles on the top and bottom and four corner. The start of the text has a handle that is empty. The bottom handle will have a plus symbol (+) if there is more text or a number symbol (#) if the file has been placed completely.

**Threaded.** All text blocks from a single file that has been placed are connected together in the order in which they were placed. Even though they have been broken into separate blocks, they are still connected or threaded together. Taking out text in the first block will shorten the length of the last text block.

**Thumbnail.** Reduced versions of the pages. These reductions are printed at such a size that 16 pages will fit on a single sheet of paper.

**Tile.** A printing technique that allows large pages to be printed with a printer not capable of printing the indicated page size. The page is broken into blocks, which are printed a sheet at a time and then manually assembled into a final page.

**View.** The size at which you view your page. On the screen, the page may be viewed at 50, 75, 100 (actual size), or 200 percent or "reduce to fit," which makes the page fit in the window at the largest size possible while still allowing you to view the entire page.

**Wordspacing.** The amount of space between words in a typeset column. There are usually minimum and maximum values for the amount of space allowed.

**Zero Point.** The point of intersection of the two zeros on the PC PageMaker on-screen rulers. These may be moved to different locations in relationship to the page.

# Product Reference

## Products Mentioned

**Adobe PostScript Fonts**
Adobe Systems, Inc.
1870 Embarcadero Rd.
Palo Alto, CA 94303
(415) 852-0271

**Amdek 410W**
**White Phosphor Monitor**
Amdek
2201 Lively Blvd.
Elk Grove Village, IL 60007
(312) 364-1180

**AutoCAD**
Autodesk, Inc.
2320 Marinship Way
Sausalito, CA 94965
(415) 332-2344

**Canon IX-12**
Canon USA, Inc.
One Canon Plaza
Lake Success, NY 11042
(516) 488-6700

**Compugraphic 400-PS**
Compugraphic Corp.
200 Ballardvale St.
Wilmington, MA 01887
(617) 658-5600

**Conographic**
**ConoVision 2800**
Conographic Corp.
17841 Fitch
Irvine, CA 92714
(714) 474-1188

**Datacopy 730, JetReader**
Datacopy Corp.
1215 Terra Bella Ave.
Mountain View, CA 94043
(415) 965-7900

**Dataproducts LZR 2665**
Dataproducts Corp.
6200 Canoga Ave.
Woodland Hill, CA 91365
(818) 888-4014

**Dest PC Scan Plus**
Dest Corp.
1201 Cadillac Ct.
Milipitas, CA 95035
(408) 946-7100

**Genius Display**
Micro Display Systems
1310 Vermillion St.
Hastings, MN 55033
(612) 437-2233

**Hercules Plus Card**
Hercules Computer Tech.
2550 Ninth St.
Berkeley, CA 94710
(415) 540-6000

**Hewlett-Packard
SoftFonts and Font Cartridges**
Hewlett-Packard Co.
Inquiries Manager
1820 Embarcadero Rd.
Palo Alto, CA 94303
(800) 367-4772

**IBM AT**
IBM Corp.
400 Columbus Ave.
Valhalla, NY 10595
(800) 447-4700

**IBM Enhanced
Graphics Display**
IBM Corp.
400 Columbus Ave.
Valhalla, NY 10595
(800) 447-4700

**IBM Model 30**
IBM Corp.
400 Columbus Ave.
Valhalla, NY 10595
(800) 447-4700

**IBM Personal Page Printer**
IBM Corp.
400 Columbus Ave.
Valhalla, NY 10595
(800) 447-4700

**IBM Solution Pac
Personal Publishing System**
IBM Corp.
400 Columbus Ave.
Valhalla, NY 10595
(800) 447-4700

**IBM Solution Pac
Personal Publishing Upgrade**
IBM Corp.
400 Columbus Ave.
Valhalla, NY 10595
(800) 447-4700

**In*a*Vision**
Micrografx, Inc.
1820 N. Greenville Ave.
Richardson, TX 75081
(214) 234-1769

**inTalk**
Palantir Software
12777 Jones Rd., Ste. 100
Houston, TX 77070
(713) 955-8800

**KroyKolor**
Kroy Sign Systems
7560 E. Redfield Rd.
Scottsdale, AZ 85260
(800) 521-4997

**Laser Connection PS Jet**
The Laser Connection
PO Box 850296
Mobile, AL 36685
(800) 441-4040

**LaserJet II**
Hewlett-Packard Co.
Inquiries Manager
1820 Embarcadero Rd.
Palo Alto, CA 94303
(800) 367-4772

**LaserJet Plus**
Hewlett-Packard Co.
Inquiries Manager
1820 Embarcadero Rd.
Palo Alto, CA 94303
(800) 367-4772

**LaserView Display System**
Sigma Designs, Inc.
46501 Landing Parkway
Fremont, CA 94538
(415) 770-0100

**LaserWriter Plus**
Apple Computer, Inc.
20525 Mariani Ave.
Cupertino, CA 95014
(408) 996-1010

**LaserWriter**
Apple Computer, Inc.
20525 Mariani Ave.
Cupertino, CA 95014
(408) 996-1010

**Linotype 100, 300**
Linotype Co.
425 Oscar Avenue
Hauppauge, NY 11788
(516) 434-2016

**Logitech Mouse**
Logitech
805 Veterans Blvd.
Redwood City, CA 94063
(415) 365-9852

**Lotus 1-2-3**
Lotus Development Corp.
55 Cambridge Parkway
Cambridge, MA 02142
(617) 557-8500

**Macintosh**
Apple Computer, Inc.
20525 Mariani Ave.
Cupertino, CA 95014
(408) 996-1010

**MacLink**
DataViz, Inc.
16 Winfield St.
Norwalk, CT 06855
(203) 866-4944

**Microsoft Mouse**
Microsoft Corp.
16011 NE 36th
PO Box 97017
Redmond, WA 98073
(206) 882-8080

**Microsoft Word**
Microsoft Corp.
16011 NE 36th
PO Box 97017
Redmond, WA 98073
(206) 882-8080

**Microtek MS-300A**
Microtek
16901 S. Western Ave.
Gardena, CA 90247
(800) 654-4160

**Mouse System PC Mouse**
Mouse Sytems Corp.
2600 San Tomas Expressway
Santa Clara, CA 95051
(408) 988-0211

**NEC Multisync Monitor**
NEC Home Electronics
1255 Michael Dr.
Wood Dale, IL 60191
(312) 860-9500

**Omnicrom Color System**
Omnicrom Systems Corporation
40 Nickerson Rd.
Ashland, MA 01721
(800) 443-4031

**PC PageMaker**
Aldus Corp.
411 First Ave. South, Ste. 200
Seattle, WA 98104
(206) 622-5500

**PC Paintbrush**
Z-Soft
1950 Spectrum Circle, Ste. A495
Marietta, GA 30067
(404) 980-1950

**PC Quik Art**
PC Quik-Art Inc.
394 S. Milledge Ave, Ste. 200
Athens, GA 30606
(800) 523-1796

**PostScript**
Adobe Systems, Inc.
1870 Embarcadero Rd.
Palo Alto, CA 94303
(415) 852-0271

**Publisher's Paintbrush**
Z-Soft
1950 Spectrum Circle, Ste. A495
Marietta, GA 30067
(404) 980-1950

**QMS PS800, PS2400**
QMS Inc.
1 Magnum Place
Mobile, AL 36618
(205) 633-4300

**Summagraphics Graphic Input Tablet**
Summagraphics Corp.
777 State St. Extension
Fairfield, CT 06430
(203) 384-1344

**Symphony**
Lotus Development Corp.
55 Cambridge Parkway
Cambridge, MA 02142
(617) 557-8500

**TI OmniLaser 2108, 2115**
Texas Instruments
PO Box 809063, H-860
Dallas, TX 75080
(800) 527-3500

**Vega Deluxe EGA Card**
Video-7 Inc.
550 Sycamore Dr.
Milipitas, CA 95035
(408) 943-0101

**Viking 1**
Moniterm Inc.
5740 Green Circle Dr.
Minnetonka, MN 55343
(612) 437-2233

**VS Softfonts**
VS Software
P.O. Box 6158
Little Rock, AR 72216
(501) 376-2083

**Windows Draw Clip Art**
Micrografx, Inc.
1820 N. Greenville Ave.
Richardson, TX 75081
(214) 234-1769

**Windows Draw**
Micrografx, Inc.
1820 N. Greenville Ave.
Richardson, TX 75081
(214) 234-1769

**Windows Graph**
Micrografx, Inc.
1820 N. Greenville Ave.
Richardson, TX 75081
(214) 234-1769

**Windows Paint**
Microsoft Corp.
16011 NE 36th
PO Box 97017
Redmond, WA 98073
(206) 882-8080

**Windows Pro 3D PC**
Enabling Technologies
600 S. Dearborn #1304
Chicago, IL 60605
(312) 427-0408

**Windows Write**
Microsoft Corp.
16011 NE 36th
PO Box 97017
Redmond, WA 98073
(206) 882-8080

**Windows**
Microsoft Corp.
16011 NE 36th
PO Box 97017
Redmond, WA 98073
(206) 882-8080

**Wyse WY-700**
Wyse Technology
3571 N. First Ave.
San Jose, CA 95134
(800) 438-9973

## LaserJet Plus Type Suppliers

**Bitstream**
215 First St.
Cambridge, MA 02142
(617) 497-6222

**CES**
509 Cathedral Pkwy. 10-A
New York, NY 10025
(800) 251-2223

**Data Transforms**
616 Washington St.
Denver, CO 80203
(303) 832-1501

**Font Center**
505 Marin St. #121
Thousand Oaks, CA 91360
(805) 373-1919

**Hewlett-Packard**
1820 Embarcadero Rd.
Palo Alto, CA 94303
(800) 367-4772

**Janus Associates**
991 Massachusetts Ave.
Cambridge, MA
(617) 354-1999

**Keller Software**
1825 Westcliff Dr.
Newport Beach, CA 92600
(714) 854-8211

**LeBaugh Software Corp.**
2720 Greene Ave.
Omaha, NE 68147
(800) 532-2844

**Network Technology Corp.**
6825 Lamp Post Lane
Alexandria, VA 22306
(703) 765-4506

**Prosoft**
7248 Bellaire Ave.
No. Hollywood, CA 91605
(818) 765-4444

**R. M. C.**
12046 Willowood Dr.
Woodbridge, VA 22192
(703) 494-2633

**SoftCraft, Inc.**
16 N. Carroll St., Ste. 500
Madison, WI 53703
(800) 351-0500

**Specific Solutions**
1898 Anthony Ct.
Mountain View, CA 94040
(415) 941-3941

**Straightforward**
15000 Halldale Ave., Ste. 115
Gardena, CA 90247
(213) 324-8827

**VS Software**
P.O. Box 6158
Little Rock, AR 72216
(501) 376-2083

**Weaver Graphics**
Fox Pavillion Box 1132
Jenkintown, PA 19046
(215) 884-9286

**Xiaphais**
13464 Washington Blvd.
Marin Del Rey, CA 90292
(213) 821-0074

## PostScript Type Suppliers

*(Note: At the time of this writing, most PostScript type suppliers are currently offering type only for the Macintosh, but have announced intentions to offer type for IBM systems. The following is intended as a reference to those companies.)*

**Adobe Systems, Inc.**
1870 Embarcadero Rd.
Palo Alto, CA 94303
(415) 852-0271

**Allotype Typographics**
1600 Packard Rd., Ste. 5
Ann Arbor, MI 48104
(313) 663-1989

**Altsys Corporation**
720 Ave. F, Ste. 108
Plano, TX 75074
(214) 424-4888

**Century Software**
2483 Hearst Ave., #175
Berkeley, CA 94709
(415) 549-1901

**Casady Company**
P.O. Box 223779
Carmel, CA 93922
(408) 646-4660

**Devonian International**
P.O. Box 2351
Montclair, CA 91763
(714) 621-0973

**Image Club Graphics**
2828-19th St., N.E.
Calgary, Alberta, Canada T2E 6Y9
(403) 250-1969

**Invincible Software**
9534 Burwick
San Antonio, TX 78230
(512) 344-4228

**Software Complement**
P.O. Box 1123
Milford, PA 18337
(717) 686-5592

**NeoScribe International**
P.O. Box 633
East Haven, CT 06512
(203) 467-9880

**T/Maker Graphics**
1973 Landings Dr.
Mountain View, CA 94043
(415) 962-0195

# Index

## A

Accelerator boards, 10
  cost of, 10
Adapters
  Color Graphics (CGA), 13
  Enhanced Graphics (EGA), 12, 13
  Monochrome Display, 12
  supported by PC PageMaker, 22
Areas, adding shading to, 193
Ascenders, 103
ASCII text files, 36, 37
  formatting features, 129
Author photographs, 62
Automatic kerning, 218-219
Automatic hyphenation, 216-217
Avant Garde type font, 113

## B

Baseline, 103
Basic report
  sample grid for, 236
  sample page for, 237
  two columns, sample grid for, 238
  sample page for, 239
Bit-mapped graphics, 42
  cropping, 174
Bleed, 173
Blocks
  of text, 177
  moving, 216
  resizing, 177
Bonding
  color, 234
  cost, 234
Boxes, adding to pages, 188
Business cards
  sample grid for, 256
  sample page for, 257

## C

Captions, 61
  wrapping around graphics, 182
Charting software, 47
Charts, 47
Circle-oval tool, 192
Clip art
  electronic, 44, 45
  software, 44, 45
Color bonding, 234
  cost, 234
Color Graphics Adapter (CGA) cards, 12
  and graphics mode, 12
Color Graphics Adapters (CGA), 13
Color graphics monitors, 12
  and graphics mode, 12
Color printing, 226
Color separations
  creating, 230-233
  creating with a color photocopier, 233
Column orientation, choosing, 145
Columns
  changing widths with text placed, 212-214
  ending flush, 185-187
  odd-sized, 211
  placing rules between, 168-170

placing text in, 165-167
variable widths, 178-182
Communication links,
    *see* Modems
Compatibles, IBM AT, 3, 9
Computer-aided publishing,
    82-84
versus manual process, 82-84
Conversions, of word
    processed text to
    PC PageMaker, 38-39
Courier type font, 112
Cropping bit-mapped
    graphics, 174
Cropping graphics, 173-174
Cropping paint graphics, 174
Cropping tool, 193
Cursor keys, 11

## D

Deck copy, 62
Descenders, 103
Designed report
    sample grid for, 240
    sample page for, 241
Desktop publishing,
    hard disks and, 23
Desktop publishing
    software, 35
Desktop publishing
    systems, 3, 7, 8, 9
    components of, 3, 9, 33-34
    cost of, 33-34
    hard disks and, 9
    hardware for, 7-9
    ideal, 23
    and mouse, 10
    peripheral hardware and, 24
    graphic input devices, 24
    RAM and, 9
    speed of with PC, 3, 9-13
    speed of with XT, 3, 9
    and support products, 7
    system approach, 8
    turnkey systems versus, 32

Devices, input, 7-8 *see also*
    Input devices
    optical character recognition
    (OCR), *see* Scanners
    output, 7-8
Diagonal tool, 192
Dictionary, 217
Digital typography, 97
Digitizers, 25
    capabilities, 25-27
Digitizing, 24
Digitizing halftones, 28
Directory,
    sample page for, 253
Directory cover
    sample grid for, 250
    sample page for, 251
Directory page,
    sample grid for, 252
Display card support, 22
Dot matrix printers, 14, 15, 16
    and pages, 139
Double sided pages,
    choosing, 145
Downloadable fonts, RAM
    space occupied by, 139
Downloadable type fonts, 49
Draw programs, 43
Drawing tools (primitives)
    in toolbox, 191-193

## E

80286 processor, 10
8088 processor, 9, 10
Electronic halftones,
    creating, 27-28
Electronic page
    assembly, 79-82
em dash, 105
em space, 105
Enhanced Color Monitors, 12
Enhanced Graphics Adapters
    (EGA), 12, 13
EPS graphics file
    formats, 197-199

## F

Facing pages, choosing, 146
Files, printing, 221-222
Flat art scanners, *see* Scanners
Flush, ending a page, 184-187
Folios, 61-62, 92
    automatic numbering, 154-157
Font (typeface), 98-101
Fonts
    downloadable
        RAM space occupied
        by, 139
    type, downloadable, 49
Formatting
    of column formats, 57, 58-59
    text into type, 122-126
    of text with word
        processing, 37-38, 121

## G

Graphic elements,
    in page grid, 92
Graphic input devices, 24
Graphic input tablets,
    24, 29, 30
    compared with mouse,
        29, 30
Graphics, 140
    cropping bit-mapped, 174
    cropping paint, 174
    crossing two columns
        rules with, 183
    enlarging on pages, 174
    as a page element, 62
    placing on pages,
        172-173, 175
    reducing on pages, 174
    resizing (cropping), 173-174
    wrapping type around,
        175-183
    wrapping type around
        abstract shaped, 182-183
Graphics boards (cards), 12
Graphics card, Hercules, 12

Index

Graphics elements, 60-61
　creation of in desktop
　　publishing, 41-47
Graphics files, 193
　formats
　　EPS, 197-199
　　TIFF, 196-197
Graphics mode, 12
　and color graphics
　　monitors, 12
　and monochrome
　　monitors, 12
Graphics software,
　see Software
Graphs, 47
Grid
　sample for
　　basic report, 236
　　basic report in two
　　　columns, 238
　　business cards, 256
　　classic newsletter, 246
　　designed report, 240
　　directory cover, 250
　　directory page, 252
　　magazine page, 254
　　modern newsletter, 242
　　modern newsletter with
　　　graphics, 244
　　report cover, 248
　　samples, 235-257
Gutters, see Page grid

**H**

Halftones, 25-27
　creating electronic, 27-28
　digitizing, 28
　electronic, 27
Hanging indents, 218
Hard disks, 9
　cost of, 10
　with desktop publishing
　　files, 23
　speed of, 10
Hardware, 7-8, 9-34

assumptions about in this
　book, and desktop
　publishing, see Desktop
　publishing systems
peripherals, 24
supported by
　PC PageMaker, 9-34
upgrading IBM PC, 10-13
upgrading PC hardware, 10-13
Hardware switching, 7-8
　with MS-DOS
　　windows, 7-8
Headlines, 56-57
　placing on pages, 159-163
　sizing on pages, 163-164
Helvetica narrow
　type font, 110
Helvetica type font, 109
Hercules graphics card, 12
　with TTL monitors, 12
High resolution monitors
　(HRM), 3, 13
High-resolution PostScript
　services, 223
Hyphen, discretionary, 217
Hyphenation
　automatic, 216-217
　prompted, 217
Hyphens, removing, 217

**I**

IBM AT, 3, 9
　advantages of in
　　desktop publishing, 78
　and desktop publishing
　　systems, 3, 8-9
　using to place photo, 74-77
　using to set type, 71-74
IBM AT compatibles, 3, 9
IBM PC, 3, 9
　and desktop publishing
　　systems, 10-13
　speed with desktop
　　publishing systems,
　　3, 9-10

upgrading hardware, 10-13
IBM XT, 3, 9
　and desktop publishing
　　systems, 3, 9
　speed with desktop
　　publishing systems, 9
Icons, 4-5, 160
Indents, hanging, 218
Input devices, 7-8
　graphic, 24
　mouse, 10

**J**

Justification, 105

**K**

Kerning, 105
　automatic, 218-219
　manual, 219

**L**

Large print runs, 225
Laser printers, 3, 14, 15
　cost of, 20
　and digital type, 97
　downloadable fonts for, 49
　maximum imagining area
　　of, 139
　page sizes supported, 139
　and pages, 139
　when to use, 226
LaserJet type
　fonts, 107-108, 119-120
LaserWriter type
　fonts, 107-118
Leading, 103
　changing, 215-216
Letter quality printers, 14
Letterspacing, 105, 219
Live area, see Page grid

## M

Magazine
  sample grid for, 254
  sample page for, 255
Manual kerning, 219
Margins, *see* Page grid
Master pages, 143
  covering elements
    of, 194-196
  left-hand, 158
  right-hand, 158
  rules between columns
    on, 183
  setting up, 148-158
Microsoft Word Version 3.0,
    formatting features, 127
Modems, 24, 31
  Hayes protocols as
    standard for, 32
  null modem cable as
    alternative to, 31
  purchasing, 32
  purposes of, 31
  telecommunications
    software for, 39-40
  and typesetting, 31
Monitor, 12
Monitor support, 22
Monitors
  color graphics, 12
  comparison of, 12-13
  Enhanced Color, 12
  high resolution, 13
  supported by
    PC PageMaker, 22
  TTL monochrome, 12
  TTL white phosphor, 12
Monochrome Display Adapter
    (MDA) cards, 12
  and graphics mode, 12
Mouse, 3, 10, 24
  alternatives to, 24
  compared with graphic
    input tablets, 29, 30
  mechanical, 11
  optical, 11

optical-mechanical, 11-12
  as primary input device, 10
MS-DOS Windows, 3-5
  using with multiple
    programs, 4-6
Multilayered pages, 140-141
MultiMate Version 3.31,
    formatting features, 128

## N

New Century Schoolbook
    type font, 116
Newsletter
  classic
    sample grid for, 246
    sample page for, 247
  modern
    sample grid for, 242
    sample page for, 243
  modern with graphics
    sample grid for, 244
    sample page for, 245
Null modem cable, 31

## O

Odd-sized columns, 211
Optical character recognition
  devices (OCRs), *see* Scanners
Output devices, 7-8
Oversized pages, producing
    with tiling feature,
    219-220

## P

Page,
  sample of for
    basic report, 237
    basic report,
      two columns, 239
    business cards, 257
    classic newsletter, 247

designed report, 241
directory, 253
directory cover, 251
magazine, 255
modern newsletter, 243
modern newsletter with
  graphics, 245
report cover, 249
Page assembly, manual versus
  PC PageMaker, 134-135
Page description language
  printers, 18, 20-21
Page files, size limits, 201
Page grid, 87-94
  columns, 91
  flexibility with, 93
  graphic elements, 92
  gutter, 89-91
  live area, 89-91
  margins, 89-91
    choosing, 146
Page numbers, 61-62, 92
Pages
  adding boxes to, 188
  adding type to, 187-188
  after first, 171
  architecture of, 55
  assembling, 48, 54
    electronic, 48
  assembly software for, 48
  bleed off of, 173
  choosing
    column orientation, 145
    double sided, 145
    facing, 146
    start #, 146
  consistency in design, 67-68
  electronic assembly
    of, 79-82
  elements of, 55-62
    author photographs, 62
    captions, 61
    deck copy, 62
    graphics, 60-61, 62
    headlines, 56-57
    page numbers
      (folios), 61-62, 92

subheads, 59-60
text, 57-58
ending flush, 184-187
enlarging graphics on, 174
horizontal (landscape) version of, 139
master, 88, 143
placing rules between columns on, 183
master left-hand, 158
master right-hand, 158
multilayered, 140-141
multipage environments, 65
multiple, 65-69
oversized, 219-220
printing, 221-222
placing graphics on, 172-173, 175
placing headlines on, 159-163
placing rules between columns on, 168-170
placing text on, 165-167
preparing for printing, 226-227
printing, 221-222
and publication design, 68
reducing graphics on, 174
resizing (cropping) graphics on, 173-174
reverse type (white type against black background), 189, 220
rules with two column graphics, 183
sample, 235-257
setting up maste pages, 148-158
setting up publication pages, 152-157
simple report versus magazine, 55-56
choosing, 145
sizing headlines on, 163-164
spread, 65-67

understanding the single page, 62
varying columns widths on, 178-182
vertical position of, 139
visual reference of, 62
wrapping captions around graphics, 182
wrapping type around graphics, 175-183
Paint graphics, cropping, 174
Paint programs, 42
Palatino type font, 115
Pasteboard, elements on, 147-148
Pasteup, 134
PC PageMaker
compared with other page assembly products, 136
cost of, 136
installation of, 137
starting, 138
Peripheral hardware, 24
communication links, 24
modems, 24
mouse, 24
mouse alternatives, 24
graphic input tablets, 24
Perpendicular tool, 192
Photocopier printing, multicolored, 223
Photographs, 25-27 *see also* Halftones
Phototypesetting, 97
Picas, 105
Pixel, 42
Pointer tool, 192
Points, 101-102
PostScript
and high-resolution services, 223
typesetting of files, 223
as page descriptor language, 18
PostScript type fonts, 107-120
Printer, choosing, 144
Printer drivers, 21

Printer spooler, 222
turning off, 222
Printer support, 21, 22
Printers, 14
comparison of dot matrix and laser output, 15-17
dot matrix, 14, 15, 16
downloadable fonts for laser, 49
laser, 3, 14, 15
and digital type, 97
letter quality, 14
memory in, 18
page description language, 18, 20-21
supported by PC PageMaker, 22
using Postscript, 18
Printing
color, 226
to disk, 222
and enlarging oversized pages, 222
large runs, 225
preparing pages for, 226-227
and reducing oversized pages, 222
two-color, 229-233
preparing pages for, 229-230
when to use a laser printer, 226
Printing oversized pages, 221-222
Printing page files, 221-223
Processors, 10
80286, 10
8088, 9, 10
Prompted hyphenation, 217
Publication pages, setting up, 152-157
Publishing, v-viii

## R

RAM, 9
  and desktop publishing systems, 9
  downloadable fonts stored in, 49
  speed of, 10
Report cover
  sample grid for, 248
  sample page for, 249
Reverse type (white type against black background), 189, 220
Rounded-corner tool, 192
Rules
  placing between columns, 168-170
  placing on master pages, 183
  reverse, 220
  with two-column graphics, 183
Running head, 61

## S

Samna Word III, formatting features, 128
Sample grids, 235-257
Sample pages, 235-257
Sans serif typefaces, 97, 99
Saving files, 158
Scanner support, 22
Scanners, 28
  cost, 28
  flat art, 28
  comparing varieties of, 28-29
  flatbed, 28
  sheetfed, 28
Serif typefaces, 97-98
Shading, adding to areas, 193
Software, 35-49, 50
  assumptions about in this book, ix
  charts and graphs, 47
  clip art, 44, 45
  conversion from word processing to PC PageMaker, 38-39
  for creating graphics elements, 41-47
  for desktop publishing, 35
  file transfer, 40-41
  functions of, 36
  capturing text, 36
  graphics, 41-47, 50
  draw programs, 43
  paint programs, 42
  graphics transfer, 40-41
  page assembly, 48
  PC PageMaker, 133
  telecommunications, 39-41
  purposes of, 39-40
  transferring files to PC PageMaker, 40
  word processing, 36-39, 50, 121
  word processing and formatting text, 37-38, 121
Square-corner tool, 192
Start page #, choosing, 146
Starting PC PageMaker, 138
Stretching text, 205-210
Subheads, 59-60
Symbol type font, 117
System, desktop publishing, *see* Desktop publishing systems

## T

Tabs, 217-218
Text, 57-58
  blocks, 177
  moving, 216
  column format of, 57, 58-59
  columns and type size of, 58-59
  formatting into type, 122-126
  placing on pages, 165-167
  preparing, 121-122
  resizing blocks of, 177
  stretching, 205-210
  type size, 57-59
Text files
  limitations to splitting, 203
  and page file sizes, 201-203
  splitting, 202-203
Text tool, 192
TIFF graphics file formats, 196-197
Tiling, 219-220
Times type font, 111
Toolbox, 191-199
  circle-oval tool, 192
  cropping tool, 193
  diagonal tool, 192
  perpendicular tool, 192
  pointer tool, 192
  rounded-corner tool, 192
  square-corner tool, 192
  text tool, 192
Toolbox drawing tools (primitives), 191-193
TTL monochrome monitors, 12
  and graphics mode, 12
TTL white phosphor monitors, 12
  cost of, 12
  manufacturers of, 12
Turnkey systems, 32
  versus desktop publishing systems, 32
Two-color printing, 229-233
  preparing pages for, 229-230
Type, 96-106
  adding, 187-188
  ascenders, 103
  baseline, 103
  changing size and leading, 215-216
  descenders, 103
  digital, 97
  downloadable fonts, 49

em space, 105
em dash, 105
font, 98-101
   changing, 214
font (typeface), 98-101
   formatting text
      into, 122-126
   justification, 105
   kerning, 105
   LaserJet fonts, 107-108,
      119-120
   LaserWriter fonts, 107-118
   leading, 103
   letterspacing, 105
   making a gauge for, 103
   phototypesetting, 97
   picas, 105
   PostScript fonts, 107-120
   reverse (white against black
      background), 189, 220
   sans serif, 97, 99
   serif, 97-99
   size of, 101-104
   wooden or metal, 96
   wordspacing, 105
   wrapping around abstract
      shaped graphics, 182-183
   wrapping around
      graphics, 175-183
Type fonts, 18, 19, 20
Typesetter support, 22
Typesetters, 139
Typesetting, 95-97
   laser printing versus, 96
   of PostScript files, 223
Typesetting devices, 14
Type size, 101-104
   changing, 215-216
   measuring in points,
      101-102

## V

Visual reference, 62
Volkswriter 3 Version 1.0,
   formatting features, 128

## W

What you see is what you
   get, 3
Widths, columns, changing
   with text placed, 212-214
variable column, 178-182
Windows, MS-DOS, 3-5
Windows Write Version 1.0,
   formatting features, 127
Word processing software,
   36-39, 50, 121
WordPerfect Version 4.1,
   formatting features, 129
Wordspacing, 105, 219
Wordstar 2000 Version 2.0,
   formatting features, 129
Wordstar Version 3.3,
   formatting features, 129
wysiwyg (what you see is
   what you get), 3

## X

XyWrite III, formatting
   features, 127

## Z

Zapf Chancery type font, 114
Zapf Dingbats type font, 118

## Colophon

All of the pages in this book were created using Microsoft Word for word processing, PageMaker for assembling type and graphics into pages, and the final pages output on an Apple LaserWriter Plus for reproduction using offset printing.

The type was set in Times Roman and Helvetica.

The cover and photographs in the book were created with conventional graphic arts methods.